The Voiceless SOUL

*How to Express and Release
Deep Fears of Unworthiness*

KELLY TALLAKSEN

BALBOA.PRESS
A DIVISION OF HAY HOUSE

Copyright © 2021 Kelly Tallaksen.

All rights reserved. No part of this book may be used or reproduced by any means, graphic, electronic, or mechanical, including photocopying, recording, taping or by any information storage retrieval system without the written permission of the author except in the case of brief quotations embodied in critical articles and reviews.

Balboa Press books may be ordered through booksellers or by contacting:

Balboa Press
A Division of Hay House
1663 Liberty Drive
Bloomington, IN 47403
www.balboapress.com
844-682-1282

Because of the dynamic nature of the Internet, any web addresses or links contained in this book may have changed since publication and may no longer be valid. The views expressed in this work are solely those of the author and do not necessarily reflect the views of the publisher, and the publisher hereby disclaims any responsibility for them.

The author of this book does not dispense medical advice or prescribe the use of any technique as a form of treatment for physical, emotional, or medical problems without the advice of a physician, either directly or indirectly. The intent of the author is only to offer information of a general nature to help you in your quest for emotional and spiritual well-being. In the event you use any of the information in this book for yourself, which is your constitutional right, the author and the publisher assume no responsibility for your actions.

Any people depicted in stock imagery provided by Getty Images are models, and such images are being used for illustrative purposes only.
Certain stock imagery © Getty Images.

Print information available on the last page.

ISBN: 978-1-9822-6031-6 (sc)
ISBN: 978-1-9822-6029-3 (hc)
ISBN: 978-1-9822-6030-9 (e)

Library of Congress Control Number: 2021903303

Balboa Press rev. date: 02/17/2021

ENDORSEMENTS

In 2016, I graduated college for Acupuncture and Oriental medicine. I had learned the ancient art of eastern medicine, and how to approach the healing and support of the body, mind and soul. I came away with an understanding of the mind and body connection, but it wasn't until I met Kelly that I would fully understand just how powerful this connection was. Shortly after our first meeting, I found myself sitting across from Kelly as a student in her hypnosis certification course, hanging onto every word as she spoke of hypnosis and soul trauma. Kelly's knowledge and understanding of human consciousness from the beginnings of life and our innate fears of nonlove brought me to a whole new understanding about how we experience life. The healing that I personally experienced from one session with Kelly was life changing. I have since referred many of my patients to Kelly who have also expressed high regards for her work.

Kelly's knowledge and skills for conveying information with examples, research and valued experience has helped transform the lives of many people and will continue to do so through this book. Kelly speaks with a compassionate voice to all those that have suffered soul trauma, leading the reader through a deeper understanding of their disconnect from their own hearts and then through a compassionate and effective healing process.

I highly recommend this book to every adult interested in what it means to truly heal the soul.

With much love,

Diane A. DiCarlo, DAc., L.Ac., Dipl. Ac. (NCCAOM), LMT, CH

***

Kelly asked me to edit her book. My editor brain did what it was supposed to, however along the way my heart - my other brain- began to open. In the process of reading this book I found myself going there, reaching back and deep within to face my own ancestral damage and just by identifying it- actually naming the shadows themselves - my own healing took place. Kelly's writing style is straightforward and sometimes brutally honest as she faces her own ancestral wounds and replies to them in heartfelt, wrenching letters. Kelly's work is probably one of the most important aspects of healing and describes what a human being can do for themselves if they truly want to heal.

Janis Seminara M.A.,Ed.

***

When typical self-help books and positive affirmations just don't cut it, turn here. Kelly provides brilliant insight to the real cause and healing of our deep-seated feelings of unworthiness.

Through real life stories and researched backed theories, Kelly guides the reader on a self- awareness and self-healing path that starts before birth. You will be amazed at what you will become aware of and then learn to release and heal. This book takes you on an amazing journey.

I highly recommend this book.

Janice Imbrogno, MS, CFCS

***

The Voiceless Soul is a worthwhile read for anyone who's willing to use spirituality and self-awareness in order to fill in the gaps that exist in today's psychological sciences. As a transpersonal hypnotist with extensive experience — as well as a real, accessible person who has worked through her own childhood trauma — Kelly Tallaksen uses clear-cut explanations, dialogues, and emotional letters to describe how readers can move from the victim mentality to a place in which they can break the chain of ancestral pain. As a writer, editor, and avid reader of the self-help sphere, I haven't found anything else out there like this, especially from such a unique perspective.

Maria Cassano, Writer & Editor

***

Kelly's book gave me new insights, perspectives and tools that I will use with my clients. Kelly shares moments of her own fears of unworthiness written in heartfelt letters from the voiceless soul of her wounded inner child, allowing the reader to fully engage with their own unhealed emotional traumas. As Kelly's soul talks to your soul in a compassionate voice, she helps you find your own voice as she guides you out of the shadows of the unworthiness trap and into your true divine self. It was not only informative, but deeply healing.

This book creates an in-depth and insightful understanding of how trauma is passed on from the wounded soul of our ancestors to our souls and so on and so forth. This creates a new pathway to heal yourself and forgive the unhealed inner child of those who hurt you and those who have hurt them as we are all stuck in the same unworthiness trap. Quite profound!

I will recommend this book to clients and colleagues!

Lynn Goldstein, LCSW

***

ACKNOWLEDGEMENTS

Writing this book has been a long emotional process that has taken me not only into the deep pain of my own voiceless inner child but into the childhood pain of those that parented me through my younger years. I realize now how important it is to understand the disconnected soul, the fears of unworthiness that keep us stuck in self-sabotage and what needs to be understood to release the innocent soul from this debilitating trap. I have learned so much on this journey and I love and appreciate all those that have supported my efforts to share this valuable information.

I want to express a special thank you to those who have acknowledged my work throughout the years and compassionately supported my efforts to take this project to completion.

To my husband Tom: Thank you for always supporting my work and especially thank you for your unremitting patience during my writing process. I appreciate all that you do for me which has allowed me the time and space to pursue my dreams.

To my family and friends: Thank you for being an advocate of my work throughout the years and supporting my long-held dream in writing this book. You have never doubted me even when I doubted myself. I appreciate your unwavering kindness, devotion and trust in my efforts and most importantly, your ongoing encouragement.

To my editor and writing coach, Janis Seminara: Thank you for your encouragement and unwavering vision to see my book published and into the hands of those who are ready to heal on a soul level. Thank you for providing your review and editing skills, your writing expertise, together with your insight and wisdom, to help bring my manuscript to completion. Your professional writing course gave me the confidence I needed to stay true to my mission.

To: Maria Cassano, writer and editor: Thank you for providing your editorial skills and continuously supporting my efforts in this project and thank you for reminding me that I share a unique message that is worthy of sharing with the world.

To my writing group, Adina Dabija, Debra Benigno and Carol Jansch: Thank you for all of your feedback and encouragement during my writing process. Your support and constructive comments were most helpful during this journey.

To my clients: A huge thank you for being so brave and courageous to enter that painful place within you and doing the necessary work to release your soul from the unworthiness trap. You have taught me so much about the consciousness of the soul and how it plays out in our physical reality.

To: Aman Aneja: Thank you for all your technical support and showing great respect for my work. You have selflessly offered your time and expertise to help me go beyond my comfort zone in social media presence so my healing work can be acknowledged on a global platform.

To my younger self: Thank you for staying strong through a difficult childhood so I could find my way back to my divine self. I love you and I am proud of your courage.

To Balboa Press: Thank you bringing this book through the editing, design, publication and distribution process. The entire team assigned to my book has demonstrated the highest levels in professionalism, competence, responsiveness and dedication to my project.

DEDICATION

This book is dedicated to all of those innocent souls that have forgotten their true value because the human experience has challenged and tested them to the point of disconnect from their own divine essence. You are all heroes. Stay strong, stay brave and stay courageous as you find your way back to the higher truth. We are all miracles in this thing called "life."

The Voiceless Soul
How to Express and Release Deep Fears of Unworthiness

Kelly Tallaksen

CONTENTS

Introduction..xvii
Chapter 1   A Conversation with Spirit................................. 1
Chapter 2   The Journey... 6
Chapter 3   How Your Life Was Created for You 12
Chapter 4   How We Get Stuck in the Unworthiness Trap......17
Chapter 5   Trauma in the Womb 24
Chapter 6   The Sensitive and Aware Unborn Child........... 35
Chapter 7   Pre-Birth Consciousness—Undeniable Evidence............ 42
Chapter 8   Sharing the Sacred Womb................................ 50
Chapter 9   The Soul's Challenges of Physical Birth 54
Chapter 10 Freeing Ourselves from Our Stories 60
Chapter 11 The Battle We Fight Inside of Us.................... 69
Chapter 12 The Heart-Shielded Adult................................74
Chapter 13 The Self-Help Era to the Rescue...................... 79
Chapter 14 Enough with the Fluffy Stuff........................... 82
Chapter 15 Levels of Soul Consciousness 91
Chapter 16 The Laws of Consciousness.............................. 95
Chapter 17 The Perpetual Trap... 102
Chapter 18 Waiting to Be Saved from Ourselves 108
Chapter 19 When Love Gets Lost Beneath the Fear..........113
Chapter 20 The Fear of True Expression 117
Chapter 21 How Emotional Immaturity Keeps Us Stuck.................121
Chapter 22 Perfect Divine Souls Wrapped Up in a Big Mess........... 125
Chapter 23 The Question You're Afraid to Ask 127
Chapter 24 No Bad Souls, Just Bad Choices..................... 129
Chapter 25 The Incomplete Stories of Our Lives.............. 132

Chapter 26	How Grown Up are the Grown-Ups in Your Life?	136
Chapter 27	The Many Wounds in the Unworthiness Trap	147
Chapter 28	Freeing Yourself from Survival Consciousness	150
Chapter 29	When the Past Keeps Calling You Back There	155
Chapter 30	The Never-Ending Need for Approval	158
Chapter 31	Seeing the Bigger Picture	162
Chapter 32	The Strength and Courage Within You	167
Chapter 33	The Source of Love You Need	171
Chapter 34	The Courage to Let Go of Your Safety Net	174
Chapter 35	A Call to the Hero Within	178
Chapter 36	Healing Ourselves Out of the Trap	182
Chapter 37	Compassion for the Wounded Child Within	187
Chapter 38	Healing Through a Psycho-Spiritual Process	194
Chapter 39	Raising Self-Awareness	197
Chapter 40	You Are Good Enough because You Are Here	200
Chapter 41	Embracing the Energetic Evolution	203
Chapter 42	Becoming the Real You	207
Chapter 43	Becoming Responsible for Your Life	210
Chapter 44	Self-Forgiveness as a Self-Healing Tool	214
Chapter 45	Compassion as the Ultimate Answer	220
Chapter 46	Reconnecting to Spirit Through the Spiritual Heart	224
Chapter 47	We are Born Creators	229
Chapter 48	Healing through Expressions from the Soul	231
Chapter 49	Embracing Your Spirit	244
Chapter 50	A Special Acknowledgement to My Clients	247

A Special Acknowledgment to the Wounded Souls of My Parents 257
A Letter to My Grown-Up Self 259
References 261

INTRODUCTION

I have often wondered how I could improve my life. I thought about ways I might be able to feel better about who I am and my reason for being in this thought-provoking, sophisticated, and enormously challenging world. I wondered why we all have different lives, even though we all live in the same world. What is the reason some of us are lucky and some of us are not? What makes us choose how we live the lives we live—or do we even have a choice?

I contemplated what it would be like if we all had our own assigned navigator who could walk us through life, so we wouldn't have so many "why" questions from the time we could speak. Some people may say that we do, and that we call this navigator God or Spirit or Higher Self. If this is so, then why is there so much confusion, distrust, and fear around the way our lives unfold? Where was our assigned navigator when we got lost in the throes of this thing called life?

In the midst of trying to figure it all out, I came across an old cliché: we are the creators of our reality. That's quite a bold and provocative statement. All I could think was *What on earth did I create?*

In following this so-called theory, I wanted to know why I had created a life that felt meaningless, empty, and void of passion, and why I was not choosing something different and better.

After years of failed efforts to improve my life—and after years of studying what makes us who we are—I learned the truth. I began to see the bigger picture. We are not the creators of our lives, at least not from the beginning. Life is created for us, and we are not aware of the energetic forces behind the way we navigate it. Nor are we aware of our ability to release their control over us.

As I dived deeper into this truth, I found myself reaching out to what I believe is my personal navigator, which is the divine spirit that lives within me. We can think of this divine source as a higher level of consciousness that lives within each of us and acts as a direct channel to the Creator. This higher consciousness sees the greatness in all of life and directs us back to the higher truth when we go off course.

For us to have the full experience of life, our Creator gave each of us our own individual soul, which takes the form of what we refer to as the "mind." The soul is the spiritual part of us having a human experience. The soul is an energy body that records each and every human experience and determines if its energetic vibration is based in love or fear.

As a certified hypnotist trained in working with the soul and spirit of human consciousness, I help people who feel lost and disconnected find their way back to the spirit within; this divine connection helps them navigate their lives from a higher level of consciousness. Before my clients can reach that higher level, they first have to heal what caused them to disconnect in the first place. As I worked with clients to help them find the source of this disconnect, I became more and more intrigued by the wisdom of soul consciousness. What I found to be most fascinating from those healing sessions was that a disconnect from spirit could begin as far back as conception. What I have discovered through my work is that the disconnect is caused by the absence of the vibration of love, leaving the soul to experience the vibration of fear as it prepares for the physical journey on earth.

Each recorded vibrational imprint of fear that is not released by the soul spreads itself into the cells of the physical body, and these energies are ultimately expressed through the nervous system. It is this collective energy that creates the consciousness that will direct our lives, unless we learn how to live from the higher vibration of spirit.

In the beginning, you came from a divine source of love. Then you entered into an unknown physical reality that was filled with fear from the people already experiencing the challenges of being human. If the flow of love did not continue as you moved from the loving energy of source into the physical world, you may have experienced a disconnect to love, which then recorded an imprint of fear.

Your first human contact is your mother. Mother's vibrational energy gets drawn into your cells as you begin to develop in the womb, thereby creating a vibrational match in your consciousness.

This became quite clear to me as several of my clients experienced emotional trauma that seemed to have its roots in mother's womb. My clients were able to verify that the emotions they were experiencing coincided with each mother's feelings about herself, as well as her life. This led me to look deeper into my own life challenges and patterns of behavior.

This book describes how we have come to be the people we are today. As I share with you some of my childhood memories that overwhelmed my soul with the vibration of fear, I also take you through the ways I was able to heal my life by regaining my trust in the spirit of who I am.

Aside from my own life experiences, I share with you a few narratives of client sessions that indicate that we are conscious and aware beings from the beginnings of life. I and also share some very compelling research that proves the theory that we are not the primary creators of our lives.

I learned, through my research and studies on unconscious human behavior, that I became a burdened soul just like the people who raised me. The people who raised me became burdened souls because of the people who cared for them. The level of consciousness we live our lives from is the energy we put out. The energy we put out easily gets absorbed into the innocent souls of those who are new to the world.

This transfer of energy is like an unavoidable trap, and there is no way out of it unless we learn how to uncreate what was created for us through this energy transfer. This trap will keep you wondering why you are not enough for this world. The consciousness of your soul will keep you working hard at getting some kind of validation for your existence. This means you forgot that you are a miracle of life, on a mission to create from the energy of the spiritual heart, which is your pathway to the spirit within. Once you get pulled into the unworthiness trap, you close off your heart to protect your soul—without realizing that you also cut off your connection to the divine.

Spirit validates you as a miraculous being of light who is simply having the experience of being human so you can use your creative energy in a physical form. When your soul continues to live in fear because of a disconnect from the love that comes from the spiritual heart, you begin to create from the energy of fear. It is the spiritual heart that allows you to remember where you came from and how loved you are by the Creator.

From the first moments of feeling unsafe, unloved, or unwanted, the soul begins to fear the unknown. This creates inner conflict as the inner wisdom that comes from the spiritual heart gets blocked and we begin to develop an ego to keep us safe in the physical world. The only way to return to the higher truth is to open our hearts and reach for divine wisdom.

During this time of spiritual growth for the entire planet, we must learn to forgive ourselves for getting caught up in the same unworthiness trap as the generations before us. We must find compassion for those who could not live by this higher truth because they lived through the energy of fear and survival consciousness. We must learn how to do better, even though the generations before could not.

Not only are we not the creators of our lives, we are a collective energetic blueprint of all the lives before us that affected our lineage.

Once we can make sense of how our lives have been created for us, for our parents, for our other primary caregivers, and for all who came before them, we will have a higher understanding about being human and how life works. Once we understand how our sense of self is distorted by the emotional energy within this collective consciousness, we can do soul-healing work and create the lives we deserve. We can start by expressing ourselves from the depths of our souls instead of allowing our pent-up emotions to express themselves through the nervous systems of our bodies.

The energetic forces of fear that have caused your innocent soul to distrust your own creative energies did not start with you. They started a long time ago and are expressed through you, just as they have been expressed through the people who passed this energy on to you. This is a generational issue of disconnect from the spiritual heart that has kept many good souls stuck in a trap, limited in life, and controlled by the fear of nonlove.

One of the ways to express the feelings of the soul and release the emotions that create fear is through writing letters. Writing letters causes you to slow your body down and lets your suppressed emotions surface from within you. As you feel the energy of each suppressed emotion rise up, you will be able to feel how heavy the energy is and realize how this energy is holding you back from your greatness. When these emotions surface and you put your feelings about them on the paper in front of you, you give them the voice you wish you'd had when you couldn't speak up or were afraid to.

Through written letters from the soul of the voiceless inner child, I allowed myself to express the pain and fears that were recorded in my soul. The emotional experiences of being cared for by adults who had failed to grow up, evolve, and live from a higher level of consciousness kept my soul fearful of a life that I longed to enjoy. After years of spiritual practice and understanding more about human consciousness, I realized that I needed to let go of old thought patterns in order to embrace this higher truth that seemed reachable yet distant from my reality.

As I wrote letters to myself and others, I started to notice how much lighter I felt. I learned that it was important to express all that I felt inside of me from a higher level of consciousness. This made writing the letters more of a therapeutic exercise for becoming a better version of myself, rather than giving power to victimhood.

When you have a part of you that needs closure with yourself or with someone else, you can find that closure through writing. By writing letters to yourself and others, you allow your voice to be heard, even if it's only heard by you. By writing letters that express all that you haven't been able to express, you release the stagnant energy caused by unresolved emotional events that keep your nervous system locked in fear. This release of energy will give your soul feelings of lightness and liberation, which then allows your nervous system to relax.

The voice is a gift from the divine. Being able to voice your feelings through writing is a physical way to express this divine gift. When you were born, you had not developed this gift yet, but your heart had been processing the energy of your feelings and emotions since its development in the womb. This built-up energy must be released from the soul if it is from the energetic force of fear, or you will continue to block access to your spiritual heart.

My hope is that we all benefit from the knowing that we are conscious and aware beings from the beginning of life. By giving our souls a voice, we can release the fear energies that hold us hostage, heal what feels broken in our souls, and release ourselves from the unworthiness trap. As you read through the chapters, you will not only gain deep insight about the connection between your patterns and the patterns of those who had great influence over you, but you may also feel unhealed emotions begin to surface. There are blank pages at the end of book, provided for the purpose of writing down any thoughts or feelings that arise as you read through each chapter. I suggest that you include in your notes which chapters brought valuable insight, so you can refer back to them as you are doing the writing exercises included in the book. The book also includes sample letters to guide you through the writing process.

As you read through this book, you will begin to realize the bigger picture and how much generational trauma plays into your life. The bigger picture not only shows you how you learned to navigate your life, but how those who cared for you learned to navigate their lives from those who cared for them. There is an untold story behind every story you tell yourself. There is a higher truth we must reach and understand about consciousness. We must realize that since we are all human, we all share the same emotional need—the need to feel worthy and acceptable to the world. The healing of ourselves and the end to this emotional trap can only come from the spiritual heart of love and compassion.

Within the higher truth is the true and essential you that is waiting to emerge. Your true self has been hidden in the shadows of fear because you have been surrounded by unconscious fears since the beginning of life. When you learn the truth behind the fears you and others carry, how these fears are unknowingly expressed into the world, and how fear changes the well-intentioned soul, you will reach an understanding that can change the way you see yourself and others. This is the higher truth for all of us. This is the understanding that will free us from the unworthiness trap.

As you read through this book, please pause when you receive any insights, aha moments, trigger flashes, or emotions surfacing from within you as you process the information. Write down what comes to you in the personal notes section. Your personal notes will assist you during the healing process provided at the end of the book.

Now, let's start this journey from the beginning.

> Deep within is our pure being which has incarnated into this body. This being is ultra-sensitive. From the moment of conception this pure being is picking up subtle impressions from the environment through the heart center of pure feeling.
>
> Dr. Mark Sircus
> *Heart Health-*
> *The Vulnerability of Being*

CHAPTER 1

A Conversation with Spirit

Spirit: Welcome to your day of conception, little zygote.
Zygote: Well, thank you. Why do you call me little zygote?
Spirit: A zygote is the cell that is formed when a female reproductive cell and a male reproductive cell join. That is what you are right now.
Zygote: Where am I? I feel like I'm in some kind of container.
Spirit: This container you refer to is a sacred place. It is the womb of the female whom you will call Mother in the physical world. You will develop in your mother's womb over the next nine months as you prepare for your entry into the physical world. During this time, you do not have a separate consciousness. Your consciousness is blended with the consciousness of Mother. All of Mother's thoughts and feelings will be yours for the next nine months.
Zygote: I hope Mother's thoughts are kind and loving. What if they are not? Will I have those thoughts also? Will I feel her bad feelings?
Spirit: Yes, little zygote. There is a good possibility that you will feel what Mother feels. Unfortunately, Mother is not aware of many of her thoughts and feelings, and also is not aware of how they affect you.
Zygote: I seem to be aware of others around Mother. Who are they?
Spirit: You already have awareness of all that is happening around you. This is called your environment. This is the environment that you will become a part of when you are born into the physical world. You are aware of the thoughts and feelings of all others Mother closely interacts with, including the male whom you will

refer to as Father in the physical world. This is the male whose cell bonded with Mother's cell to create the zygote you are now. Everything you are aware of could have a great impact on you. If the thoughts and feelings of others are kind and loving, they will have a positive impact on your well-being. If the thoughts and feelings of others are unkind, unloving, or fearful, then they could become complexes within you. Complexes become heavy burdens in your body. Unfortunately, you will not learn the words to express what you are feeling until these complexes have already become a part of you and have created what you believe is your identity. Your identity is how you view yourself and how you will present yourself to the world.

Zygote: What are complexes and burdens?

Spirit: Complexes are related emotional thoughts and ideas. Depending on your sensitivity level, they can get partly or completely suppressed in your soul, causing conflicts and unhealthy behavior. Burdens are the complexes that weigh heavy on your soul and drain your soul's energy. Many of these thoughts and feelings will be out of your awareness. They will be so deeply embedded in your soul that you will not know they are driving your behavior.

Zygote: I have a soul?

Spirit: Yes, little zygote, you have a soul. Your soul is the energy body that chose to have a physical experience with you. Your soul is the driving force behind your physical structure. It will help direct your life based on what it feels and learns from your experiences in the physical world. While you are in the womb, your soul floats in and out of your physical body and will join you fully at birth. Your soul picks up on all the impressions of your environment, which will then become imprints on your soul. Unhealthy imprints become the complexes of the soul.

Zygote: Wait! Wait just a minute! Let me get this straight. I am this tiny thing inside a big, comfy container. I have awareness of all that is going on outside this container, yet I can't communicate back? You are telling me I have a soul that seems to be like a receiver but can't reject any of the information being received? You are saying my soul can pick up complexes that don't belong to me, and I can't do anything about it? So now, tell me, if others are not aware of what they are passing on to me, how can I make them aware? How can I stop their complexes from becoming mine?

Spirit: Ah, little zygote, that is where the earthly challenges are. You may also be affected by the thoughts and feelings of your mother's mother, a woman you will refer to as Grandmother in the physical world. You see, you were just an egg in Mother's womb when Mother was in Grandmother's womb. As an egg, you were already absorbing energy that comes from the thoughts and feelings of Mother and Grandmother. Grandmother in turn is affected by the energy of her mother's and grandmother's thoughts and feelings. So you see, little zygote, much of your identity was determined way before you entered your mother's womb.

Zygote: Yikes! The physical world sounds complicated. What am I doing here, and how can I fix the mess I am getting myself into?

Spirit: You are here to learn many things. Many of these things will help you grow and develop in a healthy way, and many will stifle your ability to thrive. It is up to you to learn how to recreate the life that will be created for you by others. You must learn how to use your life experiences for learning and spiritual growth, so you can prevent the creation of a false identity.

Zygote: Well, then, that's easy. I'll just choose the thoughts and feelings that help me grow.

Spirit: Wonderful, little one. Now you're getting the idea! Unfortunately, it's not that easy. You see, little zygote, when you are born and through your childhood years, you depend on others to teach you, by their own actions and inactions, who you are and what your place is in the physical world. These others are referred to as grown-ups. Everything they teach you, whether it's right or wrong, fair or unfair, kind or unkind, or loving or unloving, becomes the truth for you. It is up to you to unlearn what you learned and relearn what you know from a higher place within you. Within you resides the truth of who you are. Your challenges will be that many grown-ups are stuck in what is called the unworthiness trap, which means they have disconnected from their true selves because they felt unworthy of love. Therefore, they have failed to act and teach from a place of love. They have complexes trapped in their souls that cause them to act and teach from a place of fear. The unworthiness trap includes many emotions that make grown-ups feel like they are not valuable enough for the world. When grown-ups feel this way, they become afraid of the world and then unknowingly teach others to be afraid of the world. When grown-ups get stuck in the unworthiness trap, they are not aware that they are pulling the souls of the people they love into the trap with them. You must learn the value of self-love before you can learn how to free your soul from this trap.

Zygote: This just gets stranger by the moment. Does every new zygote have to go through these challenges? Does life have to be so much work? I'm not sure I can handle this journey. Is it too late to turn back?

Spirit: Oh, dear one, you cannot turn back now. You were sent here by divine order for a divine purpose. Physical life can be a wild ride with many ups and downs, twists and turns, and highs and lows. You must always remain true to your divine self. You are going to be OK. Remember, you are here for a reason. You must learn to believe in yourself. You must know you are capable of all things, especially change. You must know that every difficult experience gives you an opportunity for soul growth and healing. Learning means unlearning what doesn't serve you and then learning what your soul needs for continued soul growth in your lifetime.

Zygote: That's great! Tell me how to do that.

Spirit: Be patient, little one. You must learn these things yourself. It's all part of the human experience. There is a spiritual resolution for all earthly challenges, and you must use the wisdom of your true divine self to find your answers. Your story is already in progress, and you are only the size of pea. Your story can change if you are willing to recreate it. The important part is to keep your heart open, even when life gets difficult.

Zygote: My heart?

Spirit: Yes, little zygote, you will develop a heart. The heart is the first organ to develop in the physical body. What is important to remember is that your heart is your connection to your divine self

Zygote: and infinite source of love. You must not worry, little one. I will always be here with you.

Zygote: What do you mean, *you will always be here with me*? I don't even know who you are.

Spirit: Well, little zygote, I am you. I am your spirit. I am that higher place within you that I mentioned before. I am here to help you stay connected to the love of your Creator while you take this physical journey. Please rest in the comfort of knowing that I will be guiding your soul in this lifetime. If you keep your heart open, you will receive divine guidance, but you must listen to the subtle messages. You must remember who you are. You are not the thoughts and feelings of others, but you must learn how to know the difference. You will not learn that until you are ready to grow up and become more conscious and aware. Some humans never emotionally grow up and will keep passing their complexes on to other innocent souls. You will misread and misinterpret many of your experiences with others and the world. That is the challenge. You do not have enough perceptive resources to discern between truth and nontruth while you are still in the growing phases. You must depend on others to show you the way. Many of these others are grown-ups who have failed to grow up. You have much to learn and unlearn, little one. It's important that you learn how to express yourself from the heart, even those feelings that are uncomfortable for you. If you hold them inside of you, you will get stuck in the trap. If you get stuck in the unworthiness trap, you will lose your connection to me. Stay in your heart and always reach out to me when you need guidance.

I wish you well on your journey.

CHAPTER 2

The Journey

Life can only be understood backwards; but it must be lived forwards.

-Søren Kierkegaard

So here you are in the full experience of life and all that life is: the good, the bad and the ugly. Are you satisfied with how your life is today? What are you feeling right now as you contemplate the answer? Did you smile? Did you sigh? Did you question my question?

The most important thing about living in the physical world is that you become aware enough to be able to make sense of your presence here. You are able to understand your relationships with yourself and others and honestly work toward your spiritual growth. All in check? Most likely not. Life is just too challenging to keep a steady balance with this ever-changing world filled with love, hope, fear, uncertainty, and judgment. Certainly, no life is perfect, but there are ways to make the journey a less challenging one.

The best way to navigate this world is to understand how you got where you are now. You entered into a world where you were fully dependent on the grown-ups in your life. You had no choice because you were helpless. But you're here now, reading this book, which means you survived and you are no longer helpless. That's good. What if these grown-ups didn't make you feel confident, secure, loved, wanted, appreciated, and valuable? That could be bad. Now, what if your caregiver's inability to care for you in the way you needed them to affects who you are today? That's where it may get ugly. It means you may feel cheated because you were not nurtured and supported in this lifetime the way you needed to be. This is how complexes get created and eventually burden the soul.

You may not have been given the opportunity to fully grow up if you were raised by people who didn't fully grow up. This means you may be mentally, emotionally, or spiritually suppressed through no fault of your own. Now your life is not going the way you want it to. You find yourself on an endless search for a miracle that is going to lift you out of your mediocre life.

Many of us stay stuck where we are because our energy is directed at blame. Our low vibrational energy body is expressing itself through the low vibration of judgment. If we blame our unfulfilled lives on the people who cared for us growing up, then the people we blame should blame the people who cared for them when they were growing up. The blame game can go back to the beginning of physical life. We all came into the world from a divine source of love. We lost that nurturing, warm feeling when we first experienced feelings of nonlove during our physical journey. Each generation that lived in fear unknowingly passed some of that energy on to the next generation. This makes the blame game a useless and ineffective way to feel better about our lives. It only expands the low energy that is already keeping us stuck where we are.

Maybe you blame yourself for not measuring up to those whom you needed validation from. Maybe you blame others because they have judged you, criticized you, abused you, neglected you, or just never showed up for you. Well, here's the real truth. *You can't blame anyone*, especially yourself. The way your life turned out is a matter of awareness, or lack thereof, on the part of those who have the ability to influence you. Sound confusing? Let me break it down.

Every child who comes into this world is a miracle of life. That includes you. Yes, you, the one reading this book. Now stop looking for the miracle, because you're it! You are a miracle of life, an expression of the all-loving Creator, filled with divine energy that can never be destroyed. What you need to look for is the higher truth—the part of life that you haven't discovered yet.

You see, your life is yours, and you can create it the way you want to. Here's the catch: first you have to uncreate what was created for you, because what was created for you is not the real you. The real you has yet to be discovered by you and only you. The soul of who you are has been tainted by the expectations of others, causing you to find a way to fulfill those expectations to avoid rejection by the world. When you spend your life trying to avoid rejection, you forget about the perfect miracle that you are. You devote all your energy to seeking acceptance from others, while looking to blame someone or something for your feelings of inadequacy.

The real you has become a thing of the past. You now live by your created, false self that is in conflict with the real you. It is this inner conflict that keeps you stuck in the unworthiness trap. To pull yourself out of the trap, you must heal the inner conflicts that keep you disconnected from the higher truth.

The way we conduct ourselves in this world, including how we think, act, and feel, falls under the realm of psychology. Psychology is the study of the mind and human behavior. Another word for mind is "psyche." Psyche or mind is a way to describe the place where your thoughts come from. Psyche comes from the Greek word *psyche*, which means "the soul, mind, spirit, or invisible animating entity which occupies the physical body." [1] That means human behavior is governed by an animating entity within us. What is this animating entity within us? Is it something we control, or are we controlled by it?

This animating entity within you is your soul. It is your mind on every level, your developed personality, your desires for life, your divine gifts, your energy body, and your individual divine essence. Your soul is your energy body that has been absorbing the energy of others since the

---

[1] http://www.vocabulary.com/dictionary/psyche

beginning of life in the womb. Your soul is affected by every physical and emotional trauma you have experienced since your inception. Throughout this book, I will refer to trauma as a broken connection to self, others, and spirit, causing emotional stress to the soul.

No matter what or how many soul traumas you have experienced in this lifetime, you are and always will be a pure light source of spirit energy connected to the all-loving Creator. That is the truth of who you are. When you express yourself through the energy of fear, you are expressing yourself through an energy that is not from your true energy source. It is an energy trapped inside of your true energy source.

You came into this world for a purpose, and part of that purpose is to give and receive love freely through your spiritual heart. When the spiritual heart becomes blocked by the energy of fear, the flow of love is impeded. Because of your many soul traumas and the pockets of fear energy trapped within you, you are blocked from your ability to live fully from the spiritual heart and through the soul essence of who you really are.

Your burdened soul is an energetic body filled with imprints and impressions of negative emotional experiences that keep you in an emotional feedback loop, also known as the unworthiness trap. Every negative emotion feeds the soul with more negative energy, thereby accumulating a heaviness within you. This heaviness prevents you from living life through a higher level of consciousness, causing you to unconsciously create more negative emotional energy. You have absorbed into your soul the pain of others, and then you are triggered by unpleasant childhood memories that deepen your pain.

What you may not know is that soul memories are distorted because they were recorded during a fear level of consciousness. They remain your perception of who you and others are in this world. You do not have the full story, and you cannot see the bigger picture. Trauma freezes us in our pain, creating imprints of deep emotional wounds that disturb the true essence of the soul. You only know, from the level of consciousness that you had at the time, that a situation made you feel bad about yourself or caused you to fear your new environment. This fear breaks your trust in the love that you were deeply connected to before you entered into this physical reality. Suddenly, you start to question why you have been abandoned by the loving source of the Creator. You begin to question your value.

As a fetus, newborn, or small child, you didn't have the cognitive ability to understand your environment, nor could you form words to narrate your experiences. Everything was marked into your soul as imprints. When you become an adult, your mind tries to sort them out so you can make sense of them, but it can't. There seems to be no basis for these uncomfortable thoughts and feelings. Even though they are not part of your conscious awareness, they are very much a part of your soul, and they affect the way you perceive yourself and the world.

Every decision you make is based on what you are experiencing in your soul. Most of what you are experiencing is a story that is missing pieces. Your mind fills in the blanks because it needs a narrative. You now have distorted memories causing a distorted reality that you live by. Your story becomes your version of who you are, how the world operates, and how you fit into it. Much of what is contained in your distorted version of life comes from fear-based ego consciousness.

You see, the ego mind is very clever. It can create strategies and make up stories for your protection. Even though your soul might feel broken, unworthy, and unlovable, your clever ego mind will find a way to blame others for your inability to feel whole. The blame game is the easiest way out of taking responsibility for your life. It keeps you stuck in the unworthiness trap. You get to pass your emotional burdens on to others, just as they were passed on to you.

The only way to stop passing it forward is to understand the bigger picture and realize that you are not the only one stuck in the trap. Unfortunately, many of us are stuck in the same trap. Everyone who caused you pain was in their own pain. We are all affecting and infecting each other with our soul burdens because we are all fighting for feelings of worthiness. The only way out is to grow up and take responsibility for your life. This means you will have to release yourself from the need for your life to be different than it was. When you spend all your energy trying to change what cannot be changed or wishing it were different so you could feel differently, you will eventually break down from emotional exhaustion.

Life will never be perfect. It was not perfect for those who came before us. We can hold on to what we wanted it to be and what we needed it to be, or we can look back at the past and say, "I can do better now because I know better now." This is called growing up. This is what will set you free from the prison of the falsely created self. This is what will release you from the trap.

The journey can be an interesting and enlightening experience. The only reason it may not be for you is because you are still hooked into the energy of the unworthiness trap. This energy knows no boundaries. It just traps innocent souls at their most vulnerable times in life. To create a lighter journey and a more carefree way of life, you must heal the soul and lift yourself into a higher level of consciousness. This can only be done when you can see the bigger picture around the way your life is playing out. At some point, we need to take responsibility for our lives and understand that we can't change consciousness for anyone but ourselves.

CHAPTER 3

How Your Life Was Created for You

The well-accepted theory is that we are the creators of our lives and the masters of our games. We become what we choose to become. You create vision boards, you meditate, you get energy healings, and you soak your soul in a sound bath. Wow, that stuff sure feels wonderful. It's like a cleansing of the soul. So how come you're still stuck in life?

Your conscious efforts to heal your soul and create more peace in your life are in conflict with the complexes embedded deep within your soul that cause you to believe you are unworthy of anything good. Those wonderful feelings cannot last. The unconscious feelings of unworthiness are not going to go away because you set the intention that they don't exist within you. Your conscious intentions are fighting against the unconscious feelings of unworthiness that are trapped inside of you.

You see, beautiful, divine source of love, you can't superficially heal a soul that is stuck in the unworthiness trap. The theory that you are the creator of your life has its limits. These limits are the ones imposed upon you by the grown-ups in your life because they were living through a false sense of self because of the fears surrounding their lives. Although you came to into this world as a perfect miracle, you also came into a world where many good souls live with the fear of unworthiness. They dragged you into the trap as they did their best to guide you. They were conflicted, and now you are conflicted.

The Voiceless Soul

Are you good enough? Are you truly a divine source of perfection, or has your value been compromised by what others caused you to believe? You might say that no one can devalue you, and that is true. The thing is, you have imprints in your soul that cause you to devalue you—and that is the conflict you are stuck in.

You can't create anything you want until you uncreate what keeps working against you.

Your false identity was chosen for you by the grown-ups in your life because you were too young and too unknowledgeable to create your own identity from the divine source within. You were influenced by those you trusted to teach you about who you are in this big, scary world. Those grown-ups who helped to create your identity are also physical beings with souls that have been greatly influenced by the grown-ups in their lives. And there lie the challenges of the world. The majority of the world is experiencing life from a false identity because life was created for them.

And then you grow into a teenager, searching for autonomy and your own belief system, which gets confused with the belief system already imbedded within you. Boom! You stay in constant conflict. These conflicts cause confusion for the soul. Am I safe in the world? Am I not safe in the world? Who will save me if I need saving?

We all experience life from the energy of the soul. This is where all of our unconscious thoughts and feelings are and where we hold suppressed emotions that are always seeking an outlet through us. Our thoughts and feelings are not just our own, but those that our souls absorbed along the trail of life. Our intellectual minds believe they are the boss, but they are not. That is the painstaking lesson of being human.

The ego mind, which is our protector from the cruel world of judgment and rejection, wants to run the show. The problem is it doesn't have the power over the soul that it thinks it does. The ego is that part of our personality that helps us live life through a false facade, so our perceived flaws are not seen by the world. Hats off to the ego for its strength and determination to keep us safe. What the ego doesn't do so well is gracefully handle the triggers that cause the soul to re-experience the fear the ego is protecting. Whoops! That's when we lose control of our egos, and we become reactive toward those who got under our skin and right into those cellular memories of feeling unworthy.

The ego is not a bad part of you. It is a part of you that you set up to keep you feeling safe from what you felt was an assault on your well-being. It was you who called in the ego consciousness when you needed to create an acceptable part of you to counteract the parts of you that you believed were rejected. The ego is you just playing it safe in what your soul believes to be an unsafe world.

The difficult part of soul healing is that we don't have easy access to this part of us. We placed ego walls of protection in front of those memories that caused us to feel bad about who we are. We don't know what is true and what is not. We only know that the bad feelings feel true because they are very disruptive in the thinking mind. What we don't know is how these feelings gained so much power over us. We also don't know where they began and where they gained momentum. We also don't know what complexes have been passed on to us by others who we trusted.

Guess what? It doesn't matter. Every thought and feeling you have about yourself now belong to you. No one can change any of them except you. These are heavy burdens for the soul to carry and difficult burdens to let go of. You're stuck and don't know how to get unstuck. Where does that leave you? It leaves you in a stagnant state of consciousness where you unconsciously live through repetition driven by energetic patterns embedded in the soul.

The past is over, which everyone already knows. I am not going to be the one to tell you to "let it go." Why? Because it's a useless cliché. You can't let it go—it's a part of you now. Intellectually knowing your past—including the good, the bad, and the ugly—is not the problem. The problems are the bad and the ugly imprints of energy that are still active in your soul from a long time ago. These are the energy imprints that are driving your emotions and behaviors today.

The Voiceless Soul

This does not mean you have to continuously feel like a victim in this world, nor does it mean your parents or other primary caregivers have intentionally wronged you. We are all just human beings sharing this physical world—having the good, the bad, and the ugly experiences that we let define who we are. We believe we have full control over our emotions and behaviors. Then oops, there go those funky, unwanted, knee-jerk reactions again. It makes you wonder how much control we really have. People living with unhealed trauma either become the victimizer and take control over others as a survival strategy implemented during their own experiences of trauma or they become the victim who has become emotionally weakened in the fight for acceptance, making them the perfect prey for the victimizer. I have worked with many clients whom have become stuck in the narcissist and the empath relationship that seemed to be filled with emotional instability, power struggles and a great need for self-love. Each partner is in a battle within themselves. Each partner is unaware of what drives their behavior.

We are not mindful of the driving force that controls the way we navigate our lives. We did not create the initial energy imprints within our souls, but we are reinforcing them every day. We unconsciously set up protective strategies to keep these inferior feelings about ourselves and the world out of our awareness. The same go-to strategies you used as a child will be the same strategies you call in during similar incidents as an adult. When this happens, you are an adult acting like a child. This includes running away, hiding, shutting down, or showing your badass, angry side. None of these reactions come from the spiritual heart. Reactive behavior is you not loving you. When you are not loving yourself, you are vulnerable to the less-than-love actions and inactions of others.

You were never taught to love yourself. You were taught to listen, obey, follow the rules, not make mistakes, not feel your feelings, and be like the adults in your life. You were asked to act like a grown-up by those who never grew up themselves. No wonder your soul feels confused. We are not sure how to find acceptance in a world filled with fear and judgment.

You can continue to intellectualize the reason you act the way you do, but you will not change a thing. You can do all the positive mind exercises you want, but you will just keep getting pulled back into that unworthiness trap. This is why so many people fail at making the law of attraction work for them. The universe responds to the vibrational energy coming from your soul, not the intentions of your conscious mind. The universe does not respond to what you say you want; it responds to what you believe you deserve. For the law of attraction to work for you, it's important to bring all parts of you into alignment with the higher truth. If your soul feels unlovable, then you will have unconscious beliefs that you are not worthy of what you are asking for.

The law of attraction works for everybody. If you are in alignment with your higher truth, you will experience the miracle that you are. If you are attracting negative energy into your life, then you have to heal the negative energy imprints within you for that to change. If you want radical change in your life, then you need to examine the whole picture, which is a whole lot bigger than what you can see in front of you. I am going to lay it out for you in this book, so you can make more sense of your life. Once you gain the knowledge of how life actually works, then you can use that knowledge to uncreate what has been holding you back from fully experiencing your divine essence. You will be able to navigate the journey from a higher level of consciousness instead of hiding behind your ego.

As you learn more about how you have been living through a false sense of self, you will begin to embrace the miracle that you are. As the famous cliché dictates, "The truth will set you free."

CHAPTER 4

How We Get Stuck in the Unworthiness Trap

> Forgive yourself for not knowing better at the time. Forgive yourself for giving away your power. Forgive yourself for past behaviors. Forgive yourself for the survival patterns and traits you picked up while enduring trauma. Forgive yourself for being who you needed to be.
>
> —Audrey Kitching

There is a human unworthiness trap, and many of us are falling into it. Let's start with the fact that you were greatly influenced by the grown-ups in this world, many of whom were stuck in their own emotional trauma. These grown-ups kept creating more emotional drama by not taking responsibility for the way they navigated their lives. And now *you're* the grown-up. Who is influencing your life now? You are. Now you're the one holding the trapdoor. You get to invite others in. As long as their energy bodies resonate with yours, they will walk right into the trap with you.

A soul that experiences nonlove for the first time enters the unworthiness trap without realizing it. From that very first moment of nonlove, the soul begins to search for love. Its existence in the physical world depends on it. The search becomes endless because we, as souls that need love, keep looking outside of our own divine essence to find love. We unconsciously yearn for the love of the source from which we came, but we don't always receive that love the way we need to during our physical journey. As we continue to search for love in a world of grown-ups experiencing fear, we begin to fear it is we who are unlovable. This fear energy pulls us away from our divine essence and into the world of survival that our caregivers became trapped in.

When we came into this world, we had to depend on others to show us love, because love in the physical world means the safety of our physical existence. Many of us have received the warmth and comfort of a nurturing mother or other caregiver at our start in life. As time goes on, that feeling of security begins to fade. We feel less and less of our Creator's love and depend more and more on love from those who care for us. When that love is nonexistent or becomes inconsistent, we begin to question our safety. This pulls us more and more toward survival as we experience less and less feelings of love.

Since we became stuck in survival consciousness at the first fear of nonlove, we continue to depend on others to validate us as lovable. The problem is that most of these others have also been depending on others for validation since their first feelings of nonlove. If we keep depending on others for our self-worth, then we keep searching outside of ourselves for something that is already within us.

That is how innocent souls become confused on their physical journey. We forget where we came from. We forget how loved and lovable we are. We forget that we are truly a miracle of life.

The first feeling of nonlove causes our souls to contract for safety. It's an automatic, physical response to fear. Each time we feel nonlove, the body contracts again. Eventually our physical bodies become accustomed to protecting themselves from the fear of nonlove. This fear becomes so strong that nonlove becomes an expected reality.

If we don't feel a deep sense of love for the divine beings that we are, we will keep living from our ego consciousness, looking to others for validation and acceptance. We will remain in fear of rejection and judgment. That is what will keep us stuck in the trap. We will keep our bodies contracted for safety instead of relaxed and open to receiving love.

The way out of this cycle of unworthiness is through seeing the bigger picture of your life. This means becoming aware of the patterns in your life and noticing how they lead back to the way you saw life as a child. This will give you a better understanding of where it went wrong and how you became disconnected from your true sense of self. As you started feeling disconnected from who you are, you learned to adapt to the expectations of others for safety. That was a good thing. You did what you needed to do so you could avoid possible abandonment. Although you may now know that your primary caregivers had no intentions of abandoning you, it is the consciousness of the soul that leaves the feeling of eternal love and takes the journey into a world that causes it to question its ability to be loved.

After you look at the bigger picture around your life, you will need to expand your awareness around the people who caused life to go wrong for you. These are the people who were emotionally disconnected at the time you most needed connection. There is a story that you haven't heard about their lives growing up. It includes where things went wrong for them when they needed to feel that love source, but it wasn't available.

This is why we keep falling into the trap. This is what makes us feel insecure as we seek the love source from where we came. This feels like rejection and abandonment to the soul all over again. You have never been abandoned by the all-loving Creator. You have unknowingly abandoned parts of yourself when you experienced feelings of nonlove during the physical journey.

We are all repeating the past. Each generation does better than the one before it, but these fears are so ingrained in the energy that runs through the ancestral line that it is not easy to escape.

This is why grown-ups fail to grow up. They are stuck in childhood patterns and don't realize it. Many of these grown-ups have unmet childhood emotional needs that cause them to seek ways they can get those needs met, sometimes in childish ways. They are being directed by the soul consciousness of their wounded child selves, who are desperately seeking a love source as a survival mechanism. These are the innocent, confused and conflicted souls who taught you what life is about. They are living through fear, disconnected from the higher truth, and solely dependent on their survival resources.

What we all need is the truth—not only the truth about who we are, but the truth about the experiences of those before us that took them out of their truth. The bigger story fills in the missing pieces to the story you created when you were focused on your fear of nonlove. That is the story in which you are the victim and others are to blame. If you expand your consciousness around the lives of those you blame for your unhappiness, you will see that you are feeling the same pain that they felt. The people who made you feel bad about yourself were fighting against their own distorted memories, which drove their unhealthy behaviors. Unfortunately, their pain may have been unknowingly projected onto you.

Within the bigger picture around your life are the pieces of unresolved emotional trauma that you may not be aware of. You may have the memory of these events, but the emotions attached to them are split off from conscious awareness. These split-off pieces of emotional trauma are sometimes referred to as fragments of the soul, trapped in the space and time of the emotional event. This causes us to feel less than whole without knowing why.

The feeling of being less than whole or of being completely broken up is experienced by many of us, including those adults who didn't meet our childhood needs. Many of us feel emotionally exhausted because the energy of the soul is on a never-ending search for love and safety. This is happening as we go on with our daily lives in the same routine of unconsciously seeking acceptance. It keeps us stuck in fear as we yearn for more energy to fight these debilitating feelings of unworthiness.

Your intellectual mind, which houses your ego, believes that anything that is wrong in your life has nothing to do with you. You are not responsible for it. You are doing your best, and others are not trying hard enough—they have failed you. What happens when you try to tap into those inner feelings? You may notice your mind keeps you focused on something else. Your ego is protecting you from acknowledging those painful feelings of disapproval you may have felt as a child. If your ego won't let you get in touch with the fragmented parts of your soul, then you will never heal the wounds that keep you from knowing your true, divine self. It sure feels like a trap, doesn't it?

You can leave this trap anytime you choose, but first you have to understand that the way out of the trap is through the spiritual heart of compassion. This is the source of love you became disconnected from out of your constant need for approval from sources outside of you. When you were a child, your life depended on approval from those caring for you. You knew this from a very young age. What you didn't know is that you are a miracle of life that came from an infinite source of love, and you don't need approval from anyone. How do you outgrow this false sense of self and release yourself from the energy of fear-consciousness that is permeating your ancestry and the world? It starts with understanding the higher truth.

The world of grown-ups is a challenging one. The challenges are real, and we all must experience them. To release yourself from the cycle of the unworthiness trap, you must start with learning the reasons why so many grown-ups have failed to grow up. You need to look at how their fears caused your fears. You must also look at the reasons they got stuck in that fear-consciousness and didn't seek the higher truth. This will give you the bigger picture.

The expanded picture will show you that you are not the only one who suffers from the fear of nonlove. A look into the expanded picture of trauma, which can go back many generations, means seeing the good, the bad, and the ugly in all of us. It means no more avoiding the darkness. You can't get out of the trap by pretending to be in the light of the all-loving spirit as you ignore the unhealed wounds in your soul. You must actually be deeply connected to the spirit within so you can honor the higher truth and return to your true, essential self. It is that connection that will lead you out of the trap and into the light of higher love.

We love to avoid those painful feelings. We suppressed them for a reason. When the soul is burdened with many unhealed emotions, we will do whatever we can to keep ourselves free from the daunting feelings that can turn our world upside down. We may find ourselves with addictive behaviors like excessive shopping, excessive eating, drinking alcohol, doing recreational drugs, and spending time on social media forums. None of these distraction methods will bring you the peace you desire. If we let ourselves be content in maintaining a state of being that is undisturbed and always seeking pleasure, we will never do the work it takes to heal the soul.

Many people in today's world have found peace through meditation, yoga, prayer, and energy work. These methods all bring peace to the soul, but that peace will be temporary unless the people engaging in these soul-healing activities are also in touch with the truth of who they are. If you want to bypass the feelings that are deep within you and Band-Aid yourself with spiritual practices, you will still remain stuck in the trap, always seeking love and approval. This avoidance of pain will prevent your soul from reaching its highest vibration and prevent you from exploring life like the miracle you are.

Because of the criticisms we faced as children, we live in fear of being judged. Some adults are very critical because they were heavily criticized as children. They got stuck in the pattern they grew up with. Being criticized is painful to the heart; it makes you question your value. When a child is criticized, it doesn't mean the child is not being loved. Much of a caregiver's love is blocked by their own internal fears of unworthiness, which causes them to project their criticisms about themselves onto others, unconsciously pulling those they love into the unworthiness trap.

I am not making excuses for those who are stuck in the trap and could not meet our childhood needs for love and safety. I am sharing an understanding that will help you release the pain that comes with those moments of nonlove. I am sharing the truth so you don't place the blame on yourself or on anyone else. We all need love, but fear we will never have it. This keeps us confused and conflicted about the journey we are on.

Love is our life force. The fear of not being loved and the fear of losing love are like being unable to breathe. Lacking love is like lacking oxygen. It makes you weak and vulnerable and eventually takes you down. That is why the trap is so powerful. It can suck you in the moment you feel unworthy of love.

Deep soul healing comes from knowing that your soul is worthy of the love that you wanted from others. Deep soul healing comes from the knowing that you didn't receive the love you wanted because those you wanted it from didn't receive the love they wanted. We can keep going back through all the generations, but I think you are starting to get the bigger picture.

We were all zygotes from the beginning. We all became products of those who came before us. It was important for us to come into a world filled with love so we could prosper from the light and love within us. Unfortunately, this earthly journey has many emotional challenges, and many souls got caught up in the chase for love, safety, and survival. This is where we become disconnected from ourselves and others. This is not living from the spiritual heart. This is us in a fight for acceptance in a world filled with judgment.

So now, beautiful soul that you are, it is time to learn the higher truth. It is time to realize that we are all capable of getting stuck in the trap, even though we are all deserving of love. It's time to see how feelings of nonlove make many of us believe we are the ultimate victims.

The unworthiness trap is a real human trap that holds us in a place of fear. These fears keep creating more fears. If we can understand how this trap works, then we can learn how to outwit it and stand fully in our spiritual power. When the ego is fighting with the fear of nonlove, it continues to create the fear of nonlove in others. We need to stop the moving train, dig deeper into the truth about life, and step into our fears from the spiritual heart so they can be seen for what they really are—the illusion of nonlove.

CHAPTER 5

Trauma in the Womb

The womb is a very sacred space. This space is more than just a place that provides nutrition to a developing fetus. It also serves as the space where the soul will become acquainted with its new vessel. This is the vessel that will be the physical vehicle for the soul to experience the physical world.

The soul of the unborn fetus picks up the vibrational energy that surrounds the womb. Diagram A on the following page shows how we emit a field of energy around us based on the emotional and physical state within our bodies. This energy is felt by those who are sensitive to energy—like the developing child.

Vibrations of Energy

Energy from father of child gets absorbed into the energy field of mother. The energy mother receives gets absorbed into the soul of the child.

If the energy feels threatening to the soul of the child, the child's soul records sensations of danger that stay with the soul and trickle down into the nervous system.

If the energy feels loving, the soul records sensations of safety that stay with the soul and trickle down into the nervous system.

The nervous system then responds to life based on how the nervous system receives its information from the energy body (the soul).

Diagram A
Energy Transfer to Unborn Child

The energy of a mother is affected by the environment she is surrounded by and her own thoughts and feelings about her environment. If a mother is anxious or sad because she is bearing a child without the love and support of the child's father, the unborn child's energy body will feel the lower vibrations of these feelings.

The Not So Warm and Cozy Womb Experience

My first witnessing of life in the womb was during my training in past-life regression. Since I was a womb twin survivor, the instructor asked me to be the subject for the class as he demonstrated a womb experience under hypnosis. I was both curious and afraid to re-experience life in the womb, but I reluctantly agreed.

As I sank into the big, soft, cushy chair, which allowed me to lean back just enough to stretch out and release the tension in my body, my instructor started the process. He began with soft, hypnotic words that put me into a nice, deep relaxation. He then started making suggestions for me to move back in time, which, to my surprise, quickly took me out of my body. It was an incredible feeling. I felt like I was floating and yet, at times, I could sense my physical body in the chair.

The next thing I knew, my instructor directed me to go into my mother's womb. And there I was, in the womb. It was like time didn't exist.

At first, I felt like I was being squished. I felt constricted. I couldn't see anything, just darkness. I knew I was no longer in that big, comfy chair. Suddenly, I yelled out in a frantic voice, "I need to get out of here!"

The rest went like this:

Instructor: What's happening?
Me: I'm drowning!
Instructor: Is anyone with you?
Me: Yes, my sister.

Instructor: What is your sister doing?
Me: She's in distress!

At this point, I began to feel a little anxious. Then suddenly I felt something happening. I felt an overwhelming sense of fear. I'm sure the instructor could see the tensed-up muscles through the skin on my face, because I felt like they were going to pop out of my cheeks.

Instructor: What's causing your sister's distress?
Me: Forget it.
Instructor: Forget it? What do you mean?
Me: Forget it. She's gone.
Instructor: She's gone? Where did she go?
Me: I don't know. She's just gone.

The fear grew stronger.

Instructor: Ask her why she left.

That was a strange request because I didn't think I could communicate with someone who wasn't there. I did think about what he asked because I wanted to know the answer. I did not form any words, but I could feel the thoughts coming from somewhere, like something or someone was guiding me. I wanted to know why my sister left me, so I welcomed whatever was coming through me.

And then, out of nowhere, a clear image of angel wings popped up. They were glow-like with a fiery red color and quite large. To my surprise, mysterious words came rolling out of my mouth, like a voice speaking through me.

Me: I was never meant to be on this physical plane. I only came here to guide you.

I was baffled by these strange words coming from my own mouth. I had never spoken that way before. I didn't know what made me say that. It all seemed surreal.

Instructor:	Can you tell what Mom is feeling?
Me:	She's weak. She's not a strong woman.
Instructor:	What do you mean?
Me:	She not strong. She's weak.

As I said those words, I felt a deep sadness inside of me. My whole body began to feel very heavy. This experience under hypnosis felt like I was, in that moment, inside my mother's womb. It all felt so real and yet dreamlike. Did I make it all up? It was so clear—the images, the voice, the feelings. I couldn't have made it up.

I did not question my mom about my twin sister after that session because I had heard the story many times. I knew my twin had not survived, and I knew the umbilical cord being wrapped around her throat was the culprit. I believed, during that experience, that I called my mom a weak woman because of her inability to stand up to my father. That means I was experiencing a memory from when I was older and no longer the memory of the womb. That means my conscious mind was also engaged in the process during the womb experience.

Did I use my conscious mind to create a story I was already familiar with? I could have, but the feelings in my body were strong. The anger about my sister being gone from the womb felt real. The sadness I felt when asked how Mom was feeling was real. I felt it.

The feelings of heaviness took over my entire body. Was I simply recalling a memory, or was I reliving a memory? Did I actually have conscious awareness during my time in the womb, or was I just remembering something my mother told me? I was so new to the whole experience of being in hypnosis and traveling through time that I remained skeptical for a while.

Several years later, a friend of mine was reading my astrological chart and asked, "What happened to your mother when she gave birth to you?"

I said, "She lost a daughter, so I'm sure she was very sad."

My friend emphatically said, "No, something happened to her physically."

I repeated, "Well, she had just given birth to two babies, and one of them didn't make it."

She shook her head. I was unsure of what she was getting at, but it sure made me curious. Then she asked, "Is your mom still alive?"

I answered, "Yes, she's alive and well."

My friend looked at me with a confused expression on her face.

That evening, I phoned my mom. For the first time, she revealed to me that she had gone into a life-threatening coma after she gave birth that day. A priest was called into the room to give my mom last rites. *Aha!* I thought. That had been the sadness I felt. I had known I was losing my mother.

The heaviness my body had felt in the womb was Mom's body growing weaker from the birthing process. I had just lost my sister, and now my mom was leaving me too. I knew she was weak. I felt it! It was real! The deep sadness was me feeling abandoned, alone, and afraid. I felt all of this from being guided into the womb by my training instructor.

From that day forward, I not only became fascinated by the theory of past lives, but also the theory that the unborn child forms memories.

Was this experience my first experience of feeling alone, abandoned, and unsafe? Was this my first threat of nonlove? Did I also experience Mom's sadness over losing a child? Was this why I always feared losing one of my own? Was this why I always needed a partner in life? Did my womb experience initiate the patterns of loneliness and fear of abandonment that seemed to follow me throughout my young adult life? I wanted to know everything and anything about this experience.

My twin sister died about one hour after birth. I now believe that my twin sister could not sustain life because her soul had already left the physical body when we were in the womb. That was when I felt her leave me. What compounded those overwhelming feelings was my mother going into a coma state, causing me to lose connection with her also. I was all alone.

If a mother loses consciousness during pregnancy, is it possible that the fetus feels abandoned? Did I experience the painful feelings of abandonment twice within a few hours? The feelings are real, but the voice is silent.

Past Life Theory and Womb Consciousness

I am going to touch upon the theory of souls having many lifetimes. The concept that the soul returns over and over again to experience the physical world, commonly referred to as reincarnation, is accepted by many, but is still a controversial subject.

Just as my instructor did with me, the technique for past-life regression sometimes includes taking the explorer through the womb experience before they are directed to go back into another lifetime.

In the book *Past Life Therapy*, authors Dr. Morris Netherton and Dr. Thomas Paul say that each journey begins in the womb. During the fetus's time in the womb, the unconscious mind functions alone, without the support of the conscious mind. Upon birth, the conscious mind becomes available to the newborn, and access to the unconscious mind is closed.

This means the unconscious mind of the fetus during gestation records everything in the environment around the mother. This in turn becomes the internal environment of the child. The authors also say that life patterns are determined in the womb.

In looking at your own patterns in life, you may be surprised to find out that they originated before you were born and maybe even before your mother was born. This is because your mother's inner environment includes not only the thoughts created by her, but also those that were passed down by her mother. Are you getting the bigger picture yet?

In his book *Healing Lost Souls*, William J. Baldwin discusses memories of separation. He claims that when a mother is given an anesthetic during labor, the psychic connection between infant and mother breaks. When this happens, the infant experiences abandonment.

My curiosity about my womb experience led me to learn all I could about womb memories. The more I learned, the more I was convinced that we are conscious and aware beings before our first breath in the physical world. We may not have voices, but our feelings about the experience become etched in our souls.

What if I had had a voice during those brutal moments of fear in the womb? What if I could have expressed my feelings of loneliness and fear of abandonment? If I could have spoken, I would most likely have received the support I needed to help me through my crisis.

There seems to be a universal belief that unborn and newborn children are not conscious and aware beings, making them incapable of forming memories. Science believes it has this one covered. So why do people under hypnosis have real emotional experiences when guided into the womb? If only the unborn and newborn could speak up.

Without a voice, preverbal children have no support for the feelings their little bodies take on. Many of these feelings are fear and frustration because of the confusing and sometimes unstable environment children experience in the womb and during the birthing process.

If I had had the ability to speak out during the confusion around my birth, I could have expressed my feelings and released the heavy tension that filled my little body. I could have been heard and maybe even received emotional support.

If I had been able to verbally express my feelings, it would have sounded something like this:

Dear Mother,

You left me here all alone. First my sister left, and now you are gone. Where did you go? Don't you want me? Who will care for me? What will happen to me? Why does everybody leave me?

I felt you the whole time I was there inside of you. Now I am here in the world, and you are gone. I feel so alone and abandoned. I cannot feel you anymore. We are suddenly separated, and I don't know where you are.

I spent many months with my sister next to me, and she's gone too. We shared a soul connection, and now that connection is broken.

I am afraid I'll always be alone, and I cannot survive alone in this world. I don't know anything about it. Who will be there for me?

I just need you to feel something so I can feel it too. I need to know you are there. I need to know you didn't abandon me.

There seems to be a lot of commotion going on around me. The doctors are frantically trying to save my sister. Her soul has already left her tiny little body, and they don't even know she's gone.

The doctors and nurses don't know how frightened I am. They think I have no awareness of my environment.

Everyone in the room gets quiet as the priest enters. He is going to administer last rites to you, Mom. My little body is trembling with fear, and I am so alone and scared. Where are you? They just treat me like an empty body here, like I have no soul. They are clueless.

I just wait. That's all I can do: wait. I wait for a moment of peace. I wait for a feeling of security. I wait to feel you again. Peace never comes though, because these fearful moments will always be an impression upon my soul, like a scar that never heals. I will always fear the loss and abandonment I feel now.

Sincerely,
The Daughter Who Survived

CHAPTER 6

The Sensitive and Aware Unborn Child

As I worked with clients who felt lost, disconnected, stuck, empty, or unfulfilled, I would guide them into hypnosis and have them follow their feelings to the first time they felt them. At times, my clients would find themselves in their mothers' wombs, feeling anxious, scared, and not ready to be born. As we probed into these feelings further, my clients would discover that their feelings came from something heard or felt while in the womb.

Although a fetus does not have the cognitive ability to understand what is happening in the womb, the adult re-experiences those memories and connects the energetic feeling of being in the womb with the feelings they are currently experiencing. When a client is guided back in time based on the feelings and emotions that are causing them distress in the current moment, they are following the energetic imprint of the emotions back to the original source. Although the client is reliving memories of being in the womb, they still have their adult cognitive abilities, which allow them to describe in words what their child selves felt on an energetic level.

From these sessions, many clients reported that their moms were not ready for them to be born, or their dad told their mom, "We can't afford this kid right now." Another client reported that she had sensed her mother's fear of bringing another child into the world.

One of my clients confirmed a prebirth experience of hearing her mom and dad arguing over money. My client reported back to me that her mom told her she was not planned, and money was tight. Her mother and father fought about her mother going back to work to help support the financial burden of raising a child. Her parents had many disagreements over the entire pregnancy. My client was told that once she was born, her parents relaxed and embraced their precious child.

It was a beautiful story and one that gave my client comfort. My client said she had never felt like a financial burden to her parents. She did say, however, that she found herself worrying obsessively about money. It seems that the client's soul recorded the thoughts and fears of her parents while she was in the womb, causing the client to have the same financial worries.

Another client who was regressed to the womb shared that she was excited to be born. She said she needed to take care of her mother because her mother was sad, and she could make her feel happy. My client could not confirm this story with her mother as her mother had passed away when the client was seven years old. The client did say that she recalled her mother being very distant and unaffectionate. My feeling was that her mother was a very sad woman, and the unborn fetus, as a survival strategy, felt the need to make her mother happy so her mother would accept and love the child.

During another session, a client who was regressed to the womb experienced physical discomfort as I was directing her back in time. I directed my client to go back to a time after conception but before her birth. She began to crunch the upper part of her body, and her neck became contorted. I asked if she was in the womb, and she said no. I asked if she was born, and she replied no. I then realized that she was stuck in the birth canal.

My client became terribly distressed as she re-experienced a traumatic memory of coming into the world. During the session, I told my client to keeping moving through the birth canal. I wanted my client to have the experience of coming into the physical world feeling safe, so she could become aware that the experience is now over and she had survived it. The birth trauma had become a frozen memory in her soul, which meant, on an unconscious level, she was still trying to get to safety.

When my client discussed her experience with her mother, she was told that her mother was rushed to the hospital due to going into labor without warning. My client's mother said she could feel my client begin to move through the birth canal during the ride to the hospital. My client was born with difficulty breathing and lacking oxygen. This trauma might have been the reason my client was experiencing anxiety in her adult life, which could be felt around her neck, throat, and shoulder area.

Another client was experiencing feelings of unworthiness. Our session together led her back to the day she was born. She expressed feelings that her sister didn't want her. She said her sister didn't want to hold her and just wanted to go home. She felt rejected. This story was later confirmed by her mother.

I feel that we need to change the way we treat the incoming soul. I feel we should think about the effects our thoughts and feelings have on others. Even in this day and age, when so much research has already been conducted and there is plenty of evidence of the awareness of the unborn child, there are still many practicing physicians who will not adopt this philosophy. These are the doctors who are in charge of these precious little beings as they make their entry into this world. This lack of acceptance and understanding can be damaging to the newborn's first experience of life.

According to Aletha J. Solter, author of *The Aware Baby*, any complication during labor or delivery can affect the infant. Even if the fetus was well-cared for and felt loved and wanted during the womb experience, a necessary procedure to save the child's life can cause a traumatic start.

If there is a stable and normal birth experience, but the physician is completely uninformed about the child's awareness and its initial shock of going from the warm, safe womb to bright lights and noise, the physician may unknowingly cause trauma to the newborn.

This is why it is so important to make this information mainstream.

From zygote into the world of learning and growing, we are conscious and aware beings. The experiences that have caused us stress on any level can have lingering effects throughout our lifetimes. As of this writing, I have many clients who are still amazed to learn about their womb and birth experiences during our sessions together. Most of the world has not come across this very valuable information—or if they have, they've dismissed it as fairy-tale woo-woo.

I hope that we can help bring more love and peace to the next generation by being more aware of this truth now. As an informed society, we are the hope for the future. I hope that we can create a worldwide understanding about the challenges faced by innocent and sensitive souls as they enter this physical realm.

I also hope that you can honor and accept that you are an innocent and sensitive soul as well. The world has challenged you, but you do not need to hold yourself hostage to the shortcomings of those stuck in this trap. You came into this world as a sensitive soul, and your surroundings may have caused you to believe that you do not belong here. You may have soul imprints of not feeling wanted or accepted. Your sensitive soul was picking up on the lower vibrational energies of others, and you believed you were the cause of their inability to connect with you. Your Creator wants you here because you are on a mission to learn the higher truth and live by it. That is all that matters.

We all have soul challenges, and we all try to overcome them. Many of us from the beginning of life have not been able to do that. We all have consciousness. Having a difficult life can cause that consciousness to become locked in the prison of the unworthiness trap. You deserve better.

In a 2014 TED conference, David Chalmers, philosopher and cognitive scientist, talks about the individual movie playing in our heads. He explains that our movie includes all of our senses, emotions, pain, hunger, memories, scenes from childhood, and a constant voice over narrative. He refers to this subjective experience as our stream of consciousness. Dr. Chalmers suggests that consciousness is the key to understanding the universe and ourselves.[2]

---

[2] TED Conference with David Chalmers (2014) – How do you explain consciousness? https://www.ted.com/talks/david_chalmers_how_do_you_explain_consciousness?language=en.

Dr. Peter Fenwick, neuropsychiatrist, in his discussion on near death experiences, explains his theory that the mind and brain are not the same and that consciousness may exist outside of the brain. His theory, in part, is based on patients whom have gone into cardiac arrest and the brain was no longer able to function. These patients later claimed that they were able to see themselves leaving their bodies and could witness what was happening during such life-threatening incidents.[3]

After the work I have done with my clients, I tend to believe we are highly conscious physical beings from conception, and we receive intuitive information from spirit. We have our own individual experiences that affect the way we see ourselves and the world. Some of these experiences pull us away from our connection to this higher level of consciousness. We are spiritual beings before we enter the physical body. Therefore, we are in existence before the development of a brain. We are that consciousness that exists everywhere and in everything. We are a part of the collective energy of spirit consciousness that emanated from the Creator. This means we are all a part of the all-loving, all-knowing, all-accepting Creator.

We lose the truth of who we are by not understanding our physical journey. We get caught up in the false narratives playing out in our stream of consciousness and find ourselves searching for ways to control the parts of the movie that are disrupting our peace.

Many of my clients, when guided into their mothers' wombs, have expressed that they don't want to come into the world. They feel unwanted by their mothers. They feel a sense of not belonging in this world. This does not mean that the child was not wanted or loved by the mother. It means that whatever feelings the mother was carrying became the feelings of the unborn child. If the mother felt unloved or unwanted by her own mother, then her unborn child might feel the same. This is because the mother is not fully sharing her heart with her incoming child. She is stuck in her own trap of unworthiness. These feelings become the child's fear of entering the world, a place where they feel unwanted.

---

[3] Are Mind and Brain the Same? (NDEs) (2011) by Dr. Peter Fenwick (Dudjom Buddhist & Life Enlightenment) - https://www.youtube.com/watch?v=NAn3T7MHHOM

Another interesting case was a young man who shared, during his womb experience, that his father didn't want him. I asked him what made him feel that way. He said, "He is never around; Mother is always alone."

My client was able to confirm with his mother that during the entire pregnancy, his father remained absent because he didn't want the child. The father insisted that the mother have an abortion. The mother did not share this with her son until he told her about his session with me. The biological father went in and out of my client's life and provided more heartache than happiness because of his inconsistency. My client was feeling rejected by his father way before he even met him.

What if the father was so stuck in the unworthiness trap that he couldn't even recognize the damage he was causing to this incoming soul? Are we that unconscious during the human experience? I believe many of us are, due to living through a distorted reality based in fear consciousness.

What if my client could have spoken out from the womb and expressed the pain his father was causing him as he prepared to come into the world? Would that have changed the father's feelings? Would that have changed my client? Would it have kept my client from falling into the same unworthiness trap that his father fell into?

If my client could have expressed what he was feeling from the womb instead having these energy imprints fester inside of him for most his life, it might have sounded something like this:

Dear Father,

You haven't even met me yet, but I can feel you don't want me. It's not easy to feel this way. I feel unwanted and unworthy of your love. If I come into the world without your blessing, I will feel like I don't belong here. You are not here supporting Mother during our time together. You are not here, supporting my entry into the world. I know I am a huge responsibility. I know you weren't expecting me. But I am here, and I want to be with you.

I can feel Mom's fear of not having your support. I can feel her feelings of rejection alongside my own feelings of rejection. I wish I could say this out loud to you so you could hear me. I wish you knew how much I hurt from your absence.

If you knew how much I hurt in my heart, then you might change your mind. But you can't know because I can't speak my feelings to you. I can only feel what I feel. I will carry these feelings with me for the rest of my life, but I won't remember where they came from.

I will grow up feeling half empty, with expectations of being rejected by the world.

I will fall right into the unworthiness trap that you and Mom fell into.

I will forever wonder why you didn't love me. I will forever wonder why I am not enough for you.

I will have to learn how to be in this world without you. I will have to learn how to love and honor myself, no matter how difficult that may be. I will do the best I can.

Love,
Your Unborn Son

CHAPTER 7

Pre-Birth Consciousness—Undeniable Evidence

After my own womb experience and then witnessing the experiences of my clients, I became quite curious about memories formed in the womb. I knew there was more to learn, and I was hungry for the knowledge. My yearning to find the truth led me on an extensive research expedition. Although I was convinced that we have prebirth memories which can affect the soul of who we are, I was also going against the worldwide belief that this is not possible.

I began my research by reading book after book and numerous articles on prebirth trauma. I subscribed to blogs and YouTube channels on the subject. I was obsessed with learning all I could about the conscious and aware child. I was like a kid in a candy store when I started digging into everything I could find on this subject. There was so much of it, I didn't know what to read first.

I wanted to read good, solid research by people with higher education and expertise. I wanted information that could be trusted. I wanted to know if babies actually have emotional feelings that began in the womb. Or does the mind create false memories? I wanted information from scholars who had actually studied prebirth consciousness. Like the perfect pair of shoes, I found what fit my idea of evidence.

I came across the book *Windows to the Womb: Revealing the Conscious Baby from Conception to Birth*, by David Chamberlain, a psychologist, scholar, and international lecturer. The title immediately caught my eye. I felt like I had found a bag of delicious goodies. As my hunger for knowledge grew stronger, I was excited to dig in. I skimmed through the pages with excitement. The words "birth psychology" popped out at me. Birth psychology? That must be about the mind of the newborn—which was interesting because I had always been taught that the newborn didn't have any thoughts or feelings. I had been taught—and you can still find this theory in books today—that babies are born with only two fears: the fear of falling and the fear of loud noises. I just knew the information in this book would not support that theory.

I read the book from cover to cover with chills running through me. One moment I was thinking, *This is crazy*, and the next moment I was thinking, *This is real. It's solid. It's a whole new understanding for me. I am captivated by all of it.*

In his book, Dr. Chamberlain confirms many of my experiences with clients, including his theory that the unborn child does feel emotions and that memories can be formed during the womb experience.

Several of my clients whom I have regressed back to the womb have expressed feelings of not being wanted by one or both of their parents or a jealous sibling. Dr. Chamberlain speaks of similar cases in his work. I could tell by the expression on my clients' faces that these feelings were deeply felt and painful, but because this was all so new to me, I didn't think the feelings could be real, only imagined. I wanted to believe the feelings were real, but these experiences were the opposite of everything I had been taught.

The most important piece of information I learned from Dr. Chamberlain's work was that, when a client expressed emotions from a womb memory, I could trust that they were recalling a true experience, or at least their perception of it.

As I continued to do my research, I came across a book by Wendy Anne McCarthy called *Welcoming Consciousness*. What I loved reading from Dr.

McCarthy's book was that we have memory beyond local consciousness, allowing us to function outside of time and space.

Many of my clients found themselves having an experience of coming into the world through a divine connection with their mothers, claiming that they knew who their mothers were before they entered the womb.

This is fascinating and truly debunks the theory that consciousness begins when the brain is fully formed. This tells us that we must care for our energy bodies as much as we care for our physical bodies. It is the energy body that existed first. It joined the physical body to have the physical experience. This is why consciousness is already present at conception.

There are many nonfiction books, academic studies, and professional opinions about womb consciousness that most of us have never heard of. It is said by several researchers in the field of prenatal consciousness that:

- life begins at conception
- the cells of the unborn respond to the environment
- mother and baby share experiences energetically
- consciousness can exist outside of the brain and nervous system, which means consciousness exists before birth

If this is so, then you may have been aware of your environment as far back as conception, when you were just a tiny zygote. That's incredible, right? Do you remember when you were just a tiny zygote? Of course not. But somewhere inside of you, that memory exists.

Consciousness is the energy of your soul. Your feelings about yourself, others, and the world come from everything recorded in your soul. For you to understand the force behind the way you navigate your life, you need to discover what recordings in your soul are still playing out.

I can't stress enough how soul healing is essential for a peaceful life. All that wreaks havoc on your soul must be expressed, or you will continue to feel the pressure of those energy imprints getting stronger over time. They get stronger each time you are in a similar experience, because the first impression is still being felt by the soul. The negative feelings that were experienced are in the form of a negative energy, which is a lower vibrational energy in the soul. As the soul continues to yearn for love and acceptance, the ego consciousness for self-preservation gets stronger and stronger, which then takes you further and further away from your divine healing source. You cannot connect with your true, divine self through ego consciousness. You must reconnect to the spiritual heart so you can be guided toward the higher truth.

The hard truth is that we are conscious beings from the beginning. Then we get filled up with other people's energy and lose who we really are. Is this fair? Maybe not, but it's reality. We become what others make us. We become an extension of the people who influence us. We may let go of them, but we retain some of their negative energy in our soul bodies.

From conception and all through childhood, we become less and less of who we are. A false version of self emerges from the imprints and impressions of the soul, and we identify with that false self.

Life is created for us by the thoughts, feelings, emotions, actions, and inactions of others who make impressions upon us, together with our own impressions that we formed about ourselves and the world. Does this mean we are doomed from the beginning? No, not really. We are still conscious and aware divine beings. We can use this information, learn from it, and recreate our lives.

The origin of our struggles in life could lie deep within our souls, taking root way before we could speak. Every subtle impression becomes part of us as we grow and develop in the warmth of our mothers' wombs. Are we born already afraid of the world? According to my womb experience, those of my clients, and examples I provided from my research, we absolutely are. Let's look at more research.

In the book titled *Born Scared*, Julia Ingram discusses the creation of anxiety in the womb, at birth, or in prior lifetimes. In the preface, the author explains how the root of most fears and anxiety can be discovered through the use of hypnotism. Figuring out when, how, or under what conditions such fears were created makes them easier to resolve. I have to agree.

This statement felt like a true testament and further validation of my work as a hypnotist and spiritual life coach. Once I was able to assist my clients in healing their prebirth and birth memories, they felt more peace in their souls and started living more conscious and harmonious lives. This is what I wish for you.

I didn't think I could be the only professional with clients who re-experienced womb or birth memories, but absent solid proof, I did remain skeptical of these experiences. I struggled with what I personally witnessed and the controversial statements made by professionals who claimed otherwise.

This doesn't mean you have to seek out a hypnotist and go back in time to discover where it all went wrong. As you learn more about the way life works, you will begin to release those uncomfortable feelings that you once believed defined you. You will start trusting the divine spirit within.

You will see and accept the miracle that you are.

Stanislav Grof, a Czech psychiatrist and one of the founders of the field of transpersonal psychology, in his book *Psychology of the Future*, says that traditional medicine denies that the child can consciously experience birth or record in their psyche the memory of trauma. He believes that such denial of prenatal memory is astonishing, since it is known that the capacity for memory exists in lower life forms.

In Dr. Grof's work, adult patients who reach consciousness at the perinatal level start experiencing emotions and physical sensations of extreme intensity, often surpassing anything they consider humanly possible.

In or around 1924, the book *The Trauma of Birth* by Otto Rank was published. In this book, the author suggests that the initial source of anxiety comes from the unborn child's separation from the safe place of the mother's womb and entry into the constricted space of the birth canal.

As mentioned before, one of my clients had the terrifying experience of being stuck in the birth canal, which resulted in adult anxiety. Where have we been that we are not acknowledging the significance of memories from the womb?

In this world, we are so unaware of consciousness that it's unsettling. You will see more information on the tables in the pediatrician's office about diapers and baby formula than you will ever hear about a baby's consciousness or how to honor the incoming soul. This has to change. We have got to do better.

According to Shakuntala Modi, in her book *Remarkable Healings,* reports by her hypnotized clients indicate that the fetus feels and records the mother's thoughts, feelings, and experiences and absorbs them as their own. I guess when it is said that a thing "runs in the family," it sure does, but not so much genetically as energetically. Dr. Modi also says memories are recorded in the soul because part of the soul consciousness is connected to the fetus from conception.

There is still a widespread assumption that the fetus is completely unaware of what's going on inside or outside the womb. After witnessing my clients' prebirth and birth experiences, I had to find out if expectant couples were being taught anything about the consciousness of the unborn or the newborn child. I questioned some new young mothers on this subject. They were quite shocked at the thought of their babies having any awareness during pregnancy or infancy. I believe I opened a few minds.

It's important that expectant parents, aside from receiving advice about how to physically care for themselves and their babies, be coached on how to welcome the incoming, conscious, and aware child. I'm baffled that science could be so advanced in our world today and yet seemingly unconcerned about the consciousness of the human soul.

It is widely accepted that the health of the physical body of the mother is important, as it is the mother's physical body that will nourish the fetus during gestation. What is not widely accepted is the existence of consciousness in the unborn child. I personally did not receive one iota of information on the psychological awareness of the fetus or newborn from my obstetrician or pediatrician. If I had, I would have wanted more information. I would have wanted to read books about it. I had already read books about the stages of pregnancy and the growing child, but none of those books mentioned the soul body and how it receives information based on the vibrational energy it comes in contact with. That sounds more like a sci-fi movie than science, but it's a philosophy that we need to embrace.

The Association of Prenatal and Perinatal Psychology and Health (APPPAH) has done many studies to prove consciousness exists within the unborn child. APPPAH was created for the purpose of furthering understanding of the psychology of pregnancy and birth and how pregnant mothers influence the unborn. I believe APPPAH is going to bring more awareness to the world about the consciousness of the voiceless child. Until then, I hope I can prompt you to do your own research.

Every incoming soul deserves a chance to trust their new environment and feel lovingly welcomed. Be the generation that brings this information mainstream. Let the world know that we have been aware from the beginning and are much more aware now. We need to be the voice of the voiceless. This includes being the voice of your own unheard inner child.

We need to understand that life was created for us. Since we are conscious and aware more now than ever before, we can recreate what is not working for us. We can uncreate what was unknowingly passed on to us. We can find it in our hearts to understand that we are all human souls with fears that are so deeply embedded within us that we cannot fully control how we perceive the world. It is these fear perceptions that prevent us from trusting our inner spirit and living from a higher level of consciousness. We are all capable of falling into the trap. Let's be more compassionate for those who don't know how to live beyond their deepest fears.

We are voiceless and aware souls that have lots of pain to release. This is pain that started a long time ago because much of the t world is not supported by compassion. It runs on fear and judgment. Let's stop holding back our feelings out of fear of not being heard or not wanting to be heard.

We need to be heard. We need to know that the feelings inside of us are important, no matter when they started or what these feelings are.

If we could express everything from the beginning, we would speak from this truth.

If I could have expressed my feelings from the womb, it would have sounded something like this:

Dear Mother,

Although I have not yet been born, I am here waiting for the day. Although I cannot respond to your thoughts or feelings with a voice, I can feel them in my soul. The energy of your body is now vibrating in my little body. If you feel nervous, anxious, or afraid about me coming into your life, then I may feel nervous, anxious, and afraid to enter the world.

If you believe you are not financially ready for me, then I will feel like a burden when I arrive. I won't understand your words, but I will feel your energy. I will feel the tone of your voice, and I will be aware of others around you.

My soul is blended with yours. I don't yet have my own individual consciousness. If your thoughts, feelings, and emotions are less than loving, even if not directed at me, I may interpret them as a negative reaction toward me.

When I am born, I need to feel you near me. I need to know you are there. I need to know you will not leave me. I need time to bond with you in the physical world, so I can feel safe in my new environment.

I need to know that you are ready for me, so I can feel ready for the world you will introduce me to.

Love,
Your Child

CHAPTER 8

Sharing the Sacred Womb

Sharing the womb with another soul can be a very emotional experience.

A client came to me because she felt emptiness in her life. During our discussion, she mentioned that she was a twin, but her twin brother had died at birth. This sounded all too familiar to me.

During the birth regression, she became frantic. She didn't know where her brother was. She started to cry and said, "I don't know where he is."

I asked her to recall the last time she felt his presence.

She said, "He's here."

I asked, "Where is he?"

She said, "Here, inside."

She continued to say that he was there in the womb with her. She suddenly felt very relieved as she experienced a connection with her twin brother. After working through our session together, it became apparent that my client's feelings of emptiness came from the loss of her twin brother at birth.

Another client came to me because she was experiencing panic attacks, was having difficulty breathing, and felt like she was going to die. As we did the regression work, my client found herself re-experiencing life in the womb with her twin sister. My client said her sister was not breathing correctly and was going to die. It turned out that her sister had been born with a collapsed lung and needed immediate surgery at birth. My client was mimicking what she believed her sister was experiencing in the womb. Her panic attacks came from the memory that her sister was dying. Even though her sister had been born alive, the fear of losing her sister became a frozen trauma for my client that stayed within her unconscious mind and later caused panic attacks.

As a womb twin survivor, I can vouch for the many womb sibling survivors in the world who feel an emptiness within them. My feelings of anger toward my twin as I felt her spirit slip away from her body were not imagined. I felt those feelings in my body as I re-experienced moments of trauma in the womb. The moment my sister bailed on me was the moment I experienced feelings of loneliness and a deep fear of abandonment for the first time. These feelings would control my life until I found the courage to heal the unconscious wounds of the soul through introspection and written expression of my deepest and darkest feelings.

The message here is that we are all sensitive beings. Our feelings from the very beginning of life create the foundation of how secure we will feel in the world. I now know from my experience as a womb twin survivor and my persistent research that my deepest wounds stem from losing my first contact with another human life. My sister and I shared a sacred space together for nine months. We shared consciousness with each other and our mother. We were together in feelings of oneness, and that oneness was broken. I felt like I lost half of me. I felt alone and abandoned. A part of me felt betrayed by my twin sister. These feelings became my suppressed emotional wounds, imprints on my soul, and the foundation of my emotional challenges into adulthood.

My unhealed emotional wounds helped to create my unhealthy behavioral patterns that led to more emotional chaos in my life. My behavioral patterns then influenced the people who relied on me for love and support. This is how we keep ourselves trapped and drag others into our emotional trap. This is what happens when you don't expand your awareness and see the bigger picture behind the picture in front of you. When you get locked into fear, you lose the ability to see the truth.

The womb of the mother is a warm and sacred space. Any disturbance in that divine space can create havoc in the incoming soul. A disturbance in a shared womb is a disturbance in the consciousness of the souls sharing that space.

I believe our souls are affected by everything we experience here on the physical journey, both good and not so good. Being in a deeper state of consciousness allowed me not only to recall the feelings, but to feel the feelings. What I seemed to be most affected by was the loss of connection I had felt in the womb with my twin sister. This is because we come into the world needing love and security. When we don't receive it, or it is taken away, we become lost and confused souls. I was not able to let my sister know how I felt. If I could, I would have been able to release the fear energy in my soul instead of allowing it to become a wound imprint that would disrupt my emotional well-being for years.

In healing the soul, it's important to release the energy that is disrupting the consciousness of the soul. It is never too late to express what has been suppressed, even if it goes as far back as prebirth. Although you don't remember what you felt at birth or before, you know what you feel now. Have an open mind and trust that these feelings were initially created before you could speak. Have an open heart and remind yourself that these feelings are just part of the learning experience of being human. They have nothing to do with the miracle that you are. When you were conceived, a miracle was beginning to take place in a physical body. You are that miracle. Embrace it.

I now understand the patterns in my life. I now realize that these are only patterns formed by the fear I felt around me. If I could have verbally expressed myself on the day I was born with the knowledge and understanding I have now, it would have sounded something like this:

Dear Beautiful, Divine Sister,

You left me all alone. I felt abandoned and scared. I didn't know where you went. Then Mom left. I felt so alone. You didn't want to stay here, and I understand that now. I wish you were here. We could have healed together.

We shared a soul connection, and then suddenly you were gone. I began my physical journey with pain and loss. My life script followed the theme of abandonment and loneliness. I am now learning how to heal those wounds, so I can stop fearing the loss of love.

I am learning to see the bigger picture around my fearful experiences. I am learning to stay focused on how the pain can help me learn and grow instead of focusing on how much it hurt me.

I pray your soul is at peace.

I realize now that we are not here to struggle, but to learn the valuable lessons within all of our experiences.

My dear, beautiful, divine sister, I am learning. Thank you for guiding me into this journey.

With all my love,
Your Twin

CHAPTER 9

The Soul's Challenges of Physical Birth

Birth should be a very intimate, engaging, and soul-loving experience for the newborn. Since we are sensitive and aware from the beginning, it is not usually an easy transition from the warmth and security of the mother's womb to a loud, bright, and sometimes unwelcoming physical world. The physical act of birth can be traumatizing. These memories are forever etched in the soul.

If I asked you to recall your feelings around your birth, most likely you would find the question amusing. Although you may not consciously remember what you were feeling the day you were born, those feelings are deep within your soul and expressed through your physical body. The way you move your body, the way your body tightens up in certain areas under stress, and the way you feel around loud noises could all go back to your experiences at birth.

Birth can have a negative impact on the soul if the feelings received by the newborn do not feel welcoming. This could be because the birth experience is traumatic due to birthing complications or because the newborn is sensitive to the environment around them. If a baby is born in a hospital setting, then chances are the environment was loud, noisy, and full of excitement. Sometimes the environment is one of anxiousness and fear. All of these energies are too much for a newborn to process, especially if the newborn was already fearing the world because of an unpleasant womb experience. These energies can have a long-lasting detrimental effect on the nervous system of the newborn if the experience is overwhelming.

My work with clients during a regression to the birth experience was educational for me, to say the least. What follows are some of my clients' experiences when asked to follow the source of their current challenges.

***

A client, at the age of twenty-four, came to me for a past-life regression. When I guided her to the day she was born, her facial expression immediately changed. The session went like this:

Me: What's happening?
Client: Something is wrong!
Me: What is wrong? What's happening?
Client: I don't know. I think something is wrong with my lungs. The doctor is holding me. I'm scared. I don't know where Mom is.

After the session, my client told me that she did not recall hearing anything from her mom about her lungs.

At our following session, my client told me that her mom had confirmed the memory. My client had been born with fluid in her lungs. Her mother became so hysterical over her child's trauma that the doctor had directed the nurse to sedate the mother while the doctor cleared the fluid from my client's lungs. My client's mother did not come out of sedation for a while, causing my client to feel abandoned by her mother during a time of intense fear. This separation from her mother at birth seemed to correlate with my client's anxious feelings about her mother not being there for her. It also strengthened the theory that if the mother becomes unconscious during pregnancy or at the birth of her child, the child loses its psychic connection with the mother.

Mother and child are connected through shared consciousness during gestation and the birthing process. A broken connection can feel like abandonment to the child and can affect the life of the soul during that physical journey.

***

Another client, when guided to go back to her feelings of unworthiness, recalled the moment of her first breath as she came into the world. The session went like this:

Me: How do you feel about being born?
Client: Afraid.
Me: Where do you feel that in your little body?
Client: My stomach.
Me: What is causing you to feel afraid?
Client: I'm not sure.

At that moment, I believed she could feel the feelings in her body, but didn't know where they were coming from.

Me: Can you tell me what your mom is feeling?
Client: She is overwhelmed because she does not want another baby.
Me: How does that make you feel?
Client: Sad. Unwanted.

During our work together, I had my client go deeper into the consciousness of her mother to find out what was causing her mother to feel overwhelmed. The client said her mother feared that she could not give my client everything a child needs because her mother was already raising three small children. This made my client realize that her mother's feelings hadn't stemmed from not wanting her. The worry came from her mother's fear of not being able to care for another child properly. This changed the client's perception of her mother's feelings about her and helped to heal my client's feelings of unworthiness.

After the session, my client told me she had felt her stomach churning during the session. The sensation was similar to the feeling she would get whenever she felt disapproval from her mother during her younger years. My client realized that she was not an unwanted child. She was also able to see how she turned her mother's typical parenting techniques into self-disapproval and judgment because her perceptions fed off of the birth imprint that settled in her stomach area. This connection helped my client to heal her emotional feelings of unworthiness and release the energy of the emotional imprint trapped in her stomach.

As with many unborn, newborn, and small children, my client's false perceptions caused many years of misery. These misperceptions and our personal views of the world help us create a distorted reality.

***

During an inner-child healing session, one of my clients expressed a deep fear around her birth. As we continued to work toward her feelings, she expressed that she felt like she was a mistake. She said her mother had not wanted to hold her and seemed distant and unemotional.

I had my client blend with mother's consciousness. She reported that her mother felt inadequate because her mother didn't know how to love a child. My client said that her mother hadn't felt loved by her mother, so she believed she was not capable of being a good mother.

By connecting to the soul energy of her mother during our session together, my client was able to see the bigger picture around her fears. This changed my client's perception about being loved by her mother. It also helped to repair their broken relationship caused by the deep insecurities that were etched in their souls.

***

A client came to me because she wanted to heal her overwhelming fear of death. When I guided her to go back to that feeling, she found herself alone in a crib, crying. She cried like a baby in my chair as I asked her what she was experiencing. She said that no one was coming to get her, and she felt alone and unwanted. My client was re-experiencing a traumatic time in her life as a newborn child who thought she had been abandoned and left to die because no one was responding to her crying.

I asked her to go to the moment when someone came to the crib. She stopped crying at that moment and said to me, "My mom is here." I asked her how she felt. She said, "Safe."

Those terrifying moments had been so impactful that they became an imprint on my client's soul. She held on to the fear of dying even though her mother came to get her. It was during those intense moments of crying out and not being attended to that the fear became a reality. This caused my client to believe, on an unconscious level, that she was not safe in the world. No one would come to her rescue during a time of crisis. As dramatic as this may sound, this is the distorted reality of a child who only knows survival.

***

As you can tell from these client sessions, a lot of our struggles through life started out as fears caused by misperceptions. Since we as unborn, newborn, and young children are narrowly focused on survival, we can easily misinterpret almost everything we experience that does not feel like love. These misperceptions become part of the soul consciousness that will help form negative patterns in our lifetimes. This is why understanding the whole story and seeing the bigger picture are important to our soul-healing process.

All my clients who have had the experience of recalling their birth experiences were skeptical at first. Once we connected the dots and they could see how the misperceptions of their earlier experiences created behavioral patterns later in their lives, they understood the importance of seeing the bigger picture, knowing the whole story, and understanding the higher truth.

The emotions felt by my clients during their soul-healing sessions with me were authentic feelings coming up from the memories of the soul that were now anchored in the body. The emotions attached to these earlier experiences became triggered when I guided the client through a process of locating the source of their current challenges.

What I found very interesting is that several of my clients described seeing a green light coming toward them and surrounding them during their healing work. According to many spiritualists and mystics, a green-light presence represents healing from a higher source, possibly from an angel or spirit guide. Many of my clients have described feeling the presence of guiding energy when they were regressed back to their first breath in the physical world.

I believe there is much for us to learn about life, especially life beyond our physical bodies. I think we must understand, from a higher level of awareness, the need for every soul to feel loved and connected during the physical journey. This means having more compassion for ourselves and for all those who have lost the connection to their divine selves.

The day you were born was obviously an important day because it's celebrated every year. There is more to the celebration than we realize. We are celebrating the miracle that we are. We are celebrating the days our souls fully joined our physical bodies for our adventures in the physical world. When you celebrate your special day each year, celebrate it with immense joy, because you are celebrating the miracle that you are in this lifetime.

CHAPTER 10

Freeing Ourselves from Our Stories

> Shame is the demon that keeps many of us trapped in our pain; healing comes when we gain the courage to confront our demon(s).
>
> —J'son M. Lee

Many of us have a trauma story to tell. Each story is told from a soul that feels broken, unsafe in the physical world, and lost in confusion. My story is not so pretty, but it is the story I told myself for years. It is the story I felt deep within my "fragmented" soul. It is the story that I kept alive for many years because it belonged to me and it defined who I was. It is my story, and I owned it like it was a living organ in my body. I became so attached to my story that I unconsciously found ways to recreate it over and over again in my life.

I became caught up in the unworthiness trap before I was born, and my dysfunctional childhood pulled me deeper into that trap. The only way I knew how to live my life was through the story of who I was because of the life I was given.

We hold on to our stories because our stories are all we know about our lives. A story is a set of perceptions of personal experiences wrapped up in a neat little story of me.

Growing Up Broken—My Story

It's another contemplative day as I sit and watch Mom twist a bit of her freshly washed hair and pin it to her head with bobby pins in a crisscross hold. Every day that Mom goes to work, I watch her daily routine as she beautifies herself before she leaves for the evening. I watch her carefully line the bottoms of her eyelids with a dark pencil and delicately color her lips with a bright red lipstick while her pinned-up hair is drying. She hasn't even left yet, and I miss her already. She's a gentle woman—loving and kind—and I feel a peaceful sense of security when she is home with me and my siblings. Those moments are far and few between, and I long for them often.

After Mom's hair dries, I watch her pull the bobby pins out one pin at a time. I find myself in moments of giggles as sections of her hair spring from the pins in spirally curls that bounce around on her head.

My giggles quickly turn to sorrow as Mom gazes solemnly in the mirror. She has a look of sadness in her eyes. She touches her worn, aging face as she continues to gaze in the mirror, most likely reflecting on her many regrettable years of self-sacrifice. I sit and admire Mom as only a child could. She slips into her tight black waitress uniform that sits just above the knee. She grabs her purse and scoots out the door. Her last words each day, as she leaves us to fend for ourselves, are "Be good." I'm not exactly sure what it means to be good. I only know that I want to be good because that's what Mom wants.

At the young age of six, I often questioned why Mom could not be home with us and let Dad go to work, as the other families in the neighborhood did. Our family was different. Was it because we were not good kids? I don't recall Dad ever going to work. When Dad lived with us, he spent his days sleeping and his evenings keeping us disciplined to his satisfaction. The sound of his footsteps coming toward the bedroom where my sisters and I slept was enough to make a child weep in fear. But we had to be strong; we could not weep. We had to show Dad we were good kids and were following his rules. All it took was one sibling to trigger

Dad's anger, and we would all get the breadboard spanking. Those dreaded words and his angry voice made my entire body quiver in fear.

There it is. It's time. Dad yells, "Line up!" I can already imagine the pain as his demanding voice penetrates my little body.

We all come together and form a line in the kitchen, starting with the oldest down to the youngest. I was number four in line, followed by my youngest sister. As Dad grabs the long handle of the thick, dark, wooden breadboard, I can hear my younger sister shriek with anxiety. Dad raises the breadboard up high, grasping the handle tightly. With a look of disgust on his face, he swings the breadboard down at the buttocks of my oldest sister. The screams down the line are piercing to me as I await my turn for the breadboard punishment.

Sometimes Dad would tell us who broke which rule. Sometimes the only words we heard were "Line up." I wondered why Mom was at work. She always seemed to be at work whenever I needed her to comfort me.

I need her at this moment as I shake uncontrollably. My turn in the lineup comes near. I wish Mom didn't leave us home with him all the time. Luckily my oldest sibling tries to comfort us. She takes the girl siblings into the bathroom, has us lower our pants, and looks at our swollen butts. As I twist my neck to look down at myself, I see dark blue and purple colors in a puffy circle of flesh. I'm glad it's over—well, at least for today. "You are brave," my sister says. We must be brave and always follow Dad's rules or we will be gone. I don't want to be gone. Mom would miss us, and I don't know where gone is.

Then came the day when Dad had had enough. He wanted us gone. All I can recall from the chaos of that day is Mom waking us up in the middle of the night and rushing us out the front door and into her car. It was a decently large car in a pukey green color, with the words "Plymouth Fury" written on it.

There we were, awakened from a deep sleep, all grouped together as Mom frantically and forcibly pushed us into her car. I can easily visualize the way we all stared at each other in that familiar state of confusion. The only words Mom said was that the house was filled with gas. I didn't know what she meant and I didn't know where Dad was. The confusion was overwhelming.

Mom pulled out of the driveway like a race car driver and drove what felt like two hundred miles per hour. Aside from the screeching of the tires, there was dead silence. By the looks on the faces all around me, I could tell I wasn't the only one feeling dazed and afraid. Finally, the short ride that felt like a furious spiraling roller coaster ended. We reached our destination.

It was a big building with lots of windows. The grayish color of the cement seemed darker in many spots. There was a long walkway that led up to large, daunting front doors. I almost felt like we were going to see the wizard from *The Wizard of Oz*. Would the wizard take us? Would he let us sleep there?

We followed Mom up the walkway and through the large swinging doors. My brother said he needed to use the bathroom. He broke the silence. I asked what we were doing there. Mom said she needed to talk to the police officer and that we were to sit quietly and wait. I thought, *Maybe the police officer can get the gas out of the house so we can go back to bed. I don't like it here.* We all sat huddled on a bench across from a long, high counter where a man was looking down at some papers. I don't even know if he saw us.

Mom walks up to the counter and tells the man, "I need to file a report." The man looks up at Mom. He looks annoyed. He grabs a piece of paper from a box on the counter and starts asking Mom questions. I don't know why he is so annoyed with Mom. Maybe she shouldn't have brought us here. The man keeps writing things down as Mom talks to him. She turns around occasionally to look at all of us sitting quietly on the bench. My younger sister wraps herself in her favorite blanket, which she managed to drag with her. I wish I had grabbed mine. I just need some sort of comfort.

As we are leaving the police station, Mom starts to explain to us what has happened. Our dad closed all the windows in the house. He turned up the gas in the gas fireplace in our living room as high as it could go. Then he left the house. Mom was awakened by the strong smell. Mom says the police will be looking for Dad.

I am so nervous for him. That man in the police station looked so mean. What will they do to him? Why do they want him? Will I ever see him again? All these thoughts are rushing through my head. I feel faint. I'm so tired. My siblings are fighting in the car. All this noise is hurting my head. How will we get the gas out of the house?

Mom drives a long, weary way to Grandma and Grandpa's house at the lake. She doesn't say much in the car. We all go inside and are told to find a place to sleep. Most of us sleep on the floor in the closed-in porch. Mom stays up, talking to my grandparents. We try to listen, but we are too busy talking among ourselves about what we think is happening. My oldest sister tells us to sleep, but how can I sleep? I am worried about what might happen to Dad.

Not long after that, Dad was back home. Nobody talked about that formidable day. We just stayed silent. We tried our best to be good, as Mom and Dad asked. We really did. Sometimes we would mess up. Soon thereafter, we would hear that intimidating voice again: "Line up!" Again, we would all gather in the kitchen and just wait for our punishment.

One day, not long after we received our punishment, I heard Mom walk in the door. I was so happy she was home. I needed comfort. My butt was swollen and burning. I ran to the door and said with excitement, "Mom, you're home!" I showed her my bruised butt and said, "Look what Daddy did." I just wanted her to hold me and tell me everything was going to be OK.

But she did not. Instead she said, "Well, what did you do to deserve it?"

I just shrank in shame. I did deserve it; Mom had confirmed it. I must be a very bad girl. I would always feel deep in my soul that I was undeserving of anything good in my life. "I am bad."

The Voiceless Soul

When I was about ten years old, Dad left our home for good. I felt a sense of relief. At the same time, I was scared about the change in our lives. I wondered who would care for us when Mom left the house.

I remember that depressing day. Dad backed his old, rusty station wagon up over the lawn to the stairs on the front porch. He started loading boxes. "Where are you going, Daddy?" I asked.

He answered, "I'm leaving."

My sister asked, "When will you be back?"

He answered, "I'm not coming back."

It did not take him long to pack the car with his personal things. Then he said a final goodbye—no hugs, no kisses, just "Don't give your mother a hard time."

As he drove away, my sister ran down the street, screaming, "Don't go! Don't go!" I had a weird feeling in my stomach, like someone had just punched a hole in it. I believe my soul felt that good old familiar feeling of abandonment. Dad never came home, even though a part of me always believed he would.

It wasn't easy for Mom raising five children alone. She worked hard. I remember many days kissing her goodbye as she left the house in her miniskirt and high heels. She was a very pretty barmaid, and her tips helped pay the rent. She was not liked very much by the other mothers on our block. I think that was because she was very much admired by the dads on the block. We were labeled by the other families as the "bad kids" with the "loose" mother. None of the other children were allowed to play with us. We were shunned by the neighbors for not having a dad, for having a sexy mom who had to waitress and bartend to care for us, and for spending many days without supervision. We were just a bunch of runts to them. We had no value in this world.

There goes that pain in my stomach again. This time it doesn't feel like a punch; it feels like a sword. The pain of shame and rejection have been anchored deeper in my soul.

For a short time, we spent days with Dad in a small one-room apartment he rented not too far from where we lived. I remember he would talk on the phone all the time with someone named Ann. I didn't know who Ann was, but I could tell she was important to him.

About a year after Dad left us, Dad brought me and two of my sisters to meet Ann. It was then that I found out that Dad and Ann lived in the same house. That was strange to me. My dad didn't live in our house anymore because he didn't want us. Now he lived in Ann's house. I guessed he liked her way more than he liked us.

We entered into a huge redbrick building with many windows and doors. All I could think was *Is this where she lives? This is huge!* Then we went to one specific door and Dad just walked right in. I asked Dad, "What's behind all those other doors?" and he told me other people lived there. It was the first time I had been inside an apartment building. It seemed odd to me that everyone had their own living space in this huge building with no backyard. Everything about the place seemed odd to me. Why would Dad want to live here instead of living in our house? What was wrong with our house?

Then out of another room came a tall woman with medium-length blond hair. She had dishes in her hand and was setting the table in the dining room. Dad told this woman who each of us was by name and then said, "This is Ann." He didn't seem to be excited about her meeting us. I felt a little nervous. My sisters were just as quiet as I was. I think we just didn't know what we were supposed to do. This was so different from our house. This house wasn't messy and the walls weren't cracked, and Dad seemed to like it there.

Then it came: one of the most devastating moments of my childhood, and what turned out to be a very deep impression on my soul. Out of the same room from which Ann had come ran three little children, all smaller than me. One of them ran to my dad, hugged him, and said, "Daddy, look what Mommy gave me." She held up a coloring book and crayons.

I suddenly felt sick. I felt a jolt of pain in my little, undernourished body as I heard this stranger call the only man I needed acceptance from "Daddy." I think my skinny little body went into shock as I thought, *He is not your daddy, little stranger girl. He is my daddy, and you can't have him!* I dared not say those words out loud. I had to keep them to myself.

The pain was too much to bear. I was speechless. Not only had I been abandoned, but I had been replaced. He had new kids. He didn't want us because he wanted them. He didn't want bad kids. They must be good kids. Jealousy and fear of abandonment hit me like shockwaves through my heart.

I believe my soul recorded an imprint of unworthiness that would shake my soul for the rest of my life. The abandonment imprint from birth just got stronger, and the feelings of unworthiness just kept pounding deeper into me. My soul was heavily burdened and I hadn't even hit puberty. My stomach felt like the sword had been turned in several directions. I felt weak and wounded.

Yes, those are the imprints my dad left me with. But he would not have done that if he hadn't already had those imprints himself.

That was my life growing up. That was what I knew as normal. I grew up in a world of confusion, fear, and feelings of abandonment. To some of you, this may seem like a kid's fairy tale compared to your upbringing. To others, this may rock you to your core.

From my experiences and the experiences of my clients, I now realize that we are products of the stuff people carry in their souls. Their defects turn into our defects. Our internal pain drives us to find ways to feel loved and accepted in this world. We want to feel worthy, and we want to belong. We need security, which we sometimes seek in the most unhealthy and desperate ways. Life becomes a never-ending search for safety as love takes a backseat. But you will never stop hearing and repeating the words "It's all about love." I believe many of us have lost trust in love when we lost trust in ourselves to be good enough for this world.

I have done a lot of healing work, and I still feel emotional around the experience of my younger self feeling alone and powerless around the adults in my life. I also hurt deeply when I realize how their dysfunction became my dysfunction and how I, at times, carried it forward. There is so much more going on around us and through us that we are not aware of. This has to change if we want more harmony and balance in our lives. We must get to know ourselves on a deeper level. We must become aware of the soul imprints that are disrupting our lives and our relationships with others.

Becoming aware *now* means knowing that you *were* aware all along. It means knowing that the people who hurt you are people just like you who were hurting inside. We just keep passing our pain forward like the gift that keeps on giving.

This was not an easy story to share. The difference is I don't react to it anymore. I have learned to see the bigger picture around the story created in my mind. This brought me clarity and understanding. Most importantly, it brought me to the higher truth. This higher truth is one we don't usually get to see, because we get so stuck in the pain of our story.

I had to heal the anger and resentment toward my dad or I would have continued to carry his unhealed trauma in my soul. I had to free myself from this story of pain and trauma and remember the higher truth. As souls, we are never broken—we only feel broken because of our painful experiences on the physical journey. We are always whole, forever divinely guided by the spirit within, and always loved by our Creator. We are one with our Creator, which means we are truly magnificent beings of higher consciousness that only vibrate to the energy of love and compassion. The lower vibrational energy we feel only comes from the fear of not feeling loved.

CHAPTER 11

The Battle We Fight Inside of Us

> We reenact past conflicts because this time we hope to make it come out right – we're going to win the battle. This reenactment of old, painful experiences is called "repetition compulsion."
>
> —Dr. Susan Forward
> *Toxic Parents—Overcoming Their Hurtful Legacy and Reclaiming Your Life*

When we are stuck in the trap, we believe we are in a fight with others and the world. The truth is we are fighting with our own dark feelings of unworthiness. We would like to make someone else responsible for what we feel, so we can make sense of our feelings. But others are only bringing out the pain we hid inside of us a long time ago. This is that ugly inner stuff that no one wants to acknowledge.

It's not easy to say, "I feel unworthy." Yet this is the most important thing you can do. Expression of your disowned feelings is going to help you understand yourself better. This understanding of your inner self is your pathway to healing what feels broken and disconnected within you.

Saying what you feel makes it real for you—and that is the scary part. It has to become real so you can own it, which then gives you the right to disown it once you realize it has lost its purpose. When you are fighting with feelings of unworthiness, it is the child inside of you who is reliving its first feelings of nonlove. These feelings of nonlove are based on survival consciousness, which is no longer relevant to your life now.

The battle we fight inside of us causes sensations in the body that can feel uneasy. Since we can't connect our unhealed emotions to these uncomfortable feelings, we just call it anxiety. Those uneasy feelings are the parts of us that are trying to feel safe in the world. Those parts of us feel rejected, unwanted, and unworthy. They are emotional imprints that cause you to feel unsettled. We just want them to go away.

The problem is they don't go away. They can actually get quite fierce because they are looking for expression. They need to be heard. They need to be attended to, because at a time in our earlier lives, there was no one who did attend to them. They are still looking for acknowledgment and acceptance. We refuse to notice them because we don't like these parts of us. We don't want to accept them. They feel inferior and make us feel flawed. These are the parts of us that we believe the world has rejected, so now we must reject them also.

We want to prove we are worthy of the world. At the same time, these parts within us feel unworthy of the world. The conflict that is going on inside of us will continue until we recognize these parts of ourselves. The conflict will continue until we welcome these parts into a safe and loving environment. That safe and loving environment is our spiritual hearts of love and compassion.

It is your inability to connect with these parts of you that is causing the battle within. It is your fear of getting to know these parts of you that causes you to fight against yourself and others who trigger these parts of you. You are not fighting anything outside of you. It's all happening right there within you. It is only showing up outside of you because you are reacting to the chaos within you.

Take a moment and look inside your spiritual heart. Send a flow of love from your spiritual heart into the rejected parts of you. Give them a chance to feel accepted just as they are. When you are able to do that, they will soften their need to get your attention. These may be parts of you that feel jealous, angry, resentful, betrayed, abandoned, unattractive, unintelligent, or just lonely. They are still parts of you. They are simply having an experience of feeling rejected by the world. This doesn't make them or you unworthy.

Sadly, we live in a judgmental society that furthers our need to hide any parts of us that we believe are flawed. There is added pressure to fit the required societal mold. Belonging is a humanistic need that strengthens our need for approval. Most of us live with a hidden fear of nonacceptance for who we are. This causes us to fall victim to our own egos, preventing us from loving the disowned parts of ourselves.

It's a very delicate balance to be yourself and still be a part of a judgmental society that remains stuck in its own fears of unworthiness. Once you realize that those who had the ability to make you feel bad about who you are nothing more than conditioned souls who have fallen victim to the trap, you will realize a higher truth about yourself and the world you live in.

The best way to free yourself from this trap is to recognize this truth and express on paper those feelings that you have neglected for the sake of survival in what feels like a hypercritical world. Remember, you are not fighting the world; you are fighting for feelings of worthiness against an inner voice telling you that you are not worthy.

What currently feels undesirable in your life stems from negative patterns that were formed over time from earlier experiences where you were helpless and dependent. These parts of you will continue to feel helpless and dependent and will keep running your adult life like an emotionally undernourished child, unless you accept them as valuable parts of you. This is how you help to heal the conflict that is happening within you. This is how you end the battle that started a long time ago. It is time to express yourself fully and wholeheartedly. Express your willingness to accept these parts of you unconditionally.

When you speak to those parts of you that are keeping you limited in life, you are giving yourself the voice you did not have when those feelings were too overwhelming to process. When they are processed with the love of the spiritual heart—which is the compassionate, wise, intelligent, and intuitive energy within you—your emotions feel more accepting and cared for, so you no longer feel the need to reject them. This is the only way they can heal and the only way you can return to emotional and spiritual freedom.

> Dear Jealous and Angry Parts of Me,
>
> When a stranger claimed my daddy as her daddy, I could feel the jealousy rising within me. I had to reject you. It was too much for my soul to bear. I had to swallow that hurtful feeling or I would have broken down on the floor in front of Dad's new family. I was trying to keep myself safe from further rejection, and so I rejected the jealous you.
>
> There is nothing wrong with you. It's normal to have those feelings. I only wish I could have comforted you in that moment, but I did not know how. Instead, I pushed your feelings away and left you feeling alone in your trauma. I am sorry for that.
>
> I know you needed comfort and love at that moment, but I didn't know how to do that. I know I can do that now.
>
> I now understand that Dad was not trying to replace me. Dad was trying to fill the empty spaces in his heart. We were not enough to fill his lonely, traumatized heart. His new family would also not be enough. There was nothing outside of him that was going to fill that emptiness. He didn't know that. He just kept searching for relief. He didn't know that the relief was within his spiritual heart. He had so much to learn.

Dad was stuck in very deep emotional pain that had nothing to do with me, even though it deeply affected me. My ego would not let me show jealousy, so I had to reject you as a part of me. My fear of Dad would not let me show anger, so I rejected that part of me also, only for it to show up in different ways later in life. I disowned these emotional parts of me for my own protection and safety. That was the only way I knew how to survive being a child in a world of dysfunctional grown-ups.

I want you to know that I love you and accept you just the way you are. You are valuable and significant parts of me. You deserve my love, compassion, and attention. I want you to understand that I only rejected you out of fear. I had to learn how to love and honor myself, even though I felt unworthy of it. I had to learn that it is OK to feel jealous when you feel replaced. It is OK to feel angry when you feel hurt and betrayed. It is also OK to remember that these are human emotions and can be accepted as valid feelings, so they can be properly processed through the body.

I am healing now. I no longer fear the world of grown-ups. I realize now that the only one who rejected me was myself. I let Dad's self-disdain become my self-disdain. I know better now, so I can do better now.

I would like to welcome you home. You are worthy and welcomed in this world. Come into my spiritual heart and rest your little soul energy within me. This is where you belong. You are parts of my soul, and I will never let anyone's unhealed trauma disturb my peace again.

You are safe. You are loved. You are home.

Love,
Me

CHAPTER 12

The Heart-Shielded Adult

> I've been through all of this before; he says to his heart. Yes, you have been through all this before; replies his heart. But you have never been beyond it.
>
> Sreechinth C
> *Alchemical Quotes of Paulo Coelho*

When we are born, we have open hearts that are longing for love and connection. Even if we are sad and confused about life as we enter the world, our natural response is to long for that secure feeling of safety. If we are not cared for by affectionate, loving caregivers, then we eventually become distrustful of the world and seek a way to protect ourselves from the threat of abandonment. We absorb so much negative information over our lifetimes that we can't possibly process it as fast as it's coming in. This does not stop us from yearning for love. It only keeps us distrustful of love and in conflict with our deepest desires.

I was too young to process the trauma around my birth experience, so the imprints of loneliness and abandonment became stronger as I longed for love and connection during childhood. Every child craves love and affection, but not all children receive such blessings. Unfortunately, during my childhood years, I experienced pain, violence, and fear instead of what I innately longed for. These soul imprints then influenced my behaviors throughout my life. My soul resigned itself to the belief that love does not exist. I closed my heart and learned how to function in the world without love. I showed expressions of love on a superficial level, while remaining guarded.

When we have bad experiences growing up, they create feelings of helplessness and maybe even hopelessness. We have come to depend solely on the outside world to save us, and yet we don't feel worthy of being saved. The conflicts that we have within us are keeping us locked in a prison of dark thoughts, mixed with the need to feel loved, validated, and significant. When we don't have the answers to our problems, we just keep repeating the same unhealthy patterns in the hope that something will change.

We live with shielded hearts and are always on high alert to make sure no one can cause us more pain. We remain disconnected even though it is the disconnect that keeps us stuck in the trap. We are so reliant on others for validation and safety that we have completely abandoned ourselves. We shield our hearts, we guard our souls, and we pray for connection to love. We don't even realize that we are blocking the love we need.

If we keep shielding our hearts, we will co-create more closed hearts. We will continue to struggle in our relationships with others because we won't share from our hearts, only from our ego minds that keep us at a comfortable distance.

As an aware and sensitive child, I took on all the drama in my environment. As an unaware adult who had buried all her childhood pain and blocked her heart, I had difficulty finding a way out of the trap. Instead of healing the internal wounds that started a long time ago, I let my ego take control and do whatever needed to be done to keep me safe from emotional harm. This meant I created behaviors that would stop me from having a solid and secure intimate relationship. As much as I desired it, I was also afraid of losing it once I had it.

To find more harmony in our lives, we need to find balance in our humanness. We can do this by healing the inner conflicts that were created between the true self and the false self.

The false part of the self acts like a protector, but it is protecting us from the one thing we need the most, which is emotional connection. The aware and sensitive child needs to feel loved and safe. We owe it to ourselves to give that part of us the love we need and deserve. We must stop creating more drama around our relationships and open up our hearts to the higher truth. We must learn how to grow up and become fully aware adults and live from a higher level of consciousness than our parents or ancestors could.

If we continue to shield our hearts from what we believe is a cruel world, then we will continue to create drama in our lives. We will continue to operate from an old operating system that was based in fear. We must love and honor the sensitive child within us. We must give that inner part of us what we long for. When we are able to allow love in again, we will attract more of that into our lives. That is the true law of attraction. If you keep attracting the wrong people, the wrong jobs, and the wrong intimate relationships, then chances are you are stuck in the unworthiness trap with a big shield over your heart for protection.

Step back and take a good look at the bigger picture. This will help you change that old, outdated belief system that is keeping you stuck in the past. You are still an aware, sensitive being on the inside, even if you have blocked your spiritual heart. It is that higher knowledge within you that will help you through the pain of the past and help you reconnect with your innocent soul. A hardened soul is not a happy soul. It is a soul living in survival mode. You deserve better.

If your primary caregivers closed their hearts because of unhealed trauma, then chances are you have closed your heart too. Don't let their inability to heal themselves keep you from the passionate life you deserve. Don't blame them for their inability to grow up and heal their wounded souls. Don't use blame on anything or anyone. This will only keep you stuck in the trap.

If you keep a shield across your heart, you will hold back your loving spirit, which only wants to lead you into your greatness. You may need time to remove any shields you created for yourself due to self-protection needs. You can start by expressing your need to live with an open heart so you can free your soul from the lower energies of fear.

If you speak freely from your inner child to the grown-ups in your younger years and express yourself from your spiritual heart, you will release the lower vibrational energy that came with your feelings of nonacceptance. What if you could open your heart and begin writing your deepest inner feelings from a higher level of consciousness? What if you could express your childhood needs with the wisdom you have gained through your adult years? As you read these letters, if anything comes up for you, add your thoughts and feelings in the personal note section in the back of the book.

Dear Grown-up,

I am a sensitive soul with a soft and vulnerable heart. My heart needs lots of nurturing, tender care, and love. Every time my heart breaks, it gets harder and harder to put back together. Over time, it may become so broken up that I will have to build a shield around it to protect its fragile pieces.

Once I build that shield around my heart, I may never feel comfortable removing it. As long as I keep my heart guarded from the world, I will distance myself from authentic love. That is the kind of love that comes from a higher place within me. When I guard my heart, I block the energy of my spirit, which means I block off my true self. This is not what my soul intended for this lifetime. I came here to grow, evolve, and experience love for myself and all sentient beings.

You may not be able to properly care for my heart if you have shielded your own heart. We may want to share our hearts with others, but if we are shielded, we will just keep living our lives around those fears. I don't think this is how we are supposed to navigate this journey. I don't think this is going to bring us comfort and security. I think shielding our hearts will only distance us from each other and the world.

If you are too shielded, I will need to learn how to release you from the responsibility of opening your heart to me. I will have to learn that your journey does not have to dictate my journey. I may not like the way you navigate your life, but I must learn how to release you from the responsibility of doing it well. I do not want to let shielded hearts take me away from my higher truth. I will have to learn how to open my spiritual heart and trust the spirit within. If I can't learn how to trust love from you, then I will have to learn this on my own. This will be a part of my growing up.

Most of us will have a challenging journey because of the many shielded hearts that came before us. We must learn how to evolve from the lower levels of fear. We must learn from the mistakes and fears of others.

I will learn. I will create change. I will be the hero who doesn't look back with anger and fear. I will be the hero who looks back with love and gratitude for being able to learn a truth that was not easily available to you and those before you. I will do the work that you were not able to do. The work I do is for all of us.

Sincerely,
Sensitive Me

CHAPTER 13

The Self-Help Era to the Rescue

Life seemed complicated to me, but what was so complicated? I worked, I paid my bills, I hung out with my friends, and, oh yeah, I ran like hell from intimate relationships. All normal stuff, right? I was keeping myself safe from rejection because rejection was the ultimate destroyer. "I must be tough to survive in this loveless world" was my motto. I played mindless head games with every guy I met. I had to keep testing everyone's motives and intentions. I trusted no one. I was stuck in the trap.

The running became exhausting. I felt alone and empty without true intimacy in my life. I feared the very thing I needed the most. I wanted to feel a deep connection with someone, even though I wasn't sure what that was. I prayed for something different. I prayed for something that would make me feel alive. I was losing hope and feeling lost in my own dark thoughts. And then, there it was! Suddenly, my prayers were answered.

It was during the eighties, and I was in my mid-twenties. The self-help agenda was exploding, and I was excited about it. I was finally going to rise above the water I was drowning in. I was going to be saved! Lord, let me give praise to the self-help industry!

I immediately started on a mission to heal the emptiness inside of me, find my greatness, and become the best version of me. I purchased every self-help book I could find at my local bookstore: *You Can Heal Your Life* by Louise Hay, *Women Who Love Too Much* by Robin Norwood, *When Bad*

Things Happen to Good People by Harold S. Kushner, *How to Stop Worrying and Start Living* by Dale Carnegie, and the list goes on.

But it didn't stop there. As I was searching for answers through this myriad of self-help books, motivational power seminars came into the self-help game. All I could think was that the answers must be in there somewhere. I found myself chasing the self-help industry like a tiger running after its prey. I was hungry for something to feed my soul. I needed to feel whole. I needed to feel alive. I needed to know that I was enough.

Those motivational seminars felt like a godsend. After each one I attended—and there were quite a few—I felt strong and empowered. I was going to conquer the world. I was going to show up in my amazing awesomeness. "We are born to be seen by the world" were the words of high-energy speakers who filled the atmosphere with positive energy and assured me of success. Their words, their promises, and their unstoppable enthusiasm inspired the hundreds of lost souls gathered in every large, crowded room. We all wanted that good stuff they were offering for a hefty but worthy price. All I had to do was remember how powerful I was and feel the magic inside of me.

Easy-peasy, right? Not! My new positive attitude couldn't stay positive for very long. There lies the unwanted truth: "I am a complete failure." My relentless affirmations of self-love and self-worth and all those "you can do it" self-directed power phrases were making my head spin. This was way too much work. I couldn't get my new thoughts to stick. They had no glue. They seemed to fade away as quickly as they came in. I felt like I was fighting against myself—and that was exactly what I was doing.

I became emotionally exhausted. Every time I felt a power lift, it wasn't long before I felt my whole body drop into complete and utter despair. I finally surrendered to an unwelcome reality—something was inherently wrong with me. I was a mess, and that was my destiny. After all that time and money I had spent, I wasn't even fixable. I felt like a huge disappointment to myself, to the world, and to the people who had brought me into this world.

These are the emotions that consume a soul in fear. We struggle with feelings of unworthiness and strive for validation in every aspect of our lives, until we are ready to learn the higher truth. We must remember that we are innocent souls trapped in a consciousness that is based in fear. It is not based in truth. The very people we needed to pin us with that badge of honor are stuck in a consciousness of fear, low self-esteem, and ego-based agendas. Even if someone you need to validate you seems to regard themselves highly and displays confidence and strong capabilities, just remember how important it is to save our souls from rejection. If others treat you like they are better or more important than you, it doesn't mean something is wrong with them. It means something went wrong for them, which pulled them out of their natural flow of love and sucked them into the unworthiness trap. They are overcompensating for some perceived weakness that you cannot see. This opened the door for their egos to take over and create a shield of protection, a false identity of self-assurance, and maybe even a self-important attitude. Not everyone who seems to have it all together actually has it all together. We are all human, and many of us have challenges when it comes to showing up in the world.

The self-help industry is going to keep on growing and expanding if we all keep ignoring the higher truth of who we are. Instead of chasing the answers or getting sucked into quick-fix healing modalities, endless self-help books, or power seminars, take the time to get to know yourself from the inside out. You will see and feel how beautifully innocent your soul is, even though you find yourself stuck in feelings of unworthiness.

CHAPTER 14

Enough with the Fluffy Stuff

> Neuroscience research shows that the only way we can change the way we feel is by becoming aware of our inner experience and learning to befriend what is going on inside ourselves.
>
> —Bessel van der Kolk, M.D.
> *The Body Keeps the Score*

Your new age teachers tell you that your soul is pure. You are filled with light and love, and you must let go of everything that doesn't serve you. Now, that truly is a sweet thought. So you talk to the universe, you meditate, you pray, you think positive thoughts, you say your daily affirmations, and you sleep with crystals. Good for you.

Now let's get real. This kind of stuff does not undo years of feeling unworthy. The truth is that your soul is not filled with light. It has ugly fear imprints that block your light and hold you back from the higher truth. Your soul's desire for love and truth is real, but you have a driving force within your soul that conflicts with your true nature. This driving force is called the shadow part of your soul, and it comes from the human experience of fear. You may have heard the phrase "face your fears." It means to face your shadow parts. These are the parts of you that feel unworthy of your dreams, desires, happiness, and abundance. These are the parts of you that keep you stuck in the trap.

Facing Your Shadow Self

Your shadow self needs more than all that fluffy stuff. It needs deep soul healing. The shadow parts of your soul are the parts you don't like about yourself. These are parts of you that you rejected a long time ago. You rejected them because others have rejected them when you naturally expressed these parts of you. To play it safe in the world, you keep these parts hidden.

As much as you want to get rid of these rejected parts, they are not going anywhere. They go wherever you go, just like a shadow does, always trailing behind that wonderful facade of confidence. That facade of confidence is an ego part of you that protects you from displaying the rejected parts. The ego helps you hide your shadow so you can interact with the world without feeling inferior to it.

As hard as your ego works to keep you in that place of confidence and in the self-loving character of "I am one with the light," your shadow parts keep calling you back to your fears—the dark imprints of "I am not worthy of the world" that are impressed within the soul. This is why we chase the fluffy stuff. We want more of that fluff and none of the darkness of the shadow self. We want to keep those good feelings that we get when we do spiritual healing, but we are not really doing the work that needs to be done. We keep chasing the light outside of us. This clever avoidance of our deepest fears is called "spiritual bypass," and many of us are guilty of using it.

It is understandable that we want to find a way to heal our pain without having to feel our pain. This shows us that we do want to heal. The problem is that the fluffy stuff is just a layer of icing that will dry out as soon as reality hits us again. This is because we are not using our own inner resources for healing. We are relying on outside sources to pull the darkness out of us through some spiritual work that takes you into a higher vibration. This is usually a temporary high, because the imprints that feed our souls with fear are not being attended to. They are still there in the trap. All we do is pacify them for a while. We are afraid to get up close and personal with this side of us, even though it is an important part of who we are. We caused these parts of us to fragment off of our awareness only because we couldn't process their fears. We can now. If we don't, then parts of us will be stuck in emotional immaturity. These rejected parts of us didn't get a chance to grow up with the rest of us.

Our parents and primary caregivers were no different. That is why emotional immaturity keeps us all stuck in the trap. It takes showing up and growing up to close the trap. It takes courage to go into those rejected parts of ourselves and comfort them, love them, and help them heal.

When you enter the darkness with your own inner light and all-loving spirit, you will find that the shadow parts are innocent parts of you that need your attention, your unconditional love, and your assurance of acceptance and safety. Your shadow is stuck in the darkness of fear, but this does not make your shadow a bad part of you. There are no bad parts of you. There are only unhealed parts of you that are stuck in the pain of the past. They are the parts of you that are afraid to come forward because they fear further rejection. It's an ongoing trap that we all get stuck in because we keep chasing the light. Your soul may have imprints of fear that feel like an ugly part of you, but your soul in its true form is light and love. It is the human experience that causes the soul to lose touch with its true, divine self.

Your spirit is always in the realm of light and love. Your spirit is your soul in its highest truth. Your soul becomes fully absorbed within the spirit of you when you have fully accepted all parts of you as worthy of love.

When you are able to view the bigger picture and examine how life really works, then you will spread that beautiful light within you onto those shadow parts that you mistakenly thought were inferior. When they come into the light, you will feel their pure love and innocence.

It's important for you to know that the adults in your growing-up life were not rejecting you or any part of you. They were rejecting their own shadow parts that showed up while they were caring for you. This is how we begin to see the bigger picture. We see all of us in this big mess of darkness known as the unworthiness trap. We keep reaching for the fluffy stuff as a way to ignore the pain of the soul. It is the fear of unworthiness that consumes us, causing us to focus on survival instead of love and connection to self, others, and the world.

Unfortunately, most of us do not live our lives from the spirit within. Your spirit comes from your spiritual heart. This is what some may call the higher heart. It is an energy that surrounds your physical heart. It is the channel between your soul and your spirit. If your spiritual heart is closed to ward off anyone who may hurt you, then you have blocked your spirit. The soul is no longer being guided by spirit, only by the ego and the devices of the physical being.

The shadow is everything we are not aware of within ourselves. If we do become aware of a disowned part, we may have difficulty healing and integrating it within our acceptable awareness. You can think of your shadow self as the part of you that is asleep, living in the darkness through the shadows of life. It only awakens during nightmares of being found out. There are many sleeping souls that are not seeing the bigger picture. You can be the one who does. You can become a fully awakened soul and be the light that helps others awaken from their slumber. When you open your spiritual heart, you can help others through their darkness just by being your true, loving, compassionate, and divine self.

We are all the same in our energy bodies. Physical forms are just vessels to house our souls while we take this physical journey. We are here to learn, not to hurt. Those who are fully controlled by their shadow sides have completely disconnected from their spiritual hearts. They are not evolving as they were meant to.

Many people are stuck in cynicism and despondency. Don't judge them. You will have to move on and ascend into higher consciousness without them, but always pray for their souls to heal. When you can rise up and live like the miracle you are, you will see that those who couldn't find the strength, wisdom, or courage to get out of the trap are just innocent souls, like lost little children who are still trying to find their way back to love.

As you can see from Diagram B on the following page, when the spiritual heart is blocked, the flow of energy from spirit to soul is also blocked, leaving the soul to depend on the lower energies to navigate the world, which thrive only on survival.

SPIRIT, SOUL AND PHYSICAL BODY
INTERACT WITH EACH OTHER CAUSING
HARMONY OR DISHARMONY

1. Part of your spirit is with you and the rest remains in the spirit world with your creator.

2. To connect with the love of your creator or the love of another spiritual being still in a physical body or who has crossed over, you connect through the spirit within you.

3. Your soul is your individual energy body that feels the energy of other souls and the energy created by self from experiences in the physical world.

4. Your body is the vessel for your soul and spirit. The spirit directs the soul to live its best life. The soul directs the body to have the physical experience as felt by the energy of the soul.

5. When the spirit is inaccessible due to the spiritual heart being blocked, spirit is unable to direct the soul to live through spiritual beliefs. Instead, the soul directs the body to live through the energy absorbed into the soul. This includes false negative beliefs about the self and unhealed emotions from life experiences.

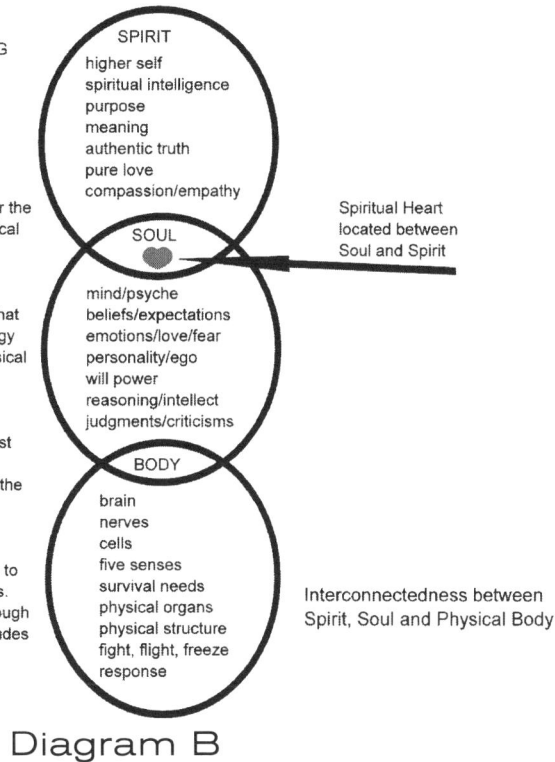

SPIRIT
higher self
spiritual intelligence
purpose
meaning
authentic truth
pure love
compassion/empathy

SOUL
mind/psyche
beliefs/expectations
emotions/love/fear
personality/ego
will power
reasoning/intellect
judgments/criticisms

BODY
brain
nerves
cells
five senses
survival needs
physical organs
physical structure
fight, flight, freeze response

Spiritual Heart
located between
Soul and Spirit

Interconnectedness between
Spirit, Soul and Physical Body

Diagram B
Interaction Between Body, Soul and Spirit

The longer we live through fear, the longer we keep our hearts closed. Unfortunately, our unending efforts to find contentment in who we are and our struggle to feel secure in the world become an exhausting pursuit. We simply can't handle all the challenges of life while our souls feel so burdened with the fear of not being enough. Since the world is filled with many rejections, we have become imprisoned by the world that we came to passionately explore.

Now listen up, beautiful spirit and miracle of life. Your soul is the consciousness that is creating your life for you. It is the driving force behind all your actions and inactions. It is making your life choices—the good, the bad, and the ugly.

When you came into being through a physical body, your soul absorbed a lot of energies that did not start with you. Once you became an adult, you became attracted to other soul energies that matched yours. You perpetuated the patterns that you want to change because of your vibrational match to others with similar soul burdens. This is how you remain stuck in the trap. Although you believe you are on a healing path because you are doing all that fluffy stuff, your soul keeps pulling you back into your shadow self because your soul has unfinished business there.

Here's the deal: you are an innocent-soul child of the Creator. Impressions run deep. You are not aware of these deep-rooted impressions that formed from before birth and on into your young childhood years. These impressions gave you information about who you are, how valuable you are, and how you fit into this big, challenging world. The information is just that: information. It gets absorbed into your soul, which then feeds that information back to you. The information is not valid; it is just a passing of information created by fear consciousness because the human experience is one of survival. The ego's job is to keep you alive and safe in a world that is filled with more fear than love. This keeps you in your guarded safe place all while keeping you from your true, divine self. Is this what you want for the rest of your life?

Your primary caregivers most likely lived more from a place of survival than a place of higher truth. How can you learn to live from that higher place if you keep aligning with those in fear? How can your caregivers hold you in that higher place if they don't know how to get there? It takes courage to step out of a comfort zone and go to a place that is unfamiliar to you. This means you have to do the real healing work. The real healing work is when you can put those ugly feelings onto paper and breathe life back into them from your spiritual heart.

We all get stuck in the unworthiness trap. We all believe someone else caused our misery and someone else is going to save us. We keep looking outside of our own spiritual hearts. We keep running toward the fluff. As we seek out the savior who is going to pull us out of the unworthiness trap, we do so with a desperate need for love and acceptance. This can only attract more drama into our lives. We need to stop feeling desperate for something that we are already deserving of. We just need to allow ourselves to feel worthy of receiving it. That means getting out of the trap because you know you don't belong there.

When all our shadow parts are healed and integrated within us, then we will navigate our world with a balance of survival and spiritual essence. We will know who we are as spiritual beings having a human experience. We will not have to keep chasing the fluffy stuff. We will know that we are miracles from a vast energy of love and compassion that came to this planet to explore it through a human body, using our higher intelligence to navigate the journey.

The eighties were all about self-improvement. It was and still is on some level a trendy phenomenon that has taken over the world, making many of us believe that there is something inherently wrong with us. This caused many people to seek the "self-improvement" formulas that the industry was selling to us. These so-called formulas are limited in their abilities to heal the soul because the soul does not need improvement. What the soul needs is compassion, love and understanding. When we hold divine truth around those parts of our souls that feel inferior, we are lifting these parts out of the darkness and into the light so they could see how perfect they really are. We don't need to improve ourselves; we need to love and accept ourselves and divine truth will emerge from that higher consciousness. We are perfect souls being challenged by the fear consciousness spreading throughout this planet because of the ancestral survival energy that continues to live through us, even though our souls have been evolving through each new generation. Instead of trying to improve yourself, lift yourself up into the higher truth and see the miracle that you are. Everything else you need to fully and lovingly accept yourself will flow from that higher state of awareness.

We fell into the trap. This is our opportunity to seek the higher truth and pull ourselves out from the shadows of darkness. Are you ready to take the leap?

CHAPTER 15

Levels of Soul Consciousness

> Life is not about becoming anything. It's about unbecoming all that is not you in order to be the true you. It's about returning to higher consciousness.
>
> —Author Unknown

Our souls are made up of layers of consciousness.

Think of the soul, which is the personality, having different layers of thought, all with different agendas and all of which are directing our lives. The levels we operate from on a daily basis are:

- conscious level
- subconscious level
- unconscious level
- higher-conscious level

The conscious level is where you are most aware of what is happening at the current moment. You are engaged with life as it is, right there in front of you. The conscious level understands linear time and is where your will power, critical thinking, planning, and ideas come from. It is also where your ego lives. The ego is that part of you that only acknowledges what is important for your safety in the world. The ego will do what is necessary to make you feel like you belong, you are accepted, and you are liked by others. It doesn't like you to be different or unique, as this may cause rejection by the world. The problem is that your soul is unique.

Since the soul has many exceptional qualities that are hidden under the ego's survival fears, you don't express yourself from your soul's higher truth. Many times, you express yourself through your soul's pain by playing it safe in the world. You don't realize you are doing this, because consciously, you desire change and growth. It is the lower levels of the consciousness that keep pulling you back to safety, which are places of familiarity.

The subconscious level is a lower, obscured level of awareness. It controls much of your life based on conditioning, memory, and the need for security. The subconscious level does not know what is true or false, right or wrong. The subconscious level doesn't know if a memory is from yesterday or from the distant past. This level of consciousness acts like a recorder; it just records all of your experiences based on how they made you feel. According to the subconscious level, everything you have experienced is still happening, because everything you have experienced is still playing out in your mind like an endless loop of recordings. This causes you to keep doing the same things over and over again, even when you are trying to change the way you live your life. You do not have easy access to the subconscious level of the soul, so it can be difficult to make the changes you want to make.

The unconscious level is a deeper level than the subconscious level and also controls much of your life based on conditioning, memory, and a need for security. At this level, you have hidden ancestral memories, past-life memories, suppressed traumatic memories, and predispositions of personality that you were born with, also referred to as personality traits. This is where our shadow parts reside. Since the shadow self is made up of the rejected parts of us, we may not even know it exists. What we do know is that we can't reach a level of peace and harmony. We don't realize that it's our shadow parts that keep calling us back to our suffering. The ego, which lies in our conscious level, keeps us busy, distracted, and yearning for improvement so that we don't have to acknowledge our shadow parts.

The higher conscious level is that of your unburdened soul, also referred to as your higher intelligence or your spirit. These are the parts of you that contain higher wisdom and spiritual gifts. These are the parts of you that live from a higher place of love, compassion, acceptance, and understanding. These are the parts of you that know you are a miracle, a gift to the world, and a being at one with the collective source of unconditional love. You may think you know this on a conscious level, but your shadow parts may be telling you something different. This is where we get stuck.

The levels of consciousness that live through us are in conflict with each other. The conflicts must be resolved for us to bring the layers of consciousness into harmony. This is what makes us feel whole and balanced.

When you acknowledge that there is more to you than a physical body that lives through a conscious level of being, you can start working with these other levels to find out which parts of you are holding you back from your greatness. Parts of you that still live in your rejected past are responsible for making you believe you are unworthy. It is these parts of you that need your attention.

Not only do we have imprints and impressions within the soul that create a false identity of the self, but we are also disconnected from the higher conscious level, where we can find the truth of who we are. Instead, we live from the conscious level, using the ego to keep us safe, as we are directed by the deeper levels of consciousness that feel unsafe.

You cannot continue to distract from your unhealed pain without consequences. That is why the burdens of the soul are like a shadow: it's always there behind you. It's haunting you like a ghost. When you experience it, you think you've been dealt a bad hand, because your life feels unstable. Well, maybe you were dealt a bad hand because you didn't pick your parents, primary caregivers, or ancestors. But darling, sweet miracle of life, you can choose to get out of the game whenever you want. You just have to decide when you are ready to set yourself free from the trap.

Many people have been transitioning from a lower level of consciousness to a more aware, intuitive, intelligent, and expanded level of consciousness. People are "waking up," as they say. This waking-up process can only feel true and complete when you can see the bigger picture. Otherwise, you are going through the motions, but you are not living in that higher truth.

It takes seeing the whole picture—letting go of everything you think you know and learning to trust the higher heart. It's not that easy to let go of what you feel protects you in this uncertain world. You need to have trust in your spiritual heart and do the soul-healing work that needs to be done. This will help you let go of the past and live more fully from the heart of compassion.

How would you like to express yourself in this world? Write your thoughts down in the note section part of this book.

> As we look around the world, we can see the myriad choices and expressions various souls can decide on. No two souls are alike; but at the core, they are the same. All souls have had different life experiences, and in a way, those experiences shape our outlook on life and the various ways to live it. Souls can express themselves through a life of compassion, tolerance, judgment, or violence.
>
> —James Van Praagh
> *Adventures of the Soul*

CHAPTER 16

The Laws of Consciousness

> Repressed and suppressed feelings require counter-energy to keep them submerged. It takes energy to hold down our feelings. As these feelings are relinquished, the energy that had been holding down the negativity is now freed for constructive uses.
>
> —David R. Hawkins
> *Letting Go: The Pathway to Surrender*

As I did my research, I thought, *It's so hard to be human.* There are many challenges we have had to face, and there will be many more throughout our lifetimes. How do we cope with difficult situations without losing ourselves in the fear of not being able to control the outcome? We must understand the Laws of Consciousness.

Many of our fears come from the fear of not being able to control things. Our sensitive souls can feel quite vulnerable at times. If we see the world through a lens of fear, then our challenges will seem much worse. We expect the conscious mind to evaluate things and protect us from exposing our negative thoughts that creep up from the subconscious level of the soul mind.

If we see the world through a lens of love, compassion, and surrender, we will meet our challenges in the best way we can. That means we need to engage the higher mind. When we surrender to what we cannot control and focus on doing the best we can to cope with difficult situations, our sensitive energy bodies will relax and we will be able to work through our challenges from our spiritual hearts. The challenge is that the ego part of our conscious mind wants to control our challenges, so these levels are working against each other instead of under the Laws of Consciousness, which call for balance and harmony.

This does not mean we should become insensitive to situations. It simply means we need to be present and aware in each current situation, so we are better equipped to handle them. The Laws of Consciousness are guidelines for understanding the human soul and what the human soul must learn, so it is not under the control of the ego mind that wants to keep the soul small and limited for acceptance and safety in the physical world.

Each level of consciousness serves a human purpose. If we were not able to suppress our emotional traumas and allow them to become unconscious, then how would we be able to function in our lives? Now that we have grown into adulthood, we have work to do to pull ourselves back into spiritual balance. The imbalance was necessary for us to continue life without breaking down the soul completely.

With the healing work I've done, I now know that the human experience can be rewarding if we learn how to navigate it through our spiritual hearts. To make the human experience a less challenging one, I believe we need to have a better understanding of why we feel the way we feel. Instead of trying to heal the symptoms of our pain, we must understand and truly accept that our inner feelings and suppressed emotions began somewhere. We must realize the human need to keep them below our level of conscious awareness. We need to accept that we did not have the mental resources to realize that we were being drawn into the human unworthiness trap. We have those resources now. As we incorporate these resources, we start to live from a level of higher consciousness. The Laws of Consciousness require us to understand that human consciousness is wrapped up in the soul and is always working to keep us safe.

The Voiceless Soul

Most of the time, we handle current situations based on the past, which means we spend a lot of time living through the lower levels of consciousness. We use strategies that we believe ensure our survival. This was a necessary coping skill when we were children. As adults, we experience each difficult situation as an uncontrollable threat, just like the ones we experienced as children.

In your younger years, you did not have the resources to find a solution to the emotional traumas you were experiencing. These emotional imprints are triggered over and over again, even though you have the resources now. When you heal what needs to be healed within you, situations that are within your control will be resolved with your current resources of knowledge and the compassion and integrity that come from the higher level of consciousness. Everything outside of your control, you will learn to surrender to so you can observe the situation with a clear mind and take any necessary steps to keep yourself and your loved ones from experiencing fear.

When you are in a place of self-love, you live from a higher level of compassion for yourself and others. This means you are no longer triggered by fears from the past, which then allows you to evaluate current situations with a higher level of awareness and composure.

The Laws of Consciousness require us to shift from lower levels of consciousness to the higher level of consciousness, so we can love and honor the miracles that we are.

We continue to remain unaware of our miraculous essence because we don't know how to fully shift to the higher level of awareness. We keep falling back into the fear of unworthiness. As we continue to look outside ourselves for love, acceptance, and validation, we continue to pretend we have reached a true sense of self-love. We are caught in this rising of consciousness without knowing how to let go of the survival strategies we set into motion as children. This keeps us out of balance and does not align with the Laws of Consciousness.

We all want to feel wanted, loved, and significant in the world. I believe this desire for acceptance begins at conception. With all the insensitive and emotionally immature beings teaching young, sensitive beings about the world, many innocent souls got caught up in the trap. This is how life works. It is the Laws of Consciousness at play, and we need to understand it better so we can use it for higher purposes.

If we experience loss of love from the beginning, as I did when my mother shut down and my twin sister made her dramatic exit, then we are already in a crisis and in need of comfort and love. If we don't receive enough love and support when we are having an emotional crisis, we may spend the rest of our lives believing no one will save us when we fall. This belief keeps us in perpetual fear and on high alert, wondering when the next stone will hit us. This causes us to put up thick walls so we can protect ourselves from the insensitivity of the world. Our innocent souls become insensitive to others because we block our spiritual hearts with our protective shields. This is how we unknowingly fall out of balance.

The Laws of Consciousness are based on the Laws of the Universe. What happens in our consciousness will be mirrored back to us through the universal source of energy, creating our reality. When our levels of consciousness remain out of balance, we have conflicts not only in our consciousness, but in our reality.

As sensitive beings in an insensitive world, we can easily get stuck in our victim stories unless we understand that insensitive souls were once sensitive souls that sought love and validation in a world filled with fear. Once we realize that we are not the only victims in the victim story, we can see the story from a different perspective and clear up our distorted reality. We can honor the subconscious and unconscious levels of soul energy as protective sources that were necessary before we gained the wisdom and knowledge of the higher truth.

When we bring balance back into the soul, we will live from the higher heart and use compassion and understanding with all the characters in our story. When we understand the laws that influence our reality, we will let

The Voiceless Soul

go of what we cannot control. We will understand how others went out of balance and why they stay stuck in the lower levels of consciousness. Only the higher truth can bring us the clarity we need. We must have compassion for those souls that could not love and honor themselves. We must understand their feelings of inadequacy because it will relieve us of ours. We must live in the higher truth even though others remain lost.

If someone in your story is too toxic to have compassion for, try having compassion for the burdened soul that has lost its connection to spirit. This means to no longer engage with or fight against the toxic person's ego mind. That is their protective self, not their true self. This doesn't mean that they are not accountable for their insensitive actions. You don't need to worry about revenge—they are already suffering. You don't see it, but the suffering is there. A disconnect from spirit means a soul in pain. Don't focus on what they have done or not done. The focus must be on your soul, not theirs. Be aware of the miracle of life that you are. Others may not see that in you because they can't see it in themselves.

No one heals by holding on to anger and resentment. Souls heal by understanding, compassion, and knowing the higher truth. Souls heal when they understand the Laws of Consciousness and heal the conflicts that keep them out of balance.

You can heal from the wounds of the past by expressing the emotions that keep you in the lower levels of consciousness. Your sensitive soul holds on to more than it can handle in this world. You must help it release the energy of feeling unworthy of the world, so you stop giving so much power to ego.

From the wisdom of the spiritual heart, write letters of higher understanding. Say all that you feel: how you hurt, how others made you feel, and how it affected your life. Say it from a compassionate level of consciousness, not the lower levels that keep you in self-protection. Say your truth without the need to defend yourself or make others wrong. Let your guard down and speak from the wisdom you have gained over the years.

These are just feelings you didn't want to feel when they were too overwhelming. These are the feelings that keep you in conflict and prevent you from experiencing a harmonious life. These are the feelings that have not been expressed because you believe they shouldn't exist, but they do. If you allow for their full expression and see them as parts of you that are innocent and deserving of love and allowed to be heard, then you won't have to hide from them anymore. You won't have to spend so much of your energy keeping them out of your awareness. When you set these feelings free from your soul, you set your soul free from the pain they are causing you. When you are free from your own pain, you no longer absorb the pain of others.

When you allow yourself to express the hurt place within you, you release all the energy that overburdened your soul a long time ago. This is how we begin the process of growing up. We give that younger part of us a chance to speak up and release those heavy feelings of unworthiness that hold us down. You will feel your innocence and your sensitivity again, but you won't be sensitive to the misguidance of others. You will be sensitive to their inability to see the truth. This will allow you to remain fully in your truth while you hold a place of compassion for those who are still in the process of learning and applying the Laws of Consciousness.

When you speak up from those hurt parts of you, you will begin to feel lighter and more connected to your higher heart. In that higher place, insensitive souls cannot pull you into their trap. Insensitive souls are not your problem. The problem is your attachment to their drama. When you understand the higher truth, you will understand that they too became attached to the drama of those who influenced their lives. We become attached to the pain of our experiences because we want to control it, yet we can't. The more we try to control the pain inside of us, the more we lose control of it. We must surrender to the pain and then love it for its experience. Let it teach you the truth about who you are instead of stealing your truth.

Your sensitive soul is the place where you hold all that you feel about yourself and the world. It is difficult to be in an insensitive world and still trust that you will be OK. When you trust that you are being emotionally challenged only because you are sensitive to the drama others are feeding you, then you can move away from their drama and seek the higher truth. That is where you will find your innocence.

Everyone's drama is about their own fear consciousness. Although you are sensitive to these insensitive beings, you are being challenged by their fears, not their true selves. Their fears become your fears when you don't understand that they are stuck in the trap. Don't close your heart because they did. They are in self-protection mode, overpowered by ego and disconnected from their love source. You don't want to go there. You don't need to engage in that consciousness. You also don't need to resent them for it. Resentment lowers your vibrational energy and opens the door for drama.

Only understanding, compassion, and acceptance are going to keep you in alignment with your higher truth. Consciousness has many levels, each with its own protective devices. When they continue to be in conflict, the sensitive soul suffers. Once you fully understand the Laws of Consciousness and apply them with the higher truth, you can live like the miracle you are.

CHAPTER 17

The Perpetual Trap

In the scenario below, you will see how our perceptions and fears create more distorted perceptions and fears and how these break down to feeling unworthy. This scenario is set in the 1800s as an example to show that not only does the trap go back many generations, it has not lost its traction even though each generation continues the search for the miracle that will release us from our suffering.

***

A small boy, born around 1853, turns eight years old. Let's call him Little Johnny. He is now considered old enough to work on the farm twelve hours a day to help keep the farm income stable. This boy lives his entire childhood under the dictates of a very demanding father, a father who relies on the farm producing enough crops to feed his family through another winter.

Little Johnny's mother spends her days making jam to sell at the local market to help offset bad crop months. Mother lives in fear of Father's rage when crops go bad. She remains quiet so as not to upset her husband, even though she feels Little Johnny is being overworked.

Little Johnny feels unworthy of Father's love because, despite all Little Johnny's hard work on the farm, Father is never happy. Little Johnny feels unworthy of Mother's attention because Mother spends most of her days taking care of his younger siblings, making jam, cooking, cleaning, and doing her best to remain unseen.

The Voiceless Soul

Little Johnny becomes an adult and labels Father as controlling and Mother as cold and distant. Little Johnny vows to be different from his parents.

What Little Johnny didn't know was that his father was raised by a man who told his sons that if they could not be good farmers, then they would be weak men. These words put fear in Little Johnny's father when he was growing up. His biggest fear was not being a good farmer and, therefore, not able to earn his father's love and respect. What Little Johnny doesn't understand is that his father lived most of his life with the fear of not being good enough. If he is not good enough for his father, then he is not good enough for the world. These fears are not in Father's conscious awareness.

Whenever there was a bad crop season, Little Johnny's father would go into a raging fear. What no one realized, not even Father himself, was that father was suffering from an unconscious fear of loss of love from his father, his family, and the world.

Loss of love means inability to be accepted. Inability to be accepted means one is unworthy. Feeling unworthy keeps you in the unworthiness trap. All of these thoughts are wrapped up in one big fear of nonsurvival.

As these thoughts crept up from the unconscious mind of Little Johnny's father, the fear of rejection by the world set in. His ego went into survival crisis, and he fought back through rage. His rage transferred to his innocent child and was received by Little Johnny as a rejection of who he was. Little Johnny continuously and desperately tried to please Father so he could win Father's love, although he felt unworthy of it.

What Little Johnny also didn't know was that Little Johnny's mother was raised by parents who said she was a mistake because they didn't want to have any more children, causing Little Johnny's mother to feel unworthy of the world. So she kept her emotions suppressed and tried desperately to please everyone. This caused Little Johnny's mother to spend her days trying to keep her husband and several children happy in a desperate attempt to earn their love so she could feel worthy of the world.

A girl, born around 1855, turns six years old. Let's call her Little Martha. Little Martha is ridiculed by Father because she is having a difficult time learning how to read. Little Martha feels stupid and unworthy of Father's love. Little Martha's mother is frustrated in helping her daughter learn to read. Over time, Mother becomes angry at her daughter for not learning as fast as other children her age. Mother has unconscious fears of Little Martha depending on a man like she had to. Little Martha feels like a burden to Mother.

Little Martha becomes an adult and labels her father as mean and her mother as impatient. Little Martha vows to be different from her parents.

What Little Martha didn't know was that her father was raised by an arrogant man who criticized his children for not being smart enough to succeed in the world. Her mother was raised by a man who treated women like burdensome subordinates. What Little Martha didn't know was that her father was living in fear of his own children not making it in the world, so he panicked when his children had difficulty in learning. Also, Little Martha didn't know that her mother lived in fear that her daughter would be treated unfairly by men because she was not educated enough to survive on her own.

Little Johnny and Little Martha meet as adults and marry. These two adults are now carrying the burdens and complexes of those who raised them, but they do not know it. They have both vowed to be different from the people who raised them. Little Johnny vows to let his children be free from household chores, and Little Martha trusts that their children will learn at their own pace. Neither Little Johnny nor Little Martha want their children to feel unloved and unworthy, as they did.

The usual honeymoon bliss follows the union in marriage of two lovers who want to be the perfect parents one day.

It's now the late 1800s. Martha gives birth to a baby boy. When the baby boy turns twelve years old, he begins to slack off on his household responsibilities, because Father never enforces them. He begins to slack off on homework because Mother never checks it. Johnny becomes angry at the boy for not doing household chores, calling him lazy and worthless.

What Johnny and the boy do not realize is that Johnny is calling the boy what he believed about himself when he couldn't keep up with his father's farming demands. Johnny's unconscious fears of being unworthy of his father's love have sneaked into his conscious mind, causing him to react toward his own son. This allows Johnny's insecurities about his worth to be passed on to the boy, causing the boy to feel unworthy of Father's love.

Martha finds out the boy is not getting his homework done. This triggers Martha's insecurities about feeling stupid, so she reacts to the boy with frustration and words of disgust. She tells her son that he will never amount to anything in this world, causing the boy to feel inadequate and unworthy of Mother's love.

***

This scenario will keep playing out over generations, showing up in different ways depending upon how each person processes their emotional experiences and feelings of unworthiness. We continue to project our suppressed emotions onto those we love because we never processed those emotions when we were children. When we get triggered by our environment, we lose control of our critical, thinking mind. Without our awareness, the emotional child within takes over.

Boy becomes adult and meets adult girl. They marry. They vow to be different from their parents. They have the complexes they picked up from their respective parents, which their respective parents picked up from their respective parents, and so on. Boy and girl's fears of unworthiness will be unconsciously projected onto their children.

Feelings of unworthiness come from the fears of others projected onto innocent, vulnerable beings. The fears were first created many generations ago.

When you look at how complexes get passed down, where in any of those generations do you notice love being expressed instead of fear? The only emotion being expressed is fear. Fear has many underlying emotions that no one is aware of, not even the one experiencing the fear. Fear keeps moving through the ancestral line, and love gets lost underneath it. Unconscious fears cause us to stop loving ourselves, which in turn stops us from loving others fully, including those we are closest to. This causes the unworthiness trap to keep growing.

We keep saying love is the answer, yet we really don't know what love is. Love is an experience, not a word. How can we experience full, unhindered, and unconditional love if we are the products of so much fear?

There is a continuous flow of unworthy feelings running through the souls of almost every human being who has ever lived, and the pain is real. It is so real that it becomes unforgivable, and that's where we get stuck. We can no longer endure the angst of others, yet we do not realize that we are stuck in the same trap. Everyone before you has experienced feelings of nonlove, and most of them were not able to heal from the deep pain of feeling unworthy.

Fear creates a continuous cycle of suffering. Life is not perfect. The people in your life are not perfect. They are human and they make lots of mistakes, many of them caused by their own insecurities. You are not the cause of their issues, but you are carrying their issues in your soul as an energetic imprint that is driving your emotional issues. This is what keeps us in the perpetual trap.

Sometimes we have overbearing parents or primary caregivers who don't give us the space we need as children. Many times, these overbearing adults were just tending to their own inner-child pain but did not know it. They saw in you their own emotional trauma and were trying to fix it. This is done unconsciously, in a desperate attempt to fix themselves. They were not trying to control you. They were trying to control the inner child in them who felt so out of control.

Don't stay angry or resentful, even if you have already decided to label them narcissistic or controlling. They are the way they are because there are parts of them that can't connect with the current reality. Be kind, for they are truly doing the best they can with what they know. They have not reached that higher truth. You can learn from their inability to see the higher truth. You can learn from the internal suffering that they could not heal. You can learn from your own self-awareness and by seeing the bigger picture.

You can bring out that hero inside of you and put an end to this perpetual trap.

CHAPTER 18

Waiting to Be Saved from Ourselves

Deep inside each of us is a younger version of ourselves that is waiting to be saved from the torment of not being good enough. This drives us to seek the big rescue, the one thing that is going to validate our existence in the world. I wonder why we never feel rescued. I wonder why we never feel validated—no matter how hard we try. I wonder why we can't find the answers we seek. Maybe it's because we are the ones who need to do the big rescue that we've been waiting for.

When we grow from childhood into adulthood with unmet childhood needs, we don't realize how important these needs are. Our higher intelligence is aware of what we need, but we are not in touch with that part of us. We are too busy trying to get our needs met in unconscious ways because the inner child is trying to feel safe and valued.

The inner child of a woman may feel like she is not pretty enough because her little brother told her she had a funny face and no one would want her. The inner child of a man may feel stupid because a teacher told him he didn't know how to use his brains. Criticisms like these cause young children to reject the criticized parts of themselves, because these parts are unacceptable to the world. As they grow into adulthood, they unconsciously find ways to overcompensate for what they believe is inadequate within them. The woman finds herself obsessed with her looks, spending large amounts of money on her appearance. The man finds himself a perpetual college student. What are they both looking

The Voiceless Soul

for? They want to be saved from their feelings of inadequacy. They want the one thing that is going to validate them as acceptable so they can feel worthy of the world.

The woman may seek out people to connect with who make her appear more appealing than the others. The man may seek out others who will make him feel superior in education and knowledge. These two people have no clue that their insecurities are directing their lives. They are being driven by their unconscious desires to fit into the world. They believe the big rescue is the people who can help them do that.

It is natural to want to be seen, heard, and valued in this world. It is unnatural to believe you are not worthy of it. The problem is many of us feel broken, and we don't know what we need so we can feel whole again. This keeps us searching for the savior who is going to fix all the broken pieces within us so we can finally live the lives we want.

We can feel that something is not right, but we don't make the connection. We don't realize that we are in conflict with ourselves. We don't see where we overcompensate for parts of us that feel unworthy. We don't see where we keep seeking validation. We don't see that we unconsciously want to be spared from our feelings of unworthiness. We are not aware of what drives us to do what we do and feel what we feel. The longer we seek a savior outside of ourselves, the longer those delicate inner parts of us suffer.

It's hard to nurture our hurt parts when we also have a critical inner voice that tells us what a mess we are. This conflict causes us to stay outside of ourselves. We don't have a clear voice speaking to us from within, because the critical voice is coming from the part of us that can't accept these wounded parts.

You will rescue your soul from the pain of unworthiness when the higher, intelligent part of you goes inside that unexplored space within you and brings love, compassion, and acceptance to the self-rejected parts of you. If you continue to stay distracted because these parts of you are emotionally overwhelming, then you will never feel free from uncomfortable feelings. They will be with you for the rest of your life. So now is the best time to do soul-healing work. Use the blank pages in the back of the book to write down all the thoughts, feelings, and emotions that show up for you while reading this book. Your feelings are important—express them as you need to.

When the hurt child within shows up, that child is voiceless, but the feelings are real. When we fight against those hurt feelings, we are fighting against an innocent part of ourselves. If we could hear our critical voices and the voices of our egos, they might sound like the familiar voices of the adults in our lives during our younger years. What if you spoke from the truth of how you feel about those parts of you, but then brought in the higher truth? You might find yourself loving these innocent parts of you.

> Dear Younger Me,
>
> I can feel your pain. It is moving through my soul like a tornado. I don't know how to stop it. I try to stay distracted and busy with everyday life to avoid the whiplash of your agony.
>
> Sometimes you are so overwhelming that it makes me want to run and hide somewhere. I wish you would just go away and leave me alone. No one ever wanted you, so why would I?
>
> Please understand that I can't keep this facade going much longer. I feel like you keep pulling me into a trap, and I don't want to be there. I want to feel significant, valued, and accepted in this world. If you keep showing up, you will prevent me from finding my peace.
>
> I suppressed you a long time ago because I didn't know how to hide your feelings of unworthiness from others. Why do you keep showing up? What do you want from me?

The Voiceless Soul

As I feel you inside my heart, I am beginning to feel your innocence. You are just a child. You couldn't have done anything wrong. You were just trying to figure it all out. You were just trying to feel wanted, loved, and accepted—and you didn't. As I go deeper into my heart, I can feel how you feel.

I am sorry you had to feel that way. I am sorry that I've been ignoring these awful feelings inside of me. You are not unworthy. You are an amazing little soul that just needs to know how perfect you are. I don't think you had enough support in your life to reach that truth.

I don't want to blame others for the suffering you feel. I believe they never reached their truth either. If I hold them responsible for what you are feeling, then I will not be able to help you heal. It seems we are all forgetting what miraculous beings we are. Maybe together we can create change for the world. Maybe we can heal together and spread the love that comes from the higher truth.

When I feel you, I now realize that you were waiting for me the whole time. I can feel you now. I am here for you.

I realize now that all you ever wanted was for me to accept you. All you ever wanted was to know that you are worthy of love, even though you don't feel that way. I am sorry for rejecting you. You deserved better, but I didn't know how to make it better. I do now.

All I ever wanted from you was for you to stop feeling so inadequate. There is nothing inadequate about you. You only felt that way because things have happened that made you believe you were. I am now aware that you are just a hurt part of my soul. I realize now that there is nothing outside of me that can heal you. All you needed was my love and acceptance. The big rescue is me loving you the way you deserve to be loved.

I am sorry I took so long to come to you. I didn't know that I was the answer to my own problems. All this time I thought these parts of me were being rejected by the world, but it was me rejecting me the whole time.

Please forgive me. You are more than enough. That battle is over now. I am here. I love you. You are whole. You are me. We are spirit.

With all my love,
Your Adult Self

CHAPTER 19

When Love Gets Lost Beneath the Fear

> When caretakers are untrustworthy, children develop a deep sense of distrust. The world seems a dangerous, hostile, unpredictable place. So, the child must always be on guard and in control. He comes to believe, "If I *control* everything, then no one can catch me off guard and hurt me."
>
> —John Bradshaw
> *Homecoming*

Every generation before you has suffered on some level from emotional conflicts. These conflicting thoughts and feelings affect the next generation. If an unborn child could speak from the womb, then maybe we could stop the madness before it starts. Since that seems like an unlikely occurrence, I think it's best to find the answer within our souls. This means you will need to let those inner thoughts and pent-up emotions be heard. You have been trying to do that in other ways without realizing it. It has to be done from a place of compassion within the spiritual heart, not through a desperate need to satisfy your childhood needs. That would be fear-based, and that is where love gets lost.

Most grown-ups who care for children are caring for them the best way they know how. Unfortunately, their best is tainted with unconscious wounds of unworthiness. Many of their actions and inactions are based in the fear of nonacceptance of who they are. This reality does not give anyone a free pass to hurt another, whether intentionally or not. What I would want you to take from this is that the reason you may feel unworthy is because there were many times love wasn't there when you needed it. The people you sought love from were stuck in their own unconscious fears and did not know how to love you the way you needed to be loved. Just as in the played-out scenarios of generational fear, love was not the guiding action.

People who don't receive the love they need tend to believe they are not worthy of love. Sadly, love gets suppressed because we fear rejection of it. When love keeps getting suppressed, our souls suffer. In turn, our bodies suffer. When love gets suppressed, the ego takes control of our lives. The ego helps us stay focused on survival, because when we disconnect from love, we disconnect from our life force, our spirit. Without connection to our spiritual intelligence, we are stuck in the lower intelligence of survival and fear. This keeps us stuck in an endless loop of unhealthy behavioral patterns.

The ego, by negating our feelings, helps us to keep our feelings suppressed. What happens when these suppressed feelings begin to surface? People change and become impostors. They become people we do not like. They become people who find ways to hurt people because they feel hurt. Some of these people are the most important people in our lives. These are the people we wish were different. Our need for our loved ones to be different than they are causes us to hold on to the past, remain in resentment, and ignore our love source. We must understand their pain so we can understand our own pain. We must stop making them responsible if they are not capable of it.

We know something has to change because we are not feeling good about the lives we are living. We want more. We need more. And yet we fear more. We stay stuck in the fear that keeps us trapped. We allow fear to take us further and further away from our love source.

Now is the time to look at the bigger picture and raise awareness of the truth. We have to stop putting love on the back burner because we don't trust it. Love is our healing power—not just love for ourselves, but love and compassion for those we have a close relationship with, even though they made us feel bad about who we are.

When you bring love to the forefront as you express all of your inner wounds, you soften the wounds and give them the space they need for healing. This includes bringing compassion into every relationship gone bad. The ugly parts of your relationships are fear energies overpowering the love inside of you. It is a difficult fight we keep fighting. It is a fight against the very things we need in this world: love, compassion, connection, and higher truth.

We only fear love because we believe it could hurt us. The pain of losing love seems to outweigh the joy of receiving love. This is not natural. This is ego-based fear—a survival strategy that is actually destroying the human spirit.

The safety of our hearts has taken priority over the love our hearts are trying to express. The only way to end this fear of nonlove that is spreading like a virus through the soul of humanity is to find our way out of the trap and seek the higher truth.

If you find yourself in fear of love, you have been deeply hurt. The thought of feeling that pain again is overwhelming. This is understandable. When you can look deeper into the pain that is now imprinted on your soul, use your higher heart and see the person who hurt you as someone who has disconnected from spirit. Take the blame off of yourself for not being able to hold on to the love. It has nothing to do with you. Write a letter to those who stole your trust in love. Speak from your hurt place while engaging the spiritual heart. There is freedom in speaking only from the higher truth.

If you find yourself hurting others because you keep running away from love, look deeper into those parts of you that fear it. Those parts of you need your attention. Write a letter to those parts of you. Remember to stay in your spiritual heart as you express the pain that caused you to fear something you naturally need and deserve in your life.

When we allow fear to keep us from the source for healing, we continue to stay in the trap and drag others into it. Notice if you are holding back on love for yourself and others because of a fear imprint of feeling unworthy of it. With so many good souls stuck in the unworthiness trap, there is much unexpressed love. Let's change that.

CHAPTER 20

The Fear of True Expression

It's difficult to express what we actually feel within us. Sometimes we don't really know what we feel. We may feel lost, confused, empty, alone, or just sad. If we actually took the time to go deep into the emotions that underlie these feelings, we would find parts of us that we probably didn't want to find.

This is what I have found in my work. My clients were in disbelief when feelings from childhood surfaced that related to their current feelings and situations.

Many of us believe our feelings don't matter. Most likely, they didn't seem to matter to anyone when we were growing up. When we are no longer small children, we have the ability to express how we feel, but we are afraid to. Our feelings were never validated, so we don't find it easy to express ourselves now. Maybe we were told to stop being so sensitive. Maybe we were told that we didn't know what we were talking about. Basically, we were told that we didn't know what we were feeling or our feelings were not important. We grow into adults and don't know how to communicate what we feel or what we need. Or we are simply afraid to fully express ourselves, out of fear of rejection.

Our inability to know how we feel on the deepest level causes us to continuously seek out something or someone to help us feel better about ourselves. This creates a world filled with shallow relationships and greatly supports the material world.

Most of us are not comfortable communicating our deepest feelings. Our fear is that we will become vulnerable beings upon whom others can prey, or that we will be called weak or overemotional. We stay with our surface feelings and dare not to go deeper into ourselves to find ugly feelings of unworthiness. We want to be accepted, so we keep a layer of protection over our hearts.

It's very risky to express yourself from that deep place within you. If you do, there is no guarantee that your feelings will be well received. If you open up your deepest feelings, you could trigger an emotional response from someone who is not ready to acknowledge their pain or yours. This could cause a reaction you may not be prepared for. This is how we go back and forth with our egos. We just don't know how to live from the higher truth. It's much safer to hold everything inside and protect ourselves with less-than-meaningful conversations.

How can we live honestly and authentically if we fear so much around our relationships with others? How can we express ourselves freely if we fear that our true feelings may be rejected, ridiculed, or just taken too lightly? We can't. This causes us to engage in shallow conversations with the most important people in our lives. The problem is these shallow conversations tend to somehow mix in deep meaning that requires a response. Sometimes we don't get the response we were hoping for. Instead, we get a reaction of fear. What now? Back to square one—afraid to communicate our true feelings.

None of this means something is wrong with you or anyone else. It just means we are stuck in the trap where the ego is keeping us safe from further feelings of unworthiness.

What we all fail to understand is that we are precious beings with many different emotions that need to be openly and honestly expressed. We need and want to be heard, but we don't know how to communicate all the heavy feelings inside of us. We want to avoid setting off our own fear reactions or those of others. It's a delicate situation when you are not speaking from that higher place within you.

The Voiceless Soul

We each have a voice inside of us that needs full expression. We are all feeling the pain of the past. We all need to know it is safe to communicate how we feel.

The only way you can speak from your spiritual heart is to know that you are always supported by the spirit of love that lives within you. There is a place of truth inside of you that has been waiting for you to call it forward. It is the higher truth that is going to get you out of the trap. It is you in moments of truth expressing feelings from your fragile heart. It is you revealing to the world who you are.

This means it's OK to say, "I feel lonely and unworthy because my mother was never there for me." That is an expression of your pain. Your feelings are real. This does not mean that the story you attached to these feelings is real. It is real for you because that is the way you experienced it. Most likely, your story is completely different from the way others in your story perceived the situation. We all create our stories based on how we perceive our experiences from a survival consciousness. What is important now is that you speak from that fragile place inside of you, always allowing the love and compassion from your spiritual heart to guide you through the healing process as you express all that you feel inside.

What is vital in expressing your deepest feelings is to acknowledge that those feelings may not actually be the higher truth of the matter. The higher truth is the removal of the ego and seeing the bigger picture from the spiritual heart. This helps you to understand the true intent of others involved in the matter. This is the story behind the story you tell yourself.

The true intent of someone not showing you love could be because they don't know how to love. They may think they are fully loving you, but you feel unloved. This may be because all they have is a limited source of love to share. Perhaps they have blocked much of their love with fear.

Speaking from your spiritual heart is about speaking with an open mind. You most likely do not have the whole story that you connect to your feelings. You only have the part of the story that you became attached to. Speaking from your spiritual heart helps you grow up from that little you inside who is stuck in the pain of the story. It also gives you a chance to see the other parts of the story that you were not aware of.

If you feel unloved, unworthy, inadequate, or any other feeling that makes you feel uncomfortable about yourself, try expressing yourself on paper. Write down everything that hurt you in the past and continues to make you feel bad. As you do that, always end your writing with the higher truth, which is the understanding that you do not know what others may have felt when their actions or inaction made you feel bad. Accept that the people who did not love you as you needed them to were most likely living life from a place of fear that originated when they didn't receive the love they needed.

When we are stuck in feelings of unworthiness because feelings of nonlove have taken us out of alignment with our true selves, we cannot find the right words to express our pain. We must align with the higher truth so we can release our deepest thoughts and feelings without fear.

Expressing yourself from the heart is part of your spiritual journey and brings you spiritual growth. When you hold back out of fear, your unhealed emotions take you further and further away from your truth.

As my soul evolved, my words to myself and others evolved. I began to write down my feelings from a spiritual place within me. There was much I didn't know when I was a little girl. The beginning of my journey had made me bitter, distant, guarded, and quite lonely. The very pain I was trying to heal, I was recreating without knowing it. Feelings of loneliness and fear of abandonment created my life script. I remained stuck in the unworthiness trap. I lived my life chasing a cure for my unhappiness.

Expressing my inner pain from a place of higher truth has helped me change the way I tell my story. I now look for the bigger picture so I can see beyond my survival fears. This doesn't mean I give out free passes for people to hurt me. What changed is that I am no longer triggered by the actions or reactions of others. I am no longer stuck in the emotional immaturity that held me in the trap for so long. I am free to walk away from what doesn't fit into my spiritual life. I hope the same for you.

CHAPTER 21

How Emotional Immaturity Keeps Us Stuck

People who are unkind, uncompassionate, nonloving, and sometimes downright mean are stuck in emotional immaturity. The part of them that didn't grow up is their wounded inner child. Instead of wondering what is wrong with them, wonder what went wrong *for* them as young, vulnerable, and innocent children. As grown-ups who have not grown up, they do not know how to nurture their wounds, so they remain disconnected from their true selves and continue to act out like children having emotional crises.

Do you ever wonder how someone could come into this world wanting to be loved but instead getting caught up in hurting others? If we can understand that there is some undetected defect in their soul that is causing them to act from a place of fear instead of love, then we can have compassion for their difficulties. It is our own emotional immaturity that doesn't want to acknowledge that others cannot meet our needs because they can't meet their own needs.

The only way out of this trap is to believe in your inherent value, to trust that you are a miraculous being deserving of full, unhindered love, and to trust that the right people will show up in your life.

If you are still trying to receive the love you need from a caregiver who failed to meet your childhood needs, then you are keeping yourself in that wounded space with them and denying yourself the happiness you deserve. If a caregiver is stuck in emotional immaturity because they have not been able to heal their burdened soul, it is up to you to understand that they are not intentionally holding back love from you. They are holding back love from themselves because they feel inadequate and flawed. If you are stuck in that trap with them, then you will attract emotionally immature people into your life.

Once you gain the higher understanding that the immature people in your life are just wounded children who don't know how to express themselves from the spiritual heart, then you will drop your expectations of them to do better and just reside in the knowing that they are doing the best they can with the wounded soul that lives within them. When you feel the need to judge, criticize, and stay angry at them for not meeting your expectations of them, then you have fallen into the same trap that they are in.

We must look at the whole picture. It is the refusal to understand what others are experiencing on a soul level that allows us to take on their stuff. We will resent them for being who they are when we don't really know who they are on a deeper level. We only know that they are not who we want them to be. If we are reacting to their behavior because we can't accept it, then we are acting from a place of emotional immaturity. This means we are not responding from a compassionate, higher heart. Responding from a compassionate, higher heart means that you understand that if they are not acting from a place of love, they must be experiencing fear. When you can do this, you have responded from a place of emotional maturity.

Nurturing our own childhood wounds and taking full responsibility for our own happiness is the way we can "adult up" and be the grown-ups we wanted others to be for us. Growing up allows us to sit in the higher truth and be in the higher love that comes from the spiritual heart.

When you trust that all souls are *expressing themselves through their own level of consciousness*, and you really understand this higher truth because you get the bigger picture, then you will rise out of emotional immaturity and connect deeper with your soul's true essence.

The emotionally immature adult lives through a false sense of self. They are controlled by self-defeating beliefs that were formed many years ago. Those beliefs include "I am not lovable," "I am unworthy of this world," No one could ever love me," I am not pretty enough," "I am stupid," and "Everyone leaves me." I can go on and on listing the ugly thoughts that are running through people's minds twenty-four hours a day. That's right: the unconscious mind never sleeps. People will act on these thoughts and beliefs, and you will wonder what is wrong with them. Many of us act on our unconscious thoughts and beliefs, but we don't realize it.

So, you see, we don't have full control over our lives the way we think we do. You gain control of your thoughts and emotions once you have healed those unhealed parts of you that are influencing your behaviors. This allows you to stop reacting to the unhealed emotions of others and respond in a responsible way. This may mean offering love and support to others, or it may mean walking away from those who are not ready to acknowledge their disconnect from love and compassion. Walking away does not always mean a physical exit from someone's life. That is not always possible. It means disconnecting from their toxic energy, not engaging with their drama, and remembering the truth of who you are.

We believe we, as well as all other adults, should be emotionally mature because we have outgrown our childhood needs. This is not true. Many of us are stuck in emotional immaturity. Our child-minded parts are still trying to get our needs met. We act out, we shut down, we run from our feelings, and we distract ourselves with mindless things. Sounds immature, doesn't it? It is—yet it is the best we can do if we did not receive the emotional connection we needed when we were growing up. This means we are still trying to connect to those feelings, but, just like a child, we do not know how. This holds true for those adults in your growing-up life, and this is why they were not capable of meeting your childhood needs. They were too focused on trying to get their own childhood needs met. Although this sounds selfish, it was most likely out of their awareness.

It's time for all of us to come back to the spiritual heart. We need to grow up and show up and be the beautiful spirits that we are. Let's step it up and become a role model for those who can't find their way out of the trap.

You have what the world needs. You were born with a guiding spirit that lives within you. Spirit brings unconditional love and shows compassion for others. Spirit has no judgments, no shame, and no guilt, just love. Your spirit can heal your wounds and bring more peace into the world. You must trust how powerful you are. In each and every one of us is a natural healer. Find that space within you.

Open your spiritual heart and allow yourself to flow into that natural inner wisdom. Get to know people on a deeper level. Get to know who they really are underneath their facade of confidence and well-being. People need people who can be compassionate and caring. Try to understand what might make them lack emotional maturity. You will find that they have a story too. They just want to feel loved. That's all they need. That's what we all need. More love—less fear.

CHAPTER 22

Perfect Divine Souls Wrapped Up in a Big Mess

Do you sometimes feel like you're just a big mess? Well, here's the deal, beautiful miracle of life. This is not one of those books that is going to tell you how you are a perfect, divine, conscious being of light and that you just need to hold a space of love around you and you will dissolve all fear. This book is not about that. Books do not always have to pamper your soul. Some books are meant to shake up and wake up your soul. Actually, this book is here to tell you what a mess you are because you are a perfect, divine, conscious being of light that came into a physical world where many people are stuck in the unworthiness trap.

The good news is you are still a divine miracle, a gift of love from above. You just need to understand how it all works. When you learn how to navigate this thing called life through a higher place within you, you will release yourself from the mess you got stuck in when you fell into the trap.

I am here to appeal to your loving and compassionate side, as you not only learn how others operate due to their inability to get out of the trap, but also to understand how you got pulled into their trap.

The adults in your life have acted out of fear more than they have acted out of love. This does not mean that they do not love you. This means they have become overwhelmed by their struggles and fears, which caused them to act from a place of nonlove. Sadly, some people have become distrustful of love because of many unloving experiences. Some people have actually become very toxic because they have never experienced love. No wonder the self-help era exploded in the 1980s. It's because we all feel like a big mess.

The challenges of life keep throwing us out of alignment with our divine selves. Those who followed self-help gurus were desperately searching for feelings of love, peace, and safety. Not much has changed. Many of us are still chasing the answers that are going to fix our messy lives.

We are walking this earth with many wounded souls. When you add into the mix the extreme pressures of today's society, you have a very toxic cocktail. No wonder the world seems like a big mess.

It takes a hero to undo the mess that has been made over the generations. One hero will help influence the emergence of more heroes. One hero will affect many generations to come. We all have that hero within us—but we must unblock our spiritual hearts and live from a higher level of consciousness. Do you have what it takes? You absolutely do.

CHAPTER 23

The Question You're Afraid to Ask

Although some of what you have read may seem a little far-fetched, it is not. You are a conscious being from the beginning, but everything you took in at the beginning became unconscious when you were born. Every feeling of nonlove during your younger years became unconscious in order to protect you from feeling inadequate and unsafe in the world. Everything that remains unconscious affects the way you live your life every day. This means most of us are living our lives unconsciously, without awareness, and basically through a false self that was created for us through a lack of knowledge of higher truth.

Some of you can read this book through and through, over and over, and still ask yourself, "Why?" Why was he so neglectful? Why did he walk out on me? Why is she so self-absorbed? Why does he get so angry? Why did she hurt me? Why does she treat my sister better? These are the questions you ask yourself. You want the answers to these burning questions, right? Actually, you don't.

What you really want is the answer to the question you are afraid to ask. You want to know what's wrong with you. Instead of asking the real question, you skirt around it, waiting to hear something that will tell you are going to be OK. You don't ask the real question because you fear the answer.

It's OK to ask the real question, but you must ask it from your spiritual heart. You have many questions, but you only want the one answer that will fix the feeling of unworthiness inside of you.

When you ask the real question from the place of real truth, then you will get the real answer.

Question: Spiritual heart filled with the love and light of the Creator, I seek the higher truth from the loving source within me. I can't help but wonder what is wrong with me?

Answer: There is nothing wrong with you, sweet miracle of life. Things have gone wrong for you because you are still learning how to love and honor yourself.

The higher truth can only come from a place of love. It is the spirit of love that we keep disconnecting from every time we rely on the physical world to validate our worthiness.

I have lived most of my life wondering what was wrong with me and how I could fix myself. What I learned in the process was that I needed to let go of what I thought life should be and just be thankful for the lessons that forced me to find the higher truth. Sometimes you have to hit bottom so you have no choice but to look up.

Many of us suffer on the inside and play the ego game on the outside. It's exhausting. It's much healthier to spend our energy on helping to create a better world by being more accepting, more understanding, and more compassionate toward ourselves and all the innocent souls that keep getting pulled into the trap.

Maybe our souls do need a shakeup, and that's OK. The suffering parts of us have been trying to get our attention. We have to look at them with an open mind, an open heart, compassion and curiosity. We have to stop being afraid of our pain. Ask the burning question that is keeping you from loving yourself and then seek the higher truth for the answer.

CHAPTER 24

No Bad Souls, Just Bad Choices

Whatever not-so-pretty story you tell yourself, you are keeping it active by believing you are your story. This causes you to unconsciously make decisions that keep you in your story. If you were cheated out of healthy parenting from your caregivers, then you probably feel that you were not worthy of their love. Chances are they were under the control of their childhood wounding, so they didn't parent you the way you should have been parented. They made mistakes. They made bad choices.

We take on so much fear as children when we are not emotionally nurtured the way we need to be. We become adults who are harboring pain from the past without realizing it. This causes us to find faults in others when they can't give us what we emotionally need. It's a very difficult process to go through. We are emotional beings with much to offer the world, yet we lose ourselves in some kind of energetic force that draws us into the trap. The feelings are real, and I am sorry for anyone who gets stuck in this debilitating trap. It's a difficult place to be and seems like a difficult place to escape from. If you fell under the control of someone else's childhood wounding, just as they did when they were young and defenseless, then you are most likely holding on to feelings that hold you back from your greatness.

When you stop holding others responsible for their inability to be in in a higher place of consciousness, you will have more control of peace in your life. Others cannot make you happy if they are stuck in unhappiness.

They will try, but they will eventually fail at it because they are making fear-based choices. You don't have to stay stuck where they are. You have the opportunity to learn and grow from their mistakes. If you label them bad, then you are stuck in ego consciousness. If you understand that they made bad choices because of their lack of higher consciousness, then you are speaking a higher truth.

I know it's a difficult process to get yourself unattached from the pain that others have caused you. Unfortunately, it is these attachments that keep you in the trap. Instead of being attached to the hurt they caused you or someone you care for, remind your beautiful, sensitive soul that you came into a world that is struggling with the fear of nonlove. This is where you can go into your spiritual heart and bring compassion to yourself and others.

Most people are not evil. They are human beings with defective soul energy that is keeping them from the full expression of love. It's important that you find a way to detach from their inability to be loving and compassionate. It is important for your own soul growth to understand their weaknesses.

A soul that suffers from the fear of nonlove may be prone to making bad choices. Everything is being done on a soul level, and we think it's an intentional choice made by the intellectual, conscious mind. This causes us to be angry at them, but our anger keeps us stuck in that same trap with them.

We can easily get hurt by the actions and inactions of others when we are still feeling the pain of past hurts that are deeply ingrained within our souls. It is not easy to become immune to the opinions of others, because we rely too much on others for validation. The approval of others is so important to our survival brain that we have instinctively become reliant on what others think. If we can see the bigger picture around the way it all works, then we can see that all souls are naturally good with good intentions. They are making bad choices based on the negative unconscious thoughts and feelings that are feeding into the soul.

When souls get lost in the challenges of the physical world, they lose sight of their miraculous spirit. This is where they go wrong. This is where they make it go wrong for others. When the bad choices of others have taken you out of alignment with your truth, it may be difficult to see what a wonderful being of light you are. We need to have compassion for the souls that can't find their inner peace so that we don't let their emotional drama disturb our peace. Ram Dass said, "You have to have a lot of compassion for the stages people are in. Souls are neither good nor evil. Actions are good or evil. Motivation is good or evil. Personalities can be good or evil. But the essence of being is neither good or evil it just is. And sometimes it has heavy stuff to work out and other times good stuff to work out." [4]

Nothing contained in this book negates the fact that some people are psychologically toxic. Some souls are so defective that they knowingly hurt others for their own satisfaction and gratification. You need to have the strength and courage to walk away from their destructive and debilitating energy. Your priority is with the health and wellness of your soul.

---

[4] https://educateinspirechange.org/spirituality/21-quotes-from-spiritual-leader-ram-dass

CHAPTER 25

The Incomplete Stories of Our Lives

Every acquaintance or close relationship you have ever had with the people in your life has given you an impression of them. Some of these impressions have helped to create the stories you tell about life. These stories are not told from a bigger viewpoint, but only from your perspective. Your impressions of others are based on how they made you feel about yourself or how they treated someone you care about. Therefore, the stories are from your perspective only, which makes the story incomplete.

The full story would include what was going on in them that caused them to make a certain impression upon you, and what was going on in you that caused you to have that impression of them. When there are missing pieces to any story, the story is incomplete. Knowing the full story will mostly likely change your perceptions and your story.

If you could understand the other parts to each story and see how those parts have nothing to do with you but came from a fear part of the other person, then you would have a better understanding of the events in the story and the people involved in it. It is the knowing that the suffering of a soul can cause suffering to another soul, not intentionally, but through the very truth that we are sensitive beings. Many of us are stuck in fear. What people say and do can affect us on a soul level if we do not stay in our higher truth. When we doubt our ability to be loved the way we need to be loved, the issues of others can easily become our issues.

The Voiceless Soul

There is a well-known truism that says, "Change your story, change your life." The problem is that it's not so easy to change a story that you have been telling yourself over and over again. Your story will change only when you can see the bigger picture, put the pieces together, and understand the story behind the story. Until you can do that, your unconscious mind will see your story only from your perception of it. Even if someone was unapologetically abusive, the story behind that story is the part you could not see or understand. That is the part where the abuser felt disconnected from love, and their frightened, angry inner child took over. There is no acceptable excuse for such behavior, but there is a reason beyond what we could comprehend. If we can see the big picture, then we can get out of feelings of victimhood and more into a heart of compassion—first for ourselves, for the suffering we endured, and also for the disconnected and confused soul that hurt us. This is the only way to disconnect from their burdens. The pain in their soul affects our soul because the lower frequencies of their actions are energetically bound to us by the emotional wounds we carry from the wrongs they have done.

Everything you put into your story is based on the emotions attached to your memories, but not the facts. What you are not aware of (because you couldn't be) are the emotions of others involved in your story. The fact is that others are suffering from feelings of unworthiness and causing emotional disturbances within you. They have failed you, and it's hurtful. As human beings, we can't help but tell the story of how we were hurt. The problem is that we sometimes get stuck in the story, and this keeps us in the trap.

Our souls remain fragmented as long as we are holding on to the emotional imprints that were caused by someone else. Our stories remain broken and incomplete as long as we stay focused only on the impressions we have of others and not the full story behind their actions. If we put the full story together, we will be able to reject the projected anger, fear, and egocentric attitudes of others, because we will realize they are suffering from feelings of nonlove.

If we are lost inside some fragmented story of victimhood and fear, we will keep projecting that out. If we are lost inside some fragmented story in which we are not allowed to be seen or heard, then we will remain invisible to the world. If we take a wider view of our story and see the bigger picture around it, we will no longer feel that others are to blame for our misery. We need to release them from our soul body so we can move on.

I hear all the time that we should be more like children because children can just shake things off. Do they just shake things off? No, they don't. Children feel defenseless against the world. They feel disempowered and controlled. They hold on to the emotions that were too intense to process. Then they grow into adults with unhealed emotions that continuously cause emotional storms inside of them.

Well, we are all like children in that we continue to feel defenseless against the world. We never shook off our childhood fears of disapproval and nonlove. We absorbed these fears into our souls, and we are now living through that reality on an unconscious level.

Let's speak from the truth: children cannot and do not shake off emotional pain. All they can do is learn how to hide their emotions to avoid further shame and rejection. As adults, they are emotionally vulnerable children on the inside, while they show a tough exterior to the world. They don't have the complete story, only the story of their fears of nonlove.

I am sorry to say it, but we do have a broken system. This broken system didn't start with you. It started way before you were born. It started way before your parents and other primary caregivers were born. This system cannot be repaired until we learn how to level up our consciousness.

If we want to feel whole and connected to the truth of who we are, it begins with putting together the higher truth, the whole story. It requires seeing the bigger picture and expressing the pain that is crushing our souls.

When we feel broken and inadequate, we have to put on a facade of confidence and security. The problem is we can't keep the facade up forever. Something always finds a way to break us down again.

I realize now how much of my pain was ignored. I kept it hidden, and I blocked all feelings toward it. I thought the traumas of my childhood were over, so I must move on. Little did I know that buried trauma drives the soul to great lengths to find ways to heal it. I just wanted to feel at peace, and I didn't know why I couldn't get there. I realize now how much my ego was in the way.

Not only was I not healing, but my soul kept creating more drama. The only way it could feel at peace was to find completion in what felt unsettled. Many times, I thought I had found serenity. Suddenly those ugly feelings started popping up again. How could I not think something was wrong with me? It was this belief that something was wrong with me that drove me into the drama. I didn't see the whole story.

It's time to untwist the stories inside us and start trusting a higher truth. There is no one in this world who is not a miraculous being of light, although many are stuck in the darkness of the trap.

When you reach the higher truth and fully embrace the miraculous light body of energy that you are, then you will no longer unconsciously create or draw toward you the drama of the world. This can only be done when you can put the whole story together, using your higher intelligence, and speak from your spiritual heart.

This book will help to guide you there.

CHAPTER 26

How Grown Up are the Grown-Ups in Your Life?

Many caregivers, however, control their children through the guise of teaching them what they think is "best" for them. But more often than not, "what's best" for a child from the perspective of a caregiver reflects the caregiver's own unresolved traumas and unmet needs more than the child's real needs or desires.

—Darius Cikanavicius
Human Development and Trauma

Many of the people you are influenced by are not living with open hearts. Who are these people you think you know? Are they harmful grown-ups who do harmful things? If they are mentally ill and maybe even psychotic, then maybe yes. These are the people who need professional help. Their souls are completely disconnected from the truth of their essence. But if you were luckier than those who had to endure extreme toxic behavior, then you probably grew up in a dysfunctional home, like most of us.

Many people didn't have *grown up* grown-ups during their young, vulnerable years. If you were one of the fortunate few to have had truly enlightened caregivers, then you have been blessed with a treasure. People who are struggling to create a better life for themselves, on any level, have

The Voiceless Soul

most likely been blessed with parents, older siblings, other family members, teachers and other influential adults who are not emotionally responsible people. Parts of them are still stuck in their unresolved childhood trauma.

Now, imagine that most of the time these influential people are influencing you, supposedly to lead you in the right direction, all while there is a fierce battle going on inside of them. When they start to lose control of their inner battle, they lose control of themselves, and you get to experience their ugly side. When this happens, you (as the child) believe you did something wrong. You think something must be wrong with you. The adult who caused you to question your lovability is not even aware of the force behind their actions. They are automatically reacting to their own fears of unlovability.

Sometimes the battle within becomes exhausting and the grown-up shuts down like a frightened child. If you are witness to this as an infant or young child, you will feel a disconnect with this person whom you regard as one of your protectors. Even at a very young age, your mind will automatically cause you to go into survival mode. This means you start creating strategies to feel safe. You may shut down to avoid the pain of neglect, or you may act out in order to get attention to regain your connection to safety. Whatever strategy your child mind invoked in order to feel safe is the same strategy you will use in your adulthood whenever you feel a disconnect from the people you look to for love, acceptance, and safety. Your soul remembers what made you feel safe and automatically defaults to that safety strategy.

Your parents and primary caregivers are doing the same thing. They are invoking their survival strategies from childhood—while they are caring for you. They are showing the parts of them that didn't grow up. Since you couldn't know that as a child, you made the decision that you were the cause of their actions or inaction. This caused you to form beliefs like "I am a disappointment," "I am not worthy of my parent's love," "I am not wanted," and 'I am the cause of my parent's unhappiness." Whatever negative beliefs you created are now imprints on your soul, playing out in your reality, easily activated by a world filled with fear.

Who are these grown-ups who have failed to make you feel loved, worthy, and secure? These grown-ups are beautiful, kind, loving souls who are fighting against the fears of not being enough. Unfortunately, their inability to resolve their inner conflicts has caused you great pain. It would be natural for you to be angry, resentful, and saddened over not receiving the love, kindness, and support you deserved as a child. By continuing to hold yourself in that energy, you are keeping that part of them inside of you. It's not serving your soul now as an adult. It is only stifling your emotional growth. When their lack of emotional maturity continues to be an issue for you in your adult life, then they have pulled you into their emotional trap.

When you look back at your life as a child, what do you notice about the grown-ups and how they conducted themselves around you? Take a moment and just observe them. Even if they have crossed over, you can still observe them in your mind. Maybe you will notice all their mistakes. Maybe you will observe where they could have done better. Maybe you will have bad feelings about them. Maybe you will just wonder what caused them to act the way they did.

We can say, on a knowledgeable level, that our parents did the best they could. We can intellectualize how they could have been overwhelmed with family issues, finances, illness, career, chores, too many children to care for, and the many other challenges that come with adulthood. What we don't do is address any of these thoughts on a feeling level. If we did, our inner child would probably show up angry as hell. That is why we don't allow ourselves to feel what we feel. We already know it wouldn't be pretty. When the world challenges us, we reexperience our childhood pain. We forget who we are and become who we believe we are. We get pulled right back into that fear of not being enough.

We are emotional beings with the ability to suppress what doesn't feel good. Yay for us! Now we get to spend most of our lives trying to figure out why we feel the way we feel. All we know how to do is keep telling ourselves that our parents did the best they could. Some of us keep telling the story of how messed up our parents are. Whatever the story may be, it is not being felt. It is being told from a place of self-protection.

The Voiceless Soul

What if you told your story from the hurt child inside of you instead of the protective adult in you?

Suppose, for example, your father left you when you were five years old. As an adult, you may be telling the story of the lowlife father who ruined your life. You may even go as far as saying, "I wish he were dead." If you could take a moment of inner reflection by moving your mind into your heart center and giving yourself a chance to feel your feelings, you might say something like this: "My father left when I was five. I felt hurt, lost, confused, and abandoned. I needed to feel loved by him to feel worthy in this world. He left me with a daddy wound the size of my heart, and I am having a hard time healing my fears of rejection, abandonment, and loneliness."

If you could gain a higher understanding and see the bigger picture around life and all of its challenges, then you would have a higher understanding of what may have caused you so much pain. You would be able to feel your feelings and bring compassion to yourself and those who could not do better. If you could be in the higher truth of the way life works, it would sound something like this: "I have been deeply hurt by my dad. He was not the father I needed him to be. I grew up feeling deprived of the love I needed for healthy emotional growth. I now understand that he didn't leave me because I was not worthy of his love. He left me because he didn't know how to be a responsible adult. He couldn't be a responsible adult because he wasn't raised by responsible people. He did not fully grow up, so he could not act like a grown-up. I forgive myself for believing I was not worthy of his love. I understand the higher truth."

This is how we express our higher truth and pull ourselves out of the unworthiness trap.

We are removed from the truth of our past, and this is why we can't move beyond it. If we can face the truth and realize that there is more to the story than we know, then we won't be wondering why we feel unworthy.

Growing up is not easy for anyone. We have to let ourselves heal the wounds that the child in us was unable to. We have to face the feelings we couldn't face when we were fully focused on safety.

You now have the opportunity to use your wise and intelligent mind with the openness of your spiritual heart to create feelings of safety around the hurt child in you. Your perceptions of your childhood experiences came from a child in need of love and safety. What may seem unimportant to you now was very important to you as a child. Your sensitivity to life comes from the sensitive child within. It is up to you to create feelings of safety by expressing feelings of love to yourself. Remember that you have always done what was best with the knowledge you had at the time. Honor the amazing soul that you are underneath all those painful experiences. Then give yourself permission to use those experiences as a way to evolve your consciousness.

It is up to you now to understand from a higher truth that the grown-ups in your life may not have been fully grown up. Their love for you was expressed in the wrong way because of it. This understanding is what will help the child in you understand that you were always safe; it just didn't feel that way at the time. If we could understand that the child mind is still living in the adult body, always seeking love and safety from the world around it, then maybe we could understand how the adults in our lives showed fear instead of love. Many of the ways in which they acted immaturely came from the memories of their child selves who were in desperate need of love, safety, control, acceptance, and affection.

The child mind is filled with imagination, curiosity, and wonder. The child mind is also wired for safety. Childhood experiences can become quite fearful if the child believes they are not loved or are unlovable. This creates fears of rejection and abandonment that consume the child's soul. When the child physically grows into adulthood, the child mind is still stuck in those fears. This creates the immature adult who doesn't feel safe in the world unless they are being shown love.

I have found in my work that a child does not perceive abandonment only in cases of actual physical abandonment by a caregiver. Emotional abandonment and neglect have an impact on the child as well. The child may feel abandoned, unsafe, and even unloved if they cannot connect with a primary caregiver. This is very common in a fast-paced world where we don't allocate enough quality time to deeply and passionately connect with those we love.

Children need to bond closely with a parent or primary caregiver for feelings of safety. If they don't feel that bond because the parent or caregiver does not make time for connection, the child may feel disconnected from love and their necessary survival source. This disconnect can show up in their adult life as feelings of unworthiness, which in turn may keep the adult desperately seeking security from others.

Here is an innocent example of a mother-child disconnect that can cause emotional challenges later in life:

A mother has to leave the home to go to work on a daily basis. This is quite disturbing to her young child, because the child needs to be with Mommy to feel secure. The child does not understand that adults go to work, so the child feels abandoned and unworthy of their mother's love. These feelings of abandonment and unworthiness then become distorted beliefs in the child's soul and create a big Mommy wound.

This is an innocent and unavoidable separation of mother and child.

The bigger issue is that the mother is busy and distracted. She does not take time to connect with her child, which would give the child a sense of security. She believes her job is to run the household and provide financial resources to the home. She does not connect with her child because she doesn't understand the importance of it. She is living in survival mode because she grew up in a home where she learned to survive her own feelings of inadequacy. Love and connection were not learned or experienced in her childhood.

The grown-ups in our lives have made childlike mistakes because they are living like children in grown-up bodies. When they feel the need to feel loved, they chase it. They don't express authentic love with the knowledge that it will come back to them. Instead, they express a desperation for love because they are like little children desperately seeking security in a world that is big and scary.

In the scenario above, the mother is seeking approval through her ability to do it all—run the household, have a full-time career, be a parent, and be a financial provider. Her reward is getting things accomplished so she can satisfy her feelings of inadequacy.

Sometimes the desperate search for love turns into desperate actions by a grown-up controlled by the fear of nonlove. It is that desperate search for love that leads to a self-absorbed way of life. This is the child mind in the adult body, still living in survival mode as they chase down love—not caring who gets hurt in the process. This is an unconscious and desperate attempt to reach a sense of safety.

In the following scenario, a child experiences actual physical abandonment and grows up with similar feelings of unworthiness as in the scenario above.

A mother left her children because she fell in love with a man who did not want her children. The memory of this is quite clear to the grown-up child: Mommy was selfish and uncaring. Yes, this is true in this situation, but what made her act this way? For the adult child to release their feelings of unworthiness and fear of abandonment, they would have to understand the motivation behind their mother's inability to love her own children.

The child (now adult) would have to become familiar with the story behind the story, or their adult self will carry childhood wounds of unworthiness that are not only soul crushing, but will cause the adult self to have intense fears of abandonment. The adult may even become very troubled.

The story behind the story of abandonment might be something like this: Mother didn't actually fall in love, but instead was feeling a desperate need for security. She was a single mom whom nobody wanted to be with. No one wanted the responsibility of her children. She let her burdens of fear overpower her love for her children. That is how powerful fear can get when it is accompanied by threats to safety and connection.

Sadly, in this situation, what the mother was unconsciously longing for was her daddy's love. The only way she could feel worthy of her daddy's love was to find a man to whom she could prove her worthiness. Although, on an unconscious level, she most likely felt guilt and shame for leaving her own children, she also had an unconscious drive to win her daddy's love. Her frozen trauma of not being worthy of her daddy's love was being played out in her adult life. Her fear of nonlove by her daddy was more powerful than the shame and guilt of abandoning her own children. She was driven by her survival mind (fear) and not driven by the love she had for her children. She could only love her children as much as she loved herself. Sadly, she did not have much love for who she was. This made it possible for her to disconnect easily from whatever love she did feel for her children.

When fear overpowers love, it means we lost ourselves in the battle.

In this latter scenario, there is a bigger picture that her children could not see. This causes her children to be pulled into her unworthiness trap. This is a mother who did not grow up because she didn't have grown up grown-ups in her life.

Does this mother deserve forgiveness for her self-centered behavior? That is up to each individual child who is experiencing the pain. The children, however, need to forgive themselves for believing that they are unworthy of their mother's love. The adult children need to find peace in the knowing that their mother was not capable of giving them the love they deserved. They must return to their souls' innocence and pull themselves out of the trap that their mother pulled them into.

A child, as an adult, after doing soul-healing work and seeing the whole picture, would reach the higher truth. This would release the negative energetic bond with the mother and give the child, now adult, emotional freedom. The grown-up child would understand that Mom was not very grown up, because she did not receive enough grown-up guidance and support. This does not make her behavior OK, but it does help to make sense of what feels like a crumbling world to the child. It helps the adult heal the childhood wounds of abandonment. It helps the adult come to the higher truth that their mother's wrongdoing had nothing to do with the child.

During my parenting years, I made my own mistakes. I tried to control situations in which I thought my children would not be safe. From their health to their happiness, I wanted to make sure I met every childhood need they had. As a young girl who was rejected by the neighbors, sent home by the school principal for looking disheveled, went days without meals, was physically sick most of the time with no one to comfort me, and lived in a home with cracked walls, mice, roaches, and broken furniture, I wanted to make sure that my children never had to endure poverty or despair.

Was it wrong to be so controlling? Maybe—but being controlling was not my intention. It was just my good intentions gone wrong. I was trying to protect my children from the pain and rejection I felt as a child. I was, without conscious thought, trying to save my own inner child from shame. My attempt to save myself was through overprotecting, overcontrolling, and overindulging my children. Many times, it was the hurt child in me making the decisions to overprotect everyone's feelings and keep them safe from what seemed like a cruel world. It was the part of me that was emotionally stifled—still stuck in the fear of unworthiness.

When I did my soul-healing work, I became more conscious and aware of my soul patterns. This helped me to let go of the things I could not control. This helped me put faith in love and the spirit within, so I could trust that my children would be OK if I let them be themselves.

Most children do not get their emotional needs met when they are raised by grown-ups who have failed to grow up. Childhood trauma affects the way we parent our own children, sometimes to their detriment. It doesn't mean we are bad parents. It just means a part of us has failed to reconnect to the truth of who we are, leaving us to feel the need to correct the parts of the past that caused us pain.

When innocent child souls become adults, they are still in need of getting their emotional needs met, causing stagnation in their growth. This creates a world of grown-ups with the emotional consciousness of small children. How do we get these adults to grow up and become responsible grown-ups? We can't. They have to figure that out on their own. The question is how do you grow up from your deficient childhood so you don't continue along their path?

The Voiceless Soul

The answer is compassion.

If we show compassion for their shortcomings, we can release ourselves from feeling the need to win their love. This allows us to accept ourselves wholeheartedly, without the fear of not being enough. When we have compassion for others, we are showing compassion for ourselves first. We are releasing ourselves from the need for their approval.

As mentioned before, toxic behavior is never acceptable. This is not about accepting bad behavior, even if it is coming from a hurt soul. This book is about healing the wounds that pulled you into the trap. It is about having compassion for the soul that doesn't know how to love. It is about having compassion for yourself because you had to endure the pain of others. It is about higher understanding.

The truth is we were taught how to navigate our lives by grown-ups who hadn't fully grown up. Many of us were raised not by mature adults but by big children. What now?

If you could have spoken to your parents or other primary caregivers before you actually learned to speak, you would have been able to express everything you felt inside. If only the feelings in your little body could have been put into words through your voice from the beginning, then maybe you would now be able to let others know when they are making you feel bad.

You couldn't voice yourself then, but you can do it now. When you voice your needs, you do so from your inner child. You can release the stuck energy of "not good enough" by putting onto paper all that your younger self has been holding in.

Always speak from your spiritual heart. If you don't, then you are just recycling anger and frustration.

If you speak from your inner child using the wisdom of the higher truth, it may sound something like this:

Dear Mom and Dad,

This is not an easy journey. I have to work hard to get your approval, and it never feels like enough. When I look into your eyes, I see your disappointment. When I look in the mirror, I see my shame. I don't know how to make these feelings go away, so I do my best to hide them.

I want nothing more than to be the perfect child for you. I try my best, but sometimes I mess up and don't know how to get it right. I am still learning how to be the child you want me to be. All I ask is that you be patient with me, so I can learn how to do that.

There is so much I want to learn from you. I don't understand the world or where I fit into it. I just know I need you to love me, so I can feel safe in a world I have yet to explore.

Please try to understand that when I disappoint you, it's not because I am not trying. It's just that I am new at this. Your love and patience are all I need. Sometimes I work too hard at trying to please you, and you get annoyed. I guess I am just so desperate for your approval that I don't know how to stop yearning for it.

Please forgive me for my mistakes. Learning is not easy when everything is so new and unfamiliar. Please be patient with me, so I don't get nervous trying to be the child you always wanted.

Please be patient with your own inner child. Your younger self needs your love just as much as I do.

With all my love,
Your Child

CHAPTER 27

The Many Wounds in the Unworthiness Trap

Life has ways of throwing many challenges our way, some of which are unavoidable. They can leave deep scars on our souls. Many of us have experienced the pain of death, divorce, poverty, bullying, and illness. These wounds can pull us into the unworthiness trap because we, as sensitive souls, believe we are the cause of the pain we experience. The pain we feel in our souls will always feel like a threat of nonlove.

The loss of a parent or other primary caregiver through death or divorce can feel like abandonment. Growing up in poverty can feel like failure. Being bullied can create feelings of shame. A serious illness in the family can cause feelings of helplessness and guilt. Being shunned by your best friend can feel like betrayal. All of these emotional traumas lead to feeling unloved and jeopardize our feelings of safety. Any one of these emotional traumas can pull us into the unworthiness trap.

The unworthiness trap is filled with many souls aching for relief. We need more understanding. We need more acceptance. We need more compassion.

I have witnessed many of these emotional traumas through soul-healing work with my clients. The way my clients were able to find peace in their challenges was to see that all of their emotional traumas are from broken expectations, self-disappointments, feelings of unworthiness, and fear of nonlove. The more they experienced emotional trauma, the more they moved away from self-love. As we worked together to bring their hearts back to their divinity, there was profound healing. My clients discovered that we are all suffering from the same delusions of unworthiness.

There are many wounds that hold us in the unworthiness trap. It is our own responsibility to get ourselves out of the trap that we were involuntarily pulled into. We have to own what we feel so we can take the steps to heal what needs to be healed. We must let go of the need for our past to be better. It had to be the way it was. It was the only way the people in your life knew how to navigate it. They did it with all their knowledge, all their conditioning, all their beliefs, and all their intentions to keep you and themselves safe. They did it with the love they were capable of, which was limited to the love they felt for themselves.

The most important part of the healing process is to feel, on a profound level (not just think it), that most of the world is trying their best with what they have learned and experienced during this journey. This is what will help us out of the trap and give us the opportunity to live in more peace and harmony.

We will love more and fear less. We will have more responsiveness and less emotional distance. We will have more empathy and less judgment. We will understand the many emotional wounds of the unworthiness trap and respond to them from a higher place of compassion and understanding.

The many wounds of the unworthiness trap are what keep the trap open for others to fall into. You are a survivor. You are here now, and you made it through many challenging years. You can stop focusing on survival now; you are safe. It's time to start focusing on the higher truth.

You were born with insight, wisdom, and spiritual knowledge that has been suppressed for too long. Open and expand your spiritual heart so you can tap into your divine gifts and release yourself from the fallacies of the past. Heal the wounds that keep you in the trap, and see the world as a place of opportunity instead of a place of fear and survival.

It's time to step into your heroic role and claim your greatness as a being of light who is here, on this big planet, for a divine purpose that serves humanity from a place of compassion and understanding. It's time to stop letting the past strip you of your right to explore this journey with the highest of love and divine truth.

Are you ready to be the one who says, "I've had enough of feeling not good enough?"

See the many wounds in the unworthiness trap, and see them for what they really are. Be the one who can love from a place of joy and freedom and not from a need for survival. Be the one who doesn't take on other people's unhealed traumas. Be the one who gets it—the one who sees the higher truth. Be the one who is no longer fooled by the darkness and can see the bigger picture.

Be your true, divine self.

CHAPTER 28

Freeing Yourself from Survival Consciousness

> Your instincts may tell you that you can't survive if you experience feelings. But they are leftover child instincts. They're the ones that first told you to freeze your feelings. They themselves are frozen and haven't grown with the rest of you. These instincts don't know that you're far more capable of learning to cope with overwhelming emotion now than when you were a child.
>
> —Maureen Brady

People who suffer from feeling unloved and, therefore, unworthy of the world live with the fear that the world sees them as inferior. This causes them to take all necessary steps to hide any perceived flaws and increase their ego power. The ego is all about showing the world you are worthy of it as you hide your self-doubt and lack of confidence.

When we are living from ego consciousness, we can exhibit confidence and strength. This is our way of fitting into the world. The moment we feel unaccepted by those we seek acceptance from, our biggest fears jump into action. We believe we are being seen for who we really are. We believe the world is turning on us because we have been found out. We fear the gig is up. Everyone can see our flaws. We may get angry. The ego gets stronger and more protective. We will express this anger at the people we feel comfortable with because we know they will take it. In turn, our loved ones will think we are not loving them and will feel unworthy of our love. This is how we pass the fear of unworthiness without realizing the damage it's doing. We are so stuck in survival consciousness that we lose our ability to see our own actions.

Our inability to see the ego for its true purpose does not give anyone a free pass to throw their anger, need for control, or self-importance at anyone. What I am saying is that, for your own emotional health, don't take ego-controlled people personally—they are just stuck in the trap. I was there for a very long time myself. I wasn't intentionally trying to harm anyone. I was just angry, afraid, and stuck in my childhood trauma.

Anger, control issues, and a superior attitude are reactions to underlying emotions that always lead back to feelings of unworthiness. When someone displays these types of attitudes, it is their way of saying, "I feel afraid." It is a childhood soul imprint that got stuck in the fear of nonlove. This is what needs to be understood. Many adults live with the fear of not being loved, not being wanted, or not being enough. They take on a big ego personality to hide these fears from others. When the anger comes through, it means the child part was triggered and the adult lost control.

Sadly, most of us believe we don't have what it takes to be loved. The only way to navigate this world is through survival, and the only way we know how to do that is to pretend we feel significant. We can't be our true, divine selves if we have to keep faking who we are. When we forget that we are truly divine beings and loved by the highest love source, we lose ourselves in the fear of nonexistence. When we abandon our truth, we abandon ourselves.

It takes a higher understanding to get out of that lower level of thinking. No one would know this unless they were living through their spiritual heart and not their ego. If others saw my anger as my plea for love and acceptance, then they wouldn't make my anger about them. They would stay in their spiritual heart and show me compassion, or maybe just let me work it out on my own. This is not something a child can do. A child becomes attached to their caregivers, and this causes them to absorb their caregiver's anger. As the child grows into adulthood, they carry their caregiver's anger inside of them. They blame themselves for not being able to please their caregivers, keeping them stuck in the anger that was passed on to them. Their ego tells them that they have the right to stay angry, because being angry gives them back the feeling of control that they lost as a child. It's a trap.

Many emotional challenges can cause us to stay in ego-based survival consciousness. We just don't know how to navigate this life without protecting ourselves from the harshness of others. People can be unkind and selfish because it's the only way they know how to protect themselves. They are fighting against a world that they believe can annihilate them for not being enough. They can't get out of survival consciousness. Don't let them take you there with them.

All the family that came before you, meaning your parents and generations beyond them, did not have the resources you have today for healing the soul. Methods of self-help were not available to them. They did not learn mindfulness techniques, because they were taught that the brain is unchangeable. Meditation was reserved for those who held the title of monk. It is only fairly new science that proves the plasticity of the brain—meaning that it is moldable and can be physically changed by new thoughts and experiences. The generations before us were mostly concerned with survival.

If previous generations were taught that they could not change their brains, which controlled their behavior, then they accepted that their lives were unchangeable. Going within to heal was something futuristic and not of the world they grew up in. The thought that we experience different levels of consciousness is still foreign to most people.

When our survival is threatened by rejection and the fear of nonlove, our unconscious mind creates a strategy to help us find a way to get the love we need. This is where unhealthy behavioral patterns begin. Some of these behaviors are self-destructive, the result of our desperate need for survival. Many of us are still locked into these unconscious survival patterns. These patterns were not just formed by you. These patterns were formed way before you were born. These patterns run through your ancestral line. Everyone keeps getting stuck in the trap. Not only did our early ancestors suffer famines, incurable illnesses, intense wars, starvation and extreme poverty, they had no outlets for their emotional suffering. The emotional suffering is what gets passed down through the generations.

You have the choice between following that legacy of fear or living through the wisdom of your higher self, creating the life you deserve.

If our ancestral lineage had flowed with an abundance of unconditional love, allowing our mothers and fathers to experience all the love they needed to feel safe in the world, then we would not be so afraid to live our lives with passion. We would feel safe being who we are. We would feel comfort in the knowing that love awaits us. This is what spirit is here to show us. This is what our souls are craving.

Each generation vows to be better parents or caregivers than the ones before them—and they usually are. Unfortunately, old, conditioned patterns do not fade away. They creep in when they are triggered by the outside environment. This causes the caregiver to react from the past, causing a moment of nonlove. The child's survival feels threatened.

We are more aware than our primary caregivers and ancestors were because we are evolving as a society. When society as a whole is stuck in a pattern of unworthiness, then it keeps us all stuck. We have more information, which gives us more knowledge, which gives us more resources, which gives us more power to change. We have more opportunities for growth and change than those before us did.

As a collective society, which has more resources than ever before, we are at a great advantage to heal ourselves out of the trap and out of survival consciousness. Human nature is not a finished product. It is more like a consciousness: meant to change, evolve, and transition into higher levels of awareness and truth. We are all changing, growing, and developing with higher understanding and the truth about human consciousness. We can only look back at the inability of those before us to live more heart-centered lives as a consciousness that was less evolved.

When you live your life from a higher level of awareness, you are able to heal your soul and help others heal as well. When you are living from a higher state of awareness, you emit more loving energy into the world. To reach that higher level, you will need to see what's going on through your current level of awareness, which keeps you stuck where you are. You will need to understand that there is a movie playing out in front of you and your soul is the director. The problem is that your soul is stuck in the fear shown in act I. It's time to close the curtain, take a pause, and then open act II. This is where the hero steps forward and brings balance back to the chaos that ensued during the first act.

Your soul is aching for one thing and one thing only: a reconnection with your true self.

Your true value is the one placed upon you by your Creator. The Creator is the one and only true source of love, and you are part of that source. Spirit is not about survival. Spirit is here to help your soul evolve into the level of spirit consciousness.

Let the love of spirit sink into your soul and hold you in your divine essence, so you can feel the purity of your soul's innocence and release the fears of unworthiness. You don't need to work so hard at survival. The soul never dies, and spirit is always with you. Let your ego relax and let love be the guiding force behind your actions.

CHAPTER 29

When the Past Keeps Calling You Back There

The past is made up of memories—some that are good and some that are not so good. Memories that continue to haunt you are memories that feel unfinished. These are the memories that hold all of those why questions. These are the memories that confuse you. These are the memories that still rock your emotional world. These are the memories that need your attention.

You have memories that keep calling you back because they are seeking completion. Parts of your past feel unfinished because you couldn't make sense of what was happening around you or the feelings happening inside of you. Because of this confusion and the fear to revisit the unknown, you chose to let these memories lie sleeping. The problem is, if you don't resolve what needs to be resolved from the past, then you are doomed to repeat it. It keeps calling you back because it needs resolution.

Due to the nature of human consciousness, we want things to feel complete before we can move forward. This is especially true when we have an emotional investment in something that remains incomplete, unresolved, and unfinished. We will always get triggered by something in our current environment that draws us right back to the memory that feels incomplete. We may not realize that this is happening, because it happens on the lower levels of consciousness, out of ordinary awareness. Completion means we found our way back to safety.

What you can learn from these memories is that you need to pay attention to what needs to be dealt with, so you can move on. You can address these unfinished tasks by bringing awareness to how you perceived these parts of the past from a place of survival. This is where you must forgive yourself for not doing better in situations that you wished you could. This is where you are grateful for the ways you were able to use your best judgment at the time. You survived, and that means you did well when navigating through the harshness of becoming an adult.

Our past can remind us how we didn't stand up for ourselves, or how we didn't fight harder for a parent or sibling being abused. Our past can remind us how we lied to get what we wanted, or how we were blamed for something we didn't do. Our unhealed emotions from the past will always involve another person or a part of ourselves. You may ask how we can complete unfinished business if the others involved are no longer in our lives. This might mean an old friend, an ex-lover, someone who has crossed over, or someone you refuse to talk to. The answer is that we do it through our own consciousness. We resolve what needs to be resolved through our own higher level of thinking. We complete what needs to be completed by seeing the past from a place of love and compassion instead of fear and survival.

The healing of your past is between your soul and your spirit. It is not with others. If you stay focused on what others did or did not do in your past, then you are going into the past with the desire to control it. Whenever you try to control something that is not in your control, it means you are actually out of control. This is the feeling in your soul that is causing confusion.

For completion of the past, you must come into the memories with love, compassion, and forgiveness for yourself and others. Instead of trying to change what happened, see the situation from your higher heart. See the damage others have caused because they were not coming from that higher place of love. See yourself coming into the memories of the past with more wisdom and knowledge than you had in the past. See yourself coming into the memories with your true divine self and love for life. See

The Voiceless Soul

yourself resolving what needs to be resolved by using your higher wisdom. This is the wisdom you didn't have as a child, but you have it now.

Remember, your fight is not with anyone else. It is with yourself. It is your ego trying to survive in a world that is challenging to the soul. It's a great disservice to your soul to continue seeking freedom from a troubled past by trying to regain control of it. Keeping your soul burdened with an unfinished past is keeping your spiritual heart shut down. This is because your past was all about survival, and now a part of you is stuck in that consciousness. There is no doubt that you have soul imprints left by someone else, or a part of you that got stuck in fear. These imprints are all in those memories. Once you complete the unfinished events in your life, those imprints will no longer need your attention. Your perceptions of your memories will change because you will see the truth within them. You will understand the reason you kept getting called back to them, and how your ego has been fighting against the emotions attached to them. Fear of nonlove is a powerful source of negative energy that keeps you away from divine truth. Fear of nonlove comes from every negative feeling you have about yourself.

The way out of that fear consciousness is to know that you are a survivor. You did it. You survived a troubled past, and now you get to go back and finish what was left undone. Completing the past can only be done through a higher level of consciousness. This is where the soul expresses what needs to be expressed, all while the spirit holds the space of love and compassion around the troubled memories.

Letting go is not easy. I am not going to give you one of those pep talks about letting it all go and watching it just dissolve. Memories are ingrained in the soul. You will keep getting pulled back to the past unless you learn how to face the past with love, compassion, and forgiveness. This is the only way to get out of your conditioned survival consciousness.

When you look back at your troubled past, you may think it would take a miracle to heal the pain you endured. Just remember that you are the miracle that you have been waiting for.

CHAPTER 30

The Never-Ending Need for Approval

> You are not lazy, unmotivated, or stuck. After years of living in survival mode, you are exhausted. There is a difference.
>
> —Nakeia Homer

My early twenties were filled with waiting tables to pay my rent and put gas in my car. Luckily, I could get free meals during break time at the diner. On my nights off, I would go to nightclubs and dance and drink until four o'clock in the morning, and then repeat the cycle of work and play without any special meaning to my life. Occasional dates gave me some hope that a nice guy was going to rescue me from my vicious cycle of emptiness. The problem was, if the guy showed serious interest, I showed no interest. If a guy was a challenge, I became intrigued by the adventure: *If I can chase this one down, I must be worthy*. I became stuck in the never-ending cycle of the games people play. We chase love, and then we run from it when it approaches.

I really just wanted someone to save me, even though I felt that no one would. There was a little me inside who was still seeking Dad's approval. Since I felt undeserving of it, I ran away when my intimate relationships became too cozy. I was afraid of abandonment once my partner got to know who I was—an unlovable girl.

The Voiceless Soul

Then a big turning point occurred in my life. My mother was tired of watching me complain about my unfulfilled life and dead-end relationships. I believe my mother was tired of watching me remind her of her own unfulfilled life. One day, with great annoyance in her voice, Mom said to me, "Why don't you just get married? That's all you want to do anyway." *Ouch, Mom, that was a hard hit!*

I remember feeling that awful stomach punch again. It was a like a giant wrecking ball that pounded right through me and into my soul. My mind was racing. I could hear my thoughts as if I were saying them over a loudspeaker. *That's all I am? I have no other ambitions? That's it?* That wrecking ball showed no mercy. I felt like a failure not only to myself, but to my mom, the foremost person I had always sought approval from. Mom had confirmed my biggest fear. I was not worthy of this world, so why was I here? At best, I could be a wife and a mother, just like Mom. I could marry a man just like Dad and raise little people like me, little people with big fears. That was all I was capable of.

Many times, I just wanted life to be done. I wanted the suffering to be gone. I felt like a failure to my mom and a mistake to my dad. My soul was done.

As terrifying as my mother's words were to me, something wonderful came out of them. A part of me had to prove something. I had to show my mom she was wrong. I just knew if I followed in her footsteps, my life would be doomed and she would see no value in me. My life had to be different.

I decided to enroll in college to prove to my mother that I could be more than what she believed I could be, even though I really just wanted to be safe. I had no interest in trying to better myself because, deep down inside, I felt incapable of it. There I was, in full survival mode. I was fighting for validation, so I could feel like I was enough for my mom and the world.

I remember walking into a huge building with people scattered all over the place. Most of them looked just as confused as I was. As I sat on one of the cold metal hallway benches in the local community college, I felt anxious. I started to sweat. Thoughts of walking out ran through my mind. I could hear my shadow parts telling me I was not smart enough for college. I tried to reject those thoughts, but they were relentless. Still, I couldn't give up. I had to prove that I was capable of more than just being someone's wife.

I engaged in the process of registering for classes while there was a remorseless battle of a need for acceptance and fear of unworthiness going on inside of me. I tried to figure out what all the brochures and forms meant. They were confusing. I wondered if the facilitators would help me or just laugh at me. Would they tell me I didn't have what it took to be a college student? Imagine me, getting higher education. I remained strong because I could hear my mother's words of disappointment running through my head. That gave me strength. I had to get her approval.

Finally, I got myself enrolled in classes. It wasn't long before I became astonishingly intrigued by the whole process of learning. What was most fascinating was that I learned I was capable of learning. I felt a glimpse of worthiness showing up from inside of me. Most importantly, I felt like I could gain some respect from Mom. I was already an unwanted child in Dad's eyes. I couldn't disappoint Mom too.

After attending college for two years and then continuing my education at a state college, I started to build some confidence. After a few decent but not very fulfilling jobs, I landed a great position in a large law firm as a paralegal. I even had my own office. There it was: everything I was looking for. I wanted to feel worthy, and a part of me did. I felt a huge burden lift from my soul when my mother told me she was proud of me.

I received cum laude honors from state college, honors I never thought my name could be attached to. My feelings about life were looking a little more hopeful. I was no longer a disappointment to Mom. This made me feel somewhat optimistic, but that was only a part of me. That was the part of me that felt capable.

Not long thereafter, there it was—my internal battle started to flare up again. There was another part of me saying, "Who do you think you're fooling?" The part of me that felt empowered for the first time in my life was battling fiercely with the part of me that believed I was a fraud, not worthy of my dad and, therefore, not worthy of success.

The need for approval is a childhood need that is almost never satisfied.

This is why so many of us fall into the unworthiness trap. When our childhood need for approval does not get satisfied by our parents or primary caregivers, we seek it in other ways. Receiving the approval of others gives us a feeling of belonging, acceptance, and value. That is why we never stop seeking approval. The fear of rejection is always lurking behind the feeling of acceptance. The feeling of rejection always pulls us back to the fear of nonlove.

My mother's words of disappointment in response to my complaints about my life left me feeling ashamed of who I was. I now know the higher truth. My mom was disappointed, but not because of my life—because of her life. The dissatisfaction that my mother expressed was not about me. It was the dissatisfaction she felt about her own life. When those same feelings showed up in me, she criticized me as if she were criticizing her younger self. My inability to make something of my life triggered my mother's inability to do something better with hers. I was her trigger, and she was mine.

Until we learn how to honor ourselves for the miraculous beings that we are, we will continue to seek approval from others. In this great time of spiritual awakening, our energy is best spent seeking the higher truth and living it.

CHAPTER 31

Seeing the Bigger Picture

The bigger picture is filled with many truths that are difficult to see when you are living from a place of survival. Most of us grew up without spiritual guidance. We did not have any tools that could help us understand that there is more to life than survival of the physical structure. We were not taught that we have souls that are sensitive to the physical world. We were only taught that we have emotional brains that we must micromanage so we can remain strong against the turbulence of the world. We did not know our sensitive souls were absorbing so many lower vibrational energies that were blocking our souls' divine essence, causing us to live in fear of death.

An important part of coming back into your true essence and being in that higher truth is to understand that there is a bigger picture that we are not aware of. Healing from the pain that has been impressed upon our souls requires that we look beyond our own lives. We must learn how the experiences of those who cared for us affected their caregiving abilities. What soul imprints were directing their actions and inaction, and how did that affect us? How far back through our lineage do we need to go to find the true culprit of our emotional wounds? We don't have to know everyone's story. What we do need to know is that their experiences with their caregivers have affected the way they care for others. It is deeply healing when you, with a compassionate heart, understand the stories of the two generations before you.

The Voiceless Soul

If you have a parent who grew up with an alcoholic and abusive father, you may have been cared for by a parent who didn't know how to connect with children. If you have parent who lost their mom at a very young age, you may have been cared for by a parent who lacked nurturing skills. Their deficiencies easily became your deficiencies—not on purpose, but through the consciousness that lives within our souls.

Once we see the bigger picture, it will be easier to see how we lost our true sense of self and adapted to the expectations of others for our safety and well-being. We were born with amazing survival skills, and these skills remain with us during the physical journey. When we cannot care for ourselves, our survival depends on our ability to be accepted by those who keep us alive. We do not want to battle with those who feed us. Our parents, grandparents, and all those before us did what they had to do for survival. This survival energy gets passed through the generations and shows up differently for all of us.

If we really get this concept, then we might be able to release those who cared for us from the responsibility of making us feel worthy of them. It had to be the way it was because most people don't know how to raise their consciousness and navigate their lives with self-awareness, especially the people who came before us. Most people don't know how to get unstuck, so they struggle with their inner conflicts as they try to create their dream lives. They want better lives than they had growing up, and they usually try hard to make that happen. They will make mistakes and will unknowingly hurt others because old, negative patterns are working against their highest intentions. This is true for all those who came before you, as life was not easy for most of our ancestors.

Many people in prior generations had to suffer in silence with unsettled emotional trauma, survival fears, and a desperate desire for love, significance, and value. They had to suck up all those difficult emotions and get on with life. If they told a therapist how they felt, they were probably treated for emotional instability or even mental illness. If they asked a doctor for help, they got a pill to suppress their emotions even more. Yes, your parents and all the people in your life that you feel did not live up to your expectations are human beings with complexes and burdens and little help to understand or process their experiences. They had no alternative but to rely on physical and mental health practitioners.

There was little opportunity for them to heal their souls, because the word "soul" was not part of their vocabulary. They had minds, and if the mind was not able to cope with life, then the mind was sick and needed medical treatment.

These people have said and done things that may have hurt you. They may have caused you to not love yourself. That was not fair to you. You can basically say they ruined your life. Or you can say, "They didn't do better because they didn't know better. Thankfully, I do." If they had been able to learn what I am sharing with you now, then chances are they wouldn't have blamed themselves for not being enough. They would have had a better understanding of why they felt the way they felt, which means they would have been better caregivers for you. It's sad for you as well as sad for them. Someone has to start the healing process for the next generation. Will that be you?

If anyone has intentionally hurt you and maybe even continues to hurt you in some way, then they have a troubled soul and they need help. Their soul has been so burdened with trapped emotions that they have lost their ability to cope. They want to hurt because they are so hurt. This is how human beings who cannot experience love on any level continue to cause pain for others.

We need to step it up with our understanding of human consciousness and the energy body. People stuck in low vibrational energy have many pockets of negative energy that can get charged up at any time, causing mayhem for those around them. They will react to these charged emotions through their ego consciousness, because that's how they protect themselves from further harm. It is all part of being human. We have to know from a heart-level consciousness that there is something we don't understand about internal suffering. We need to expand our awareness around these unseen parts of the picture and see the truth behind a soul's inability to harmoniously engage with life.

The Voiceless Soul

People in conflict seem to cause more conflict. People in pain seem to cause more pain. People who feel unloved find it hard to love another. The more we learn, the better choices we will make when engaged with those who are disconnected from their spiritual hearts.

We are all reacting and responding to life based on our feelings of self-worth. It feels like nonlove toward you when you are experiencing the pain of others, but it is not.

When will the madness stop so we can love those who are hurting, including ourselves? When can we stop the judgments and finally free ourselves from this debilitating trap? I hope you are beginning to see the bigger picture. I hope you realize that the negative beliefs that have been running through your ancestral line are nothing more than beliefs based in fear—and we are all wasting our beautiful lives trying to figure out why we are not enough.

Your past experiences are your teachers, not an indication of who you are. If you view any of your negative past experiences as things that have ruined your life or taken from you what you need, then you have fallen into the trap. No person and no experience can take from you your true, divine self.

When you can observe the bigger picture, you will learn how easy it is to get stuck in the trap and all the negative experiences that come along with being held in an emotional place of nonlove. The only escape that people use is avoidance of the feelings that pulled them into the trap in the first place. Those painful feelings are avoided because they feel like a truth that can bring you to your knees. Yet there is absolutely zero truth in the belief that anyone is unworthy. This is what you must learn as you become more and more aware of the bigger picture around you.

Expressing all that you have suppressed is a way to feel heard and a way to release the heavy energy that is holding you down. If you want to get unstuck from the untruth that you have become attached to, then you have to speak from a higher place within you. Speaking about your unhealed pain from a place of higher truth allows you to speak it without reinforcing the trauma you want to heal. By allowing yourself to speak with compassion for those who could not be the people you wanted them to be, you release the anger, resentment, and sadness you built around your story. You get to tell your story from the spiritual heart, which only knows nonjudgment, compassion, and love.

You want to be heard, you need to be heard, and you deserve to be heard. When you express yourself from a fear place wrapped in ego consciousness, you add more negative energy to the story. When you speak from higher knowledge that is gained by seeing the bigger picture, you are speaking through a higher vibration—a frequency of understanding and compassion.

When you speak from the higher truth, you allow the healing energy of your spirit to take you back to your true self. This is where the story of how perfect your soul is, how perfect the souls of all others are, and how perfect the love of spirit is starts to unfold. You finally get to see the bigger picture. This is the picture that shows you how fear has obstructed our deep love for each other and the world.

Don't stay in the trap. It's filled with so much fear. Be the true hero that you are. The world is waiting for more heroes to step forward.

The bigger picture shows you how others became disconnected from love in the first place. It wasn't you who caused the disconnect. You are just part of the bigger picture. You must be willing to see the whole picture, so you can know the real reason you are stuck in the same trap with the people you feel disconnected from.

CHAPTER 32

The Strength and Courage Within You

Grown-ups have a lot to learn, and I am one of those grown-ups. I am learning, and I am sharing this because we are just little children who didn't fully grow up. Our failure to grow up has created much pain and stress for ourselves and those we love. We have forgotten our true value in the process of trying to prove ourselves worthy.

Let's change this. Let's give a voice to the parts of us that couldn't speak, but felt the pain of rejection, loneliness, unworthiness, and abandonment. I survived and so did you. Maybe you didn't get all your needs met, but you did get enough needs met to be here now. Celebrate that! You stayed strong and brave through every childhood wounding, and you are now an adult who can help yourself through the pain of the past, become a responsible grown-up, and live like the miracle you are.

It's time to give a voice to the parts of you that need your attention. You need to speak up and speak out from your heart. When you speak up, you are telling your story from that courageous place within you. When you speak from the heart, you bring compassion to the story that caused you conflict, confusion, and emotional pain.

Going deep within yourself to locate the true source of your suffering is frightening. Most likely, we are afraid to see an ugly part of ourselves. As ugly as these parts of us may seem, they are just ugly feelings about ourselves. They are not who we are. What we don't realize is that anything that doesn't come from a place of love is not truth. When you express what you feel inside and you see yourself in this convoluted scenario with others, you will get a bigger picture of the past.

Use your heart instead of your head to seek the higher truth. This will lead you to the spirit of oneness. You are a brave soul in many ways. Just because you have been hurt doesn't mean you were not strong. You survived the pain of the past, which means you want to be here in this world. You want to do the work you came here to do as a loving soul. You have so much to celebrate about your life here, but you must know that you are being held back because of your inability to release yourself from the unworthiness trap.

We all pledge to do better than what was provided to us, and that is where we are showing our strength and courage. Unfortunately, we keep ourselves small in the process because we are still seeking validation from others. Since we know more than our ancestors knew, we can do more than they could do. We can break the cycle. First, we must understand how we unconsciously keep the cycle going.

We can't keep waiting for the big rescue. We must be the ones to do the big rescue. We need to bring forward the strength and courage we had growing up in an uncertain world filled with fear. We have grown through our desire to heal the past. We are ready to enter that higher place within us and celebrate our truth.

I have faith in you, me, and all those who can make the pledge to do better by being aware of what the bigger truth. We can acknowledge that there is a bigger picture. Victims create more victims. Emotionally responsible adults create more emotionally responsible adults. Let's grow up!

I changed how I saw my story, and so can you. I am celebrating my bravery and determination to step back into the higher truth that I disconnected from a long time ago.

The higher truth is that I was not abandoned by my mother; she abandoned herself. I was not abandoned by my twin sister; her soul was not ready for this troubled world. I am worthy of my father's love, although his soul was too damaged to provide it. This is the way it is. It couldn't be any other way. I just had to understand that. Nothing that happened to me can steal my value, my strength, or my courage.

Now, when I look in the mirror, I can honestly say, "You are a miracle of life." I did the big rescue. I have not fully embraced my awesomeness yet, but I am definitely more aware and more connected to my all-loving spirit. I know I am worth the time and effort it takes to fully heal my soul.

Can you say that about yourself? If not, then it's time to start looking at the bigger picture. Use your voice to express all the feelings you have been avoiding. Be strong, be courageous, and express every ugly feeling inside of you. Always close your letters with love from your higher heart.

Dear Mom and Dad,

I am scared. I feel unwanted. I feel like a burden. All I want is to be able to please you, so you will love me. If I don't feel worthy of your love, I may never feel worthy of anyone's love. When you set me free into that big, scary world, how will I survive if no one can love me? How will I stay safe if no one will care about me? What is wrong with me? What do I need to fix? How do I prove I am valuable so others will accept me? I feel lost and confused.

These are the expressions of my younger self. That is the part of me that has not healed from the pain of feeling unworthy. I am older now, and I remain stuck in that confusion.

Now, as an adult, I believe you are loving me the best way you know how. That doesn't seem to be enough for my younger self, who is still trying to figure out how to feel loved enough to feel safe in the big world. This part of me keeps me from loving who I am.

My memories of our lives together are fuzzy. Many of my low-energy thoughts consume my mind. I can't seem to remember the good days. The bad days are so overwhelming.

I hope one day I can sort this all out. I hope one day I can understand these feelings. I hope one day I can live my life knowing that everything is going to be OK. I hope I can express my pain without fearing it.

As confused as I am on this journey, I know there is wisdom in my soul. I know that I have to learn many things on my own. I know that I cannot rely on others to teach me how to lovingly navigate my life if they can't lovingly navigate their own.

I realize now that I am the only one who can heal the little girl in me. I am the only one who can save her from her pain. I am willing to learn how to do that.

As I do the work to heal my soul, I will keep you in my heart. I know you wish to heal as well, even if you don't know how to.

Love,
Lost and Confused Little Me

CHAPTER 33

The Source of Love You Need

When you are able to, take a moment and look in the mirror. Ask yourself who decided that you weren't good enough. You will see your own image, the true culprit. You made this decision when you trusted that others had the right to define your worth.

No matter what your primary caregivers did or didn't do, their actions don't show you who you are—they show you who the caregivers were in that moment. They do not own you, so they cannot know your value. You own you, and only you can decide your value. They did not create the true you. The true you was created by divine love for a divine purpose.

Your parents gave you physical life here on this planet. They created a human body for your soul to use for a physical experience. Others have participated in the creation of *who you think you are* because the biggest influencers in a child's life are the parents and other primary caregivers. Since you were initially created from a source of pure love, you are an integral part of that pure source of love. Any beliefs about yourself that are not in alignment with that truth are false beliefs. This means that you do not have to seek love from anywhere else, since it is already there inside of you.

Unfortunately, in the human experience, we get caught up in everyone's fears. Instead of looking inside ourselves—because it's *not* how we were taught—we continue to look outside of ourselves, just as our primary caregivers did. It's hard not to look outside of ourselves, because all we knew as young, needy children was to look to our caregivers for safety.

Many people, especially the generations before us, were not aware enough to understand that there is more to us than our physical bodies. If they provided a child with food, shelter, water, education, and medical care, then they did their job as caregivers. This is how they love. This is what they learned about human needs. To generations past, this is love because this is caring.

To the child, it's usually not enough. The child needs consistent reassurance that they are loved. It's a difficult balance for parents and primary caregivers, and many times mistakes will be made. Caring adults will not always be able to meet all the needs of the child, especially if they have been deprived of their own emotional needs. Aside from what children are taught by their caregivers, cultural and societal rules play into the way our lives are structured. This is why we must let go of blame, resentment, old conditioning, and the fears others have projected onto us. We have to love ourselves enough to take responsibly for our own lives. It starts with knowing that we have the highest source of love within us.

Because the child always seeks love and approval, it is easy for the child to feel nonlove in the most innocent of situations. When a parent gets angry, the child thinks they are the cause of it. When a child is reprimanded, the child believes they are a disappointment to their caregivers. These are all moments that feel like nonlove during the "normal" growing-up process. These feared moments of nonlove during childhood keep you wondering if the world will reject you or accept you. These feared moments keep you from fully loving yourself. Even though the adult self knows that these are not indications of nonlove, the adult is carrying the energy of child consciousness.

We keep forgetting who we are. We keep falling back into the trap of the false created self. We have unknowingly allowed fear patterns to be formed that we can't seem to break. It is these fear patterns that wall off the love source within us.

The Voiceless Soul

You see, beautiful spirit being, your soul does not know how to release these fear patterns without your help. If you keep trying to ego-think your way out of the trap, you will fall deeper into it. If you want to change the way you think, feel, act, and live your life like the miracle you are, then you may have to struggle with that uncomfortable feeling of getting to know the hurt parts of you. These hidden parts of you need your authentic love above all else.

Spirit lives in your spiritual heart. Your spirit is always ready and willing to lovingly guide your soul through the physical journey. You only need to look within to remember how amazing you are.

You are the source of the love you need.

Start expressing yourself from the deepest part of your soul through your spiritual heart. All you need is pen, paper, and the wisdom and intelligence that comes from the spiritual heart. That is where the magic begins. It starts with you and the higher truth.

CHAPTER 34

The Courage to Let Go of Your Safety Net

> Although healing brings a better life, it also threatens to permanently alter life as you've known it. Your relationships, your position in the world, even your sense of identity may change. Coping patterns that have served you for a lifetime will be called into question. When you make the commitment to heal, you risk losing much of what is familiar. As a result one part of you may want to heal while another resists change.
>
> —Laura Davis
> *The Courage to Heal Workbook*

Human beings need certainty because knowing what might happen to us feels safe. Because of this, we desperately cling to what is familiar to us, making it difficult to change the course of our lives.

To navigate your life in a different direction means you have to become unattached to what you are comfortable with. This may feel risky because you have no certainty of where a new direction will take you. This is what holds you back from making that big step forward.

The drama from the past keeps drawing you back for more. It's a place that you know you can navigate because you have done it many times before. It's not that easy to let go of that safety net, especially when your soul is controlled by an ego that is focused on survival.

The Voiceless Soul

I followed my path of certainty for many years. It felt safe. I was not happy, but I was attached to the life that was familiar to me. I wanted to believe there was a better way. Hence, I spent my life savings on useless self-help books and power seminars. I just couldn't get to the next level.

I was so determined to get my mother's validation that I forced myself out of my safety net to enroll in college. I didn't do it because I was brave enough to let go of my familiar way of life. I did it because I was scared. I was afraid of being my mother. I was afraid of living the life she lived. I forced myself away from my safety net of familiar drama when my mother brought to my attention, in her usual direct and stoic manner, the fact that I was wasting my life.

That was the beginning of my new path. That path turned into a very challenging but worthwhile journey. I am more at peace and more in touch with my higher wisdom. I rely on my own personal navigator, which has never failed me. It may have taken me through challenges I wasn't prepared for, but those challenges were lessons for growth. It may have turned me in directions I didn't want to go, but I was being led toward something better. I have learned to trust the guidance of spirit because spirit is always guiding from a place of love.

Once you see the bigger picture, you will become aware that you have been holding on to the pain of the past because of your need to stay in a safe and familiar place, one you feel you can control. Instead of trying to control it or wishing it were different, look at it from a higher level of understanding. Our unconscious attempts to avoid pain also drive us to repeat it by pulling us into the same old drama. Some of us might be as lost as the people who made us feel bad—it just shows up differently in each of us.

Letting go of your safety net is about trusting that there is a better way. The past has taught you many valuable things. Everything you have learned can be used to help you grow. What will stifle your emotional and spiritual growth is wanting others to change so you can feel better about yourself. The most difficult part of the journey is surrendering to what is. It is accepting that people will not always meet your expectations. It is knowing that emotionally immature people are just lost little children trying to find a way to feel validated. Once you can trust that this is how it works, then you can let go of the safety net of familiar drama and raise your level of consciousness to a place of higher understanding, higher compassion, and higher truth. This is the soul work we all need to do if we want to make better life choices and live more purposefully.

The first step before any soul-healing work is remembering that you are a miracle of life. The life that you have been given is precious. Keep it precious. Keep it free from the projected fears of others. Remember that love is the ultimate answer for all of us.

Love comprises higher understanding, compassion, acceptance, forgiveness, and truth.

Understanding the truth has helped me see the possibility of creating a better version of myself. Although our souls do not need improvement, our souls do need compassion. This is where we better ourselves—we live through the spiritual heart instead of the ego. My life changed when I looked deeper into my emotional challenges. I took the time to understand where it went wrong for me and where it went wrong for the people who influenced me. Although the fear of losing my mom's love pushed me into something new and unfamiliar, I still had to learn how to trust that I was safe on this new journey. I didn't believe in myself until I learned how to use my higher consciousness. I had to clear the burdens of my soul, so I was no longer blocked from seeing the higher truth. This helped me let go of the safety net and step into other unknown territories.

I feel like I reinvented myself by embracing uncertainty. It's not the easiest thing to do, as we are hardwired to keep ourselves safe from harm. If we don't know what is around the corner, we enter it with caution. That's a good thing, but only when you are truly in danger—otherwise, it's just a conditioned response to fear of the unknown. It's holding you back from living the life you want.

You do not have to wait for someone to provoke your shadow side to see the higher truth. Your shadow parts are being triggered all the time. It is your reaction to them that you must notice. If you are being triggered, you are stuck in the drama of the past. If this is happening, then take a deeper look into your life and see where you keep repeating those old patterns. Notice where you might find it hard to let certain things go. These are the things that you wanted to control at an earlier time, but you couldn't. Now your ego mind is trying to control the situation so you don't end up in harm's way. If you stay in your familiar life when a part of you is longing for growth and expansion, then you are clinging to a safety net that will keep you stuck in the trap.

If you let go of this familiar game and take a chance on learning the higher truth, you will find that you have the courage to let go. You will get to know how these drama stories stay alive because you unconsciously choose to participate in them.

You can begin to walk out of the trap by acknowledging that it is the drama that keeps you there. It is you in that familiar way of life that is certain, predictable, and safe. You must find a way to feel safe enough to let go. You must trust the spirit within, which is the part of you that has been calling you to step into your transpersonal power and release your gifts into the world.

The safety net you held on to for so long deserves applause. It was there to keep you feeling safe. It was not there to hold you back—even though it did. It was there for your highest good at a time when you needed safety first. It was there when you were not evolved enough to know how to navigate this world via your inner spirit.

You are evolving now. It's OK to say goodbye to the safety net of survival and step into your true, divine self. This is where you can look at the whole picture and see where you got stuck and what kept you there. This is where you can see that others are still stuck, but they don't know it. Let them be where they are. Just hold that space of lightness around them. They mean no harm to you. They are just playing it safe.

Having the courage to let go of your safety net also deserves applause. This is you taking a step into your higher knowing. This is you moving toward the freedom of your soul. Applaud your courage.

CHAPTER 35

A Call to the Hero Within

Do not be dismayed by the brokenness of the world. All things break. And all things can be mended. Not with time, as they say, but with intention. So go. Love intentionally, extravagantly, unconditionally. The broken world waits in darkness for the light that is you.

—L. R. Knost

The one thing I learned from my unsuccessful journey to heal myself was that books and power talks do not heal layers of pain. They are Band-Aid approaches to deep inner wounds that cut you at your core. These methods only teach you how to manage your emotions instead of exploring them.

Unlike other books that promise a quick fix for your life challenges, this book gives you a dose of reality. There are no quick fixes for a soul burdened with pain. There is a process of healing that begins with seeing the bigger picture and expressing yourself openly and honestly from your burdened soul through your spiritual heart.

This book has given you some insight into how your life was created for you. It is meant to show you how there was never anything wrong with you, even though things went wrong for you. You have an opportunity to recreate your life when you are ready to release others from the responsibility of being the grown-up. Emotional immaturity is like an epidemic that no one wants to face. Be the hero who says, "I can do better because I know better." Be the grown-up that others could not be.

Only you can decide when it's time to release your primary caregivers from any anger and resentments you may have toward them. They do not heal that way, and neither do you. You cannot change or heal anyone except yourself. Anyone who is stuck in the unworthiness trap has to find their own way out. What you can do is have compassion for them and maybe even share your light so they can see their way out. But if you are trying to change them, heal them, or wake up their consciousness when they have resistance to a new ideology, then you are wasting your energy.

Your energy should be spent on recreating the life you deserve.

Take your need to receive anyone's validation off your priority list. Their acceptance of you is not necessary for your spiritual growth. Your acceptance of you is.

There is a hero inside of you. It was there all the time. It was just waiting for you to step into your greatness and realign yourself with your highest truth. You can, right now in this moment, decide if you want to rise above your current level of consciousness and see your world for what it is. Or you can stay right where you are, wishing things were different. You can continue to live your life mostly from an unconscious state of mind, or you can live life through your wise, divine self.

This book is a call to the hero within you.

Things won't be different until you make the choice for things to be different. When you raise your level of awareness—when you practice understanding, acceptance, and compassion instead of anger, resentment, and fear—you choose for things to be different, not for others, but for yourself.

The world needs more heroes. Let your soul feel compassion for yourself and for those who remain stuck. Let your soul know that you care by expressing your genuine love and acceptance for yourself and all you had to endure while you were learning about life. Let your soul know that you refuse to continue taking on the pain of others. Remind yourself that we all get caught up in fear. Understand how pain enters the soul and takes over its good nature. Reach the level of truth where you understand that all souls go through a growing process, but some of them are stuck in stagnation. The soul's intention on this journey is to learn, grow, and evolve with each human experience. When this doesn't happen, it means there are unseen forces within them that are holding them back. These forces are fragmented parts of the soul that got caught up in the fear of nonlove.

Our first intention was always love. We let the fear of others drive us into safety consciousness. Only a hero can undo this mess.

You may notice that many of the people around you are living from a level of frustration, fear, and self-neglect. Don't judge them—let them be. The only way you can help those lost souls is by coming back to your true, essential self and pull yourself from their trap. If they see you rise into the true, divine being that you are, they may want to follow. If they don't, they are stuck. You cannot pull them out of the trap; you can only lead them out by example.

The more love and light you spread throughout the world, the better chances lost souls have of finding their way back to their true selves.

We all wonder why people do the things they do. We all wonder why they can't heal and move on with life. We all wonder what keeps people so stuck in their misery. We all wonder why others didn't love us the way we needed them to. We don't need to keep chasing the answers to find peace within ourselves. We just need to step into our own higher awareness and understand the consciousness of the soul. We can stop supporting the already highly profitable self-help industry that cannot deliver lasting peace. All it does is take your money and give you empty promises.

It's important to start supporting your own divine self and dig deeper into the truth about who you really are on this journey. Learn why other

The Voiceless Soul

souls unknowingly strayed from their divine selves, relying on ego to guide them. Only a hero can do this. A hero is a soul that has returned to the divine truth and is ready to lead the world instead of being stuck in the fears of the world. A hero is someone who can accept the higher truth, live by it, and spread it on to those who are lost. A hero is ready to heal their soul so they can spread the light of love that lives within them.

Express all that you hold inside of you. Let it be released with love. Be the one in your family line who does the soul-healing work that stops the madness.

Be the hero of your lineage. Be who others were afraid to be. Be the hero who changes the course for future generations, so these souls can be free to live like the miracles they are.

CHAPTER 36

Healing Ourselves Out of the Trap

If you want to get out of the trap, you must be willing to release your attachments to your pain. In other words, stop wishing it didn't happen. It did—and now it's over. By wishing it were different, you stay focused on it. You know what I'm talking about. It's that feeling of unworthiness you got stuck in because a lover was unfaithful, a dad abandoned you, a mother criticized you, a teacher ridiculed you, a boss degraded you, or your neighbor bullied you. These are the kinds of challenges that the soul must face. Instead of looking for some quick fix by a healing method that does not reach the level of the soul, go within yourself and find the pain you swallowed a long time ago.

The heavy burdens that you have been carrying around will not get lighter until you get serious about your healing work. The only way out of that miserable trap is to face what pulled you into it in the first place.

Here's the thing, beautiful soul: all those life disappointments, unmet needs, broken expectations, and unfulfilled desires have not only been experienced by you. If there is dysfunction in your family line on any level, then chances are that dysfunction is part of an ongoing trail of unworthiness that started way before you were born. Stop blaming others and yourself for the reason you feel unhappy. Blame only blocks the healing process and keeps you from seeing the bigger picture.

The Voiceless Soul

The inability to see the higher truth perpetuates emotional suffering. There are defects that live deep within the many good and innocent souls that you come across every day. If you think they are consciously choosing to live dysfunctional lives, then you are not living from the higher truth. Your healing will take place when you realize that soul consciousness has many levels. Those who are stuck at the lower levels need more empathy, not judgment.

Compassion is a big part of recreating your life.

We are all miracles of life. We have to honor and respect ourselves and others. That is what a true grown-up would do.

If your soul has been heavily damaged by parents or caregivers who were lost in their feelings of brokenness, then maybe they will never reach the higher truth. Don't continue to resent their inability to grow up or change their understanding of life. Release yourself from your attachment to them by knowing that you are a true miracle of life, and they have failed to see that. It's not easy to give up on the connection you have always longed for. For your own soul growth, you can't let others who are stuck in the trap hold you back from your divine truth. The most important connection is with you and your spirit.

It's OK not to love a parent or primary caregiver like a child would. It's OK if they never gave you any reason to have compassion for them. It's OK if you feel they don't deserve any attention from you. It's OK to emotionally detach. If you are showing emotions of hate or resentment toward them, then you are still attached. The higher truth helps you release those negative attachments, so you can be free to move on with your life.

You will grow from the understanding that you were loved with all the love they were capable of. Now it is up to you to give yourself the love you deserve.

You heal your way out of the trap by giving yourself permission to feel what you feel. You heal your way out of the trap by expressing everything that is weighing heavy on your soul. You release yourself from the trap when you can look back at those painful memories and remind yourself that you were brave and you survived. That is because you knew in your spiritual heart that you would rise above your soul traumas someday. Today is that day.

You can speak up now as if you had a clear voice from the beginning. You can begin to unburden your soul and live in spiritual freedom. You can heal your way out of the trap by acknowledging that your life was not what you wanted it to be. You can express all your fears, needs, and love. Healing your way out of the trap and into the truth of who you are requires no holding back.

Express your way out of your pain by writing letters. Say what you feel. Say what you needed and didn't get from those who cared for you. Express how others affected you and how you may have passed your unhealed trauma on to others. Express with certainty that you are evolving out of the drama that others are stuck in. You are expressing the truth of your feelings. You are expressing all of your soul's pain and confusion. You have the right to speak up.

To fully heal your way out of the trap, so that you don't get sucked back in, you will need to finish your letters with love and compassion from your spiritual heart. This will give your soul the closure and comfort it needs. You need to return to the truth of who you are.

Expressing all of what burdens your soul through the physical act of writing allows you to release the feelings of unworthiness from your soul onto the paper. By ending your story with higher understanding and higher compassion, you leave your soul in a place of acceptance and peace. When you release all negative attachments to those who pulled you into their traps, you lighten the energy in your soul. You deserve this.

Dear Dad,

You hurt me. You always made me feel like I was a burden to you. I could never please you. I never felt like I was enough, and I blame you for that.

We lived in a messy house. I never had nice clothes. Most of the time I looked homeless. I felt ashamed of who I was. You didn't care. You were so wrapped up in your own personal struggles that you didn't notice I was struggling myself. You didn't see me. You didn't hear me. I felt so alone.

I was small. I was vulnerable. I was defenseless. Although I was new to this thing called life, I was already preparing for my survival. I never felt protected.

You passed much of your pain on to me. I had to carry your burdens for a long time. That was unfair. They were so heavy for such a little body to carry. They held me back from loving and honoring who I was.

As an adult, I lived with many inner conflicts. My repressed anger showed up when others triggered my insecurities. I secretly blamed myself for not being enough for your love, although I outwardly blamed you for your parenting deficiencies. I repeated many of your mistakes without realizing it. I wanted to be different from you, and yet in many ways I became you.

I get it now, Dad. I did the work. I saw the bigger picture that was not available to me while I was stuck trying to survive your need to destroy the good in life. I can see it now. I can see what you could never see. You were stuck in the unworthiness trap. You didn't know how to get out of it, so you took me in with you.

I know you didn't mean to hurt me. You were just stuck in your childhood pain. You never reached inside your heart. You lived a hard life, and you died a hard death. I am sorry for your suffering. I am sorry for the little me who suffered with you.

I will do better than you could do. I will find the hero in me, so I can break the cycle of unworthiness that crucified our family line.

I hope you rest in peace and the angels of love surround you. I hope you find the peace that you unknowingly resisted your whole life.

Blessing for a rested and renewed soul.

With all my love,
Your Daughter

CHAPTER 37

Compassion for the Wounded Child Within

When you read the letters in this book, you are hearing my soul speak. Some of my childhood wounds may trigger yours. That is because we are innately compassionate human beings who never want to see a child suffer.

I would like for you to also consider that the adults you grew up with and the adults in your life now all have memories from childhood. Many of them have memories that make them believe they are unworthy of love. A soul in pain will react in many different childish ways, some of which we cannot understand or even tolerate when they show up in an adult. This doesn't mean we need to cater to the childish attitude of the adults we care about, but maybe we can be more understanding and compassionate. If we are comfortable with the person, maybe we can ask if they need to talk about something when they start acting fearful, shut down, sad, or angry.

Most importantly, these letters are meant to help you reconnect with your own inner child. These letters are meant help you become aware of your inner child's needs. Your inner child is just as worthy of love, respect, nurturing, and care as those other little suffering children that you feel compassion for. The reason you don't feel the same compassion for your own inner child is because you have dissociated from your hurt child parts.

If I can do anything in this book to help you start your soul-healing work, it is to appeal to the compassionate soul that you are. I would love for you to bring out those stifled childhood parts when you write your letters.

These hidden parts of you are parts of your soul; they belong to you. They are afraid to be seen or heard. They feel rejected by the world because they felt rejected by those they needed acceptance from. It wasn't because you were not a good child. It wasn't because you were an unlovable child. It wasn't because you were not enough for those whose acceptance you needed. It was because you were not guided through life by grown-ups who had fully grown up.

You didn't receive the validation you needed because the grown-ups in your life were not capable of seeing the divine spirit in you. This is because they could not see the divine spirit in themselves.

If you are in a place where you can close your eyes and go within to a deeper level of consciousness, take a moment and do that. As you close your eyes, breathe deep inside your heart and connect with your spiritual essence. As you go within, let your imagination take you to any caregiver who criticized you or made you feel bad about yourself as a child. Then see that caregiver as a child not getting the love and attention they needed from their caregivers. See that child as an innocent child who craved love but spent many years feeling unloved. This causes a disconnect from oneself, a fragmentation of the soul. The fragmented soul does not fully connect with others, even though it wants to.

This does not mean that a child was not loved. It just means that there are so many fears around life that a sensitive child grows up in fear even when they are being loved. These are the fears that get passed on to other innocent children like you. Unfortunately, we all carry the burdens of generational fears.

In essence, we are all little children in adult bodies, trying to find our way back to love.

The Voiceless Soul

Every grown-up who has not fully grown up has a repressed childhood part in them that is running their lives. That is why grown-ups can be loving and compassionate one day and raging bulls the next. These are the emotionally immature parts showing up. These are their hurt child parts that they rejected a long time ago. These are the parts of themselves that they dislike. These are the parts of them that they project onto others, causing more childhood wounds. We must find a way to stop the ongoing fear of nonlove.

Phrases such as "You should be ashamed of yourself," "Don't be a crybaby," "I don't want to hear it," "You make me sick" and "What the hell is wrong with you?" are common. These are the disempowering words that many of us have grown up with, including our parents, primary caregivers, and generations past. We are simply parroting our caregivers without realizing the damage being done to the innocent child. We lose so much of who we really are when we get stuck in the burdens and fears of others. Growing up with emotionally immature grown-ups is the biggest emotional challenge we will ever face in our lives. We cannot keep ignoring the hurt and rejected child within us.

We don't know anyone's story behind the story they tell. I am not saying you didn't suffer or that your life was not difficult. Many children suffer from not getting their emotional needs met. Holding on to your resentment about it is what keeps you stuck in your woundedness. What I am saying is don't blame yourself for your caregiver's inadequacies. These wounds you are feeling did not start with you. They are wounds of the past that are kept alive because the unworthiness trap is not easy to get out of. It takes strength, courage, higher understanding, acceptance, compassion, and authentic love. We are all capable of reaching that higher level, but the problem is we don't think we are worthy of it.

When you expand your awareness, you allow the picture of your life experiences to include the experiences of your parents and other caregivers, including the wounded child within each of them. Expand your awareness to understand how their traumas have completely changed who they are compared to the type of parents and caregivers they wanted and intended to be. Broaden your perception of where it may have gone wrong for them as young children. Unfortunately, most people don't understand that they need emotional healing, so they just carry on through life without realizing that they are fighting against their own inner reality.

I know it might be difficult to release yourself from your negative emotional attachments because you really needed the love that you didn't feel. It's heartbreaking for all those who feel unworthy. This means it goes beyond our own pain. It goes deep into the world, including our own family line. If you keep holding others responsible for you not getting your needs met, then you won't be able to meet those needs for yourself. You deserve better.

It takes true understanding and compassion to help heal this world. It starts with showing enough compassion for ourselves and the people we blame for not being the people we needed them to be. This must be accomplished by understanding the pain that lives within these wounded souls. Although it may seem logical that difficult people should be able to see themselves as difficult, most of them do not. They live their lives mostly from a low level of awareness. If you could feel their souls by going inside your heart and imagining them as hurt children, you would understand the true reason they were deficient in their caregiving. Then you would no longer blame yourself or them. You would understand that this is a generational issue, which became a world issue. The world needs more heroes to help end the emotional chaos.

There are numerous studies showing that forgiveness helps us heal. If forgiveness were an easy thing to do, then more people would be able to forgive others and there wouldn't be so much pain in the world. When people say they have forgiven someone, I don't think they actually release the hurt they feel inside. I think people just rationalize that it's the right thing to do, when the truth is they don't want to forgive. They think they do, but the hurt part of them is still holding on to what it believes is unforgivable.

Instead of rationalizing that you need to forgive them so you can move on with life, feel the forgiveness and what that really means. It means you do not personalize their soul burdens. It means you know their wrongdoings have nothing to do with you. You know from a higher level of understanding that you are not forgiving someone for doing something wrong; you are forgiving them for not knowing how to do better.

You are not forgiving their unkind acts. You are not forgiving their neglect or abuse. You are forgiving them for not being able to reach a higher level of understanding and compassion. You are forgiving them for being stuck. You are forgiving the hurt and rejected child within them. You are forgiving their soul for not having the strength, courage, or knowledge to get out of the unworthiness trap.

Your compassion is not for them or what they did or didn't do. It is for the suffering child within them who never healed. It is that suffering child within them who caused the grown-up not to grow up and be the person you needed them to be.

For your soul to heal, your soul must feel compassion for the suffering soul that caused your soul to suffer. This includes understanding that there is a wounded child in them. This is what caused the wounded child in you. The woundedness we all feel comes from generations past. We were not able to live from a place of higher understanding when we were children. We need to do that now, as responsible adults.

Having an understanding and compassionate level of consciousness *does not* in any way whatsoever condone any physical or emotional neglect or abuse from anyone against anyone. There are some very toxic people in the world. Their protective egos run the entire show. These people will hurt anyone who gets in the way of their need to feel good about themselves. These people are so deep in the trap that they don't know any other way to live.

This isn't about creating a pity party either. It's about having the real story behind the story we tell ourselves. It is about understanding that you were innocent from the beginning, as were your parents, caregivers, and ancestors. It is the fears that we let consume us that eventually destroy our good nature.

Do not confuse acceptance of a burdened soul with the acceptance of bad treatment. Please understand that acts of unkindness come from a soul in pain. These are acts of unkindness from someone who does not like who they are or someone who feels that their well-being is under attack. This is a sickness in the mind. It can create havoc in your mind if you don't accept that it has nothing to do with who you are. By not accepting that these are defects in the soul of another, you continue to let others create your life. As a child, you had no choice, but now you do.

With this hard truth, what will you choose for your soul's experience here on the earth plane? Will you choose to stay in the lower energies of victimhood, or will you rise up and be the creative, compassionate, and loving soul you came here to be?

The wounded child within you needs you to do the soul-healing work. The innocent and precious child soul needs you to be their guiding spirit. Be the wise grown-up who helps to change the life of one innocent child—the child within. This is how you create change within yourself and the world. You start from healing the wounds of your younger self. You accept that the pain of others is the wounded child in them. These are just child energies making waves because they want to be heard, acknowledged, and valued.

Speak to your wounded younger self from your spiritual heart. The wounded child parts within you need to reconnect with the higher truth so these parts of you can grow up with the rest of you. Only you can make yourself feel whole again.

Dear Little Me,

> You are just starting out in life, and you are already feeling bad about who you are. This is not what I wanted for us. When you are sad, I feel sad. All of your feelings affect me as an adult. I want you to remember who you are so I can remember who I am. You are innocent, lovable, and wanted. You belong in this world. You were sent here to do great things. I want you to live the life you deserve. I want you to heal so I can heal.

The Voiceless Soul

I know you needed more than you received. I know the grown-ups in this world can seem very intimidating when you are so small. Please know that when grown-ups are not responsive to your needs, it's because they are not being responsive to their own needs. They get lost in the fear of not being enough. When that happens, they say and do things that come from a hurt place inside of them. Many times, the people we need to validate our worth are wrapped up in their own pain of unworthiness. Sometimes they are just trying to protect us, but they do it in desperate ways. Sometimes they shut down because the child within them is feeling sad.

I need you to know that their burdens have nothing to do with you. Their burdens were with them before you came into their lives. You are the blessing of love they needed, but maybe they didn't see that.

I know you don't understand this now, but I do because I have learned so much about the world of grown-ups. That is why I am sharing this with you. I am sharing this so you understand that you are not inadequate or unworthy. You just feel that way because the people you relied on did not support your emotional needs. I don't want you to be stuck in their trap, which is flooded with fear. I want you to be the happy child that you deserve to be.

I love you, little one. I am here to help you through your pain and help you reconnect to your true, divine self. You are a beautiful soul filled with light and passion. I am ready to help you discover those amazing parts of you. I want you to be curious about life, not fear it. I am always here for you.

Love,
Your Grown-Up Self

CHAPTER 38

Healing Through a Psycho-Spiritual Process

Allowing your younger self to be heard by your adult self is an important step in your soul-healing process. The expression of your inner pain helps the emotions become unattached from your soul, where they felt stuck and alone. When these unhealed emotions come forward from the frightened inner child within you, you have an opportunity to bring much-needed love and compassion to those inner child parts.

When you express the feelings that you have been holding on to for so long, you begin to stir up emotions that have been buried deep inside of you. This is what you have been avoiding, and this is why you are not healing. When you write your letters, these emotions start pouring out of you. You are giving them the freedom to be heard. You are no longer stifling those parts of you. This is freedom.

When you express yourself from these hurt parts of you, you need to address the people who you believe are responsible for the way you feel. You don't need to do this in their physical presence. This is not about making them recognize their faults. Demanding recognition just means you need validation from them. If they hurt you in any way, intentionally or not, it was wrong. You can't fix what went wrong for them in their lives. That is their work, not yours. You can only heal where it went wrong for you because it went wrong for them. You are releasing your energetic entanglement with them by expressing how their deficiencies affected you. You are now choosing compassion over judgment.

When you express yourself from the soul while engaged with your spiritual heart, you are expressing your feelings and emotions through a childlike psychological process, but from a higher level of consciousness. This is because you are no longer that little child, but a part of you is stuck in that childhood emotional trauma. This psycho-spiritual healing process allows you to bring your higher mind into those inner child parts that lost connection to self, significant others, and the divine spirit within. This is where soul meets spirit and there is a reunion of love, compassion, and understanding. The only one who needs to validate your existence, your worth, and your place in this world is your divine self.

The more we hang on to how it should have been, the more we block the energy to our higher heart. This means we are allowing the lower energies to steal our connection to the divine energy of pure love. There must be a connection from the lower self to the higher self through the spiritual heart so there is always loving guidance, even when we are being greatly challenged. We must know who we are even when we feel defeated. It is this divine connection that will lift us back up and remind us of who we are. We must never forget our divine truth.

Allowing the hurt child parts to be heard while you hold a space of divine love is the psycho-spiritual process that is going to heal your soul burdens. It is where you can fully express yourself with the love and support of your Creator. As you open your spiritual heart to the hurt child within you, the flow of energy from the divine source of love pours through you and into your soul. This is where you are reminded of the miracle you are, no matter what you have experienced in life. This is where you speak from that divine energy and bring the words of comfort to the hurt parts inside of you. This is where you get to forgive yourself for believing that you had to prove your worth to receive love. You don't have to prove yourself to anyone. You are a part of the divine creation of love. There is no other love that is more important than the love your Creator has for you. You are a part of that divine energy, which means loving yourself for the divine spirit you are. It's important to stay connected to that love source.

This is how you engage in a soul-healing journey. This is the gift of healing you give to yourself.

CHAPTER 39

Raising Self-Awareness

You can truly live like the miracle you are, but there is a catch. You need to get out of the "but I needed" or "they should have" or "why me" self-torment. I know; I've been there. It's not that easy, but it will free your soul and take you into a level of higher consciousness.

We all need to feel loved, worthy, wanted, and safe. We need to feel that we matter in this world. If we don't feel that way, then we will struggle in life. If you hold on to the belief that your miserable life is the fault of another, then you will continue to struggle. When you give others the power to validate you, you will never be free to validate yourself.

You want others to change so you can change. Those others also want to be validated by the people whom they blame for their unhappiness. This trap is so powerful that we can't think our way out of it. We have to heal the pain that entrapped us in the first place. This means taking back the power to heal yourself instead of relying on others to fill the holes in your heart.

That misery you are feeling was felt by the same people you are blaming for your misery. The big issue is that no one knows that they are being controlled by the burdens of the soul. Now your life is filled with layers of pain that started way before you were born. This makes you believe that life has let you down and there is nothing you can do about it. Life feels challenging for many people because they can't face those ugly feelings of unworthiness. They would rather spend their energy proving that they have some value to contribute to the world, while they continuously fight against their inner fears of rejection. This keeps them in the trap.

The real issue is the lack of knowledge and available information about how we became the way we are and why we feel so lost on the journey. We can't keep suppressing our unhealed emotions and unconsciously continue to engage in destructive behaviors to distract ourselves from what needs our attention. Chasing the light is not the answer. The answer is bringing your divine self into those parts of you that can't see the light.

When you are ready to give up the new age "all is light and no darkness can exist within us" theory, then you are ready to heal. We are filled with light when we live from the spiritual heart, but we are also filled with the shadows of darkness from our wounded past. Even after healing our shadow parts, we will still live in a world of emotional challenges. We are not forever armored from emotional trauma. When we heal old wounds, we are better emotionally prepared to handle a current crisis.

If you want to keep chasing the light, then you will continue to run away from your own healing capabilities. If you don't want to explore what is keeping you from your greatness, then you will never shine like the miracle you are.

You can reach your full, unhindered potential when you are ready to face the truth about human consciousness. That is why I am giving you research-backed concrete information that brings real hope and real healing possibilities. I want to help raise awareness of the higher truth, and I would love for you to do the same. This is the only way we can help others see their true value. We must learn how to live from our spiritual hearts and prove that compassion is the answer for all of us. This is all part of growing up and living from the heart.

This game of chasing the light within us is getting old. You must also be willing to enter the darkness and get personal with its destructive energy. Your true, divine self is really needed right now—not only for yourself, but for the disconnected world.

The Voiceless Soul

It's time to raise awareness of who you were before others told you who you are. This means reconnecting with the divine spirit within you. This means loving and honoring all parts of you. This means knowing that no matter how your life unfolded—how mean, neglectful, abusive, narcissistic, or unreliable your primary caregivers were—you are still and always will be a miracle of life. Your Creator did not send you here to hold the pain for others. You are here to learn from the pain of others. You are here to raise self-awareness, to know who you are, to love who you are, and to be who you are. When you become self-aware, you begin to receive higher messages of love from the divine essence within you.

No one wants to be wrapped up in feelings of unworthiness. Unfortunately, most people don't realize that they are. That means the ego is doing its job. Becoming self-aware means giving yourself permission to be aware of the ego's protections and to realize that they no longer serve a purpose for you.

Self-awareness is about bringing forth your disowned feelings and accepting them as valid feelings that deserve comfort and love. When you can look inside of yourself without judgment or fear, you will become aware of your innocence. This will help you come back into energetic balance because you will no longer feel the need to fight against these parts of you.

When you can expand your awareness into understanding that others are reacting to their own inner fears and not attacking you, then you will have raised your self-awareness. This means you get it. You understand the origins of dysfunction. You understand that not everyone has the inner strength to pull themselves out of the trap. You understand that this is not your issue. You know, from your spiritual heart, that some people are fighting against themselves, and you do not have to engage in that battle.

When you raise your self-awareness, you will notice when you are reacting to life instead of responding to life. You will notice when ego wants to take control. You will turn toward the spiritual heart for guidance.

You are ready for a true transformation. It all starts with raising your self-awareness to a level of higher understanding and true compassion.

CHAPTER 40

You Are Good Enough because You Are Here

If your heart resonates with what I am sharing with you, this book will help you find the passion and desire to recreate your life the way you want it to be. My goal is to help you build more compassion for yourself and the suffering world you came into.

The people of the world have been stuck in survival consciousness for centuries. The compassion and love of our collective spirit has been layered over with fear. Our souls have become drained and weakened from the many challenges of the physical world.

Once you understand that life is meant to teach you, not torture you, then you will begin to accept that there is a higher purpose for your life. Ask yourself how you would like to contribute to the world. What are you here for? What can you give of yourself to help the world evolve into a higher level of consciousness and a more compassionate way of life? What have your experiences taught you that you can now share with others? Whatever comes up for you, write it down in your personal notes.

You are a precious soul filled with light frequencies that emit a force of love energy through the heart. Don't ever forget that. You are simply experiencing feelings of "not good enough" because you have been influenced by other "not good enoughs." The whole world is filled with them. These influences have stifled your spiritual development. It's time to come back to your truth.

What is Real?

What is real and what is not has yet to be discovered by you. You are still living through your false narrative because you don't know any other way to see yourself. You have become blinded by the fear of not being accepted for who you are.

I not only had to learn how to accept the fact that the man who brought me into this world wanted to eliminate me from the world, but I also had to learn how to separate myself from his burdens of pain. I had to learn how to accept myself even though I felt deeply flawed and unwanted. Believe me, no pity here. I have grown and evolved from my life experiences, and I have learned how to find my true self. I found ways to understand the pain of the people who have hurt me. By understanding their pain, I realized it wasn't my pain. It didn't belong to me. I realized I was worthy of this world, even if others didn't make me feel that way.

I gave myself permission to heal the wounds of the past by letting go of my attachment to my pain. I gave myself permission to let go of what was familiar. I began recreating the life I deserve. My hope is that you do the same. You belong here, and so do I. We are all divine beings. Those who can't find a way to reconnect with the spirit within are fighting against their greatness with their unrelenting feelings of unworthiness. They need compassion. They need heroes like us to help them see the higher truth.

So many faulty beliefs and unhealthy patterns are stored in the souls of so many good-hearted people. Let's be more compassionate with ourselves and others, as we all come from the same source of love.

Remembering What Love Is

Every person who has or continues to walk this planet is here to learn about love. Those who can't get to that higher level are those who are stuck in feelings of nonlove. Some of us will grow up and some of us will not. Some of us will remain attached to our pain, and some of us will free ourselves. Not everyone will reconnect with who they really are.

You are no longer under the power of your caregivers. Restore the power that you gave up a long time ago by stepping fully into your miraculous self. Follow the pathway out of the unworthiness trap by entering the realm of the spiritual heart.

You belong. You are loved. You are a miracle. If you are reading this book, then you have been chosen and challenged to meet your true mission. You are here to learn how to heal the burdens of the soul so you can live by your divine truth.

Pampering yourself while you deny your feelings of unworthiness is not self-love—it is self-denial. Real, honest, and authentic love is loving all parts of you because all parts of you are from an energetic, divine source of love. When you are loving yourself fully and authentically, you are automatically sending that love vibration out into the world. When you have rejected parts of yourself that keep holding you in the trap, then you are holding back on love.

Your Creator sent you here to help spread love. You are here because the world needs you.

CHAPTER 41

Embracing the Energetic Evolution

> Transpersonal Power can be found in everyone. It is based on empathy, detachment, and going beyond ego to find your deeper Identity.
>
> —Deepak Chopra
> *The Soul of Leadership*

Without the new science and new age phenomena, prior generations had very little choice of how to heal their suppressed trauma due to unmet needs. They had no idea that their emotional needs were just as important as their physical needs. As long as their physical needs were met, then there wasn't anything they should feel bad about. The problem is that there was a lot to feel bad about. They did not feel loved, wanted, or valued. It was rare for our ancestors to experience an intimate connection to their primary caregivers. This may have caused them to feel like burdens to society. These are the emotional burdens that have been passed on to for generations.

Since expressing negative emotions about one's life seemed abnormal, irrational, and socially unacceptable, most people in generations past did not feel it was safe to express their true feelings. Those who could not hold back their emotional distress were labeled unstable, an emotional train wreck, and even incurably insane.

The reason we are better at navigating life than those who went before us is because we are transitioning from the "survival of the fittest" principle into emotional expression and spiritual growth. This gives us a sense of freedom, autonomy, and inner connectedness. We are no longer strangers to ourselves. This is a huge step forward for humanity. We are collectively thinking at higher levels of consciousness. We are collectively feeling at deeper levels of our souls. We are becoming more in tune with our needs, desires, and purpose. We are moving away from the opinions of others and trusting ourselves more. We are no longer easily persuaded to give up our power.

There is a huge shift in the collective field of thought processes, and you are a big part of that shift. You are here to help create a flow of more love, compassion, and acceptance. You have a great advantage over those who raised you into your adulthood. You are growing up; they were not able to grow up. You came into this world as a miracle and entered into a struggling humanity. Start showing up in your miraculous light, and stay true to your mission.

We can continue to grow more consciously by increasing our appetite for transformation. We can allow ourselves to evolve to a level of compassion that brings not only deep inner peace for ourselves, but more peace for our collective society. We can help heal the mental and emotional wounds of others by healing ourselves first. If we carry that high-vibrational energy of self-love, then we can pass that energy on to those we come in contact with. We can help others grow up and connect with their own inner spirit by living from our higher truth.

You can be the change the world needs. You can live from a place of higher understanding so you don't get absorbed into that lower level of consciousness. You can take advantage of this energetic expansion into truth and move with it instead of against it. It's time to heed the calling of a more compassionate and loving society. It's time to evolve into your higher knowing and save yourself from the damage done by generations living in fear of nonlove. It's time to embrace the energetic evolution.

The Voiceless Soul

By living from your spiritual heart, you hold compassion for those who did not have the opportunities you have today and those who are blind to the higher truth. This allows you to live more peacefully because you have a higher understanding of what the real mission is about. This is what growing up is. This is what being more conscious and aware is. It is living life without judgments, criticisms, and disregard for one's inability to find oneself. It is you embracing the energetic evolution because you are a part of the energetic shift into higher consciousness. You are a hero.

Each new generation is more evolved than the one before it. We are reaching higher levels of awareness as more internal wisdom is embraced and shared.

Many of those experiencing this energetic shift are still held back by feelings of unworthiness. This locks them into an immobilized state of consciousness and greatly slows down the movement. This is because everyone is pampering themselves with fluff. A real shift will take place when they allow their shadow parts to be seen and heard, so they can be healed with the source of authentic truth and love.

To raise awareness for others, we have to be in that awareness ourselves. When we still have unhealed pieces of our soul directing our lives, we are not in our highest awareness. We are still carrying the energy of past wounds that are seeking our attention. We have to stop letting the past control our future. The only way we can do that is to heal all the emotions that keep calling us back to the trap. Once we do that, we step out of the trap. We see the world from a higher level of truth, compassion, understanding, and acceptance. We regain the power of the divine light within us.

Since we are experiencing an energetic evolution, it is easier than ever before to put an end to our debilitating fears of unworthiness and start creating the life we deserve. We have the wisdom and compassion it takes to put our high-vibrational energy into motion and start recreating our lives.

You can't go back and change the lives of your ancestors. Their experiences were part of their soul's growth and a learning experience for you. What you can do is help transform the energy that moves through your ancestral line to a more compassionate and loving energy by seeing your ancestors as innocent souls that didn't know how to get out of the trap. From where you are now, in a higher level of consciousness than those who came before you, you can heal your soul burdens and help change the future of the world. When generational trauma is halted, it allows a healing of society. If you trust that we are all one collective energy, then when we heal, the souls of our ancestors will feel the break in the cycle of lower consciousness, allowing their souls to rest more peacefully.

In this time of energy transition, we are all being called to rise up and be the hero of our heritage. We are needed here and now to help stop the madness and bring this world to a compassionate level of energetic bonding. Those who are not able to rise up and step out of the trap will continue to struggle. We must accept this without judgment.

We must take advantage of this energetic evolution and the increasing opportunities that offer us a chance to take back our power and recreate our lives. This is the only way we can contribute more compassion to a love-diminished world. We must be the heroes who let go of what we cannot change and embrace what we can change.

It's not easy being the awakened one in your lineage, but you were called here at this time to take on this difficult task. Take it on with courage, compassion, and love. This will provide the strength you need during your intense energetic transition.

We all deserve to live a life we love. Let's not deny that to anyone who is stuck.

CHAPTER 42

Becoming the Real You

People are naturally loving and compassionate, but traumatic experiences can cause guarded hearts and limited trust in people and the world. Just because you don't see their wounded souls doesn't mean they are not suffering.

It's hard not to call out a narcissist as selfish and uncaring. It's hard not to call out an angry father as controlling and unloving. It's hard not to call out a mother who is depressed as unaffectionate and self-absorbed. We have a tendency to believe that people can switch off those traits if they want to. That is where we get stuck in a lower level of consciousness. We lack the higher knowing that others are living from their wounded selves, completely disconnected from their spirit—just like the child who feels unworthy of Mom or Dad's love cannot switch off those feelings of unworthiness. This is how adults become people who do not like themselves and then develop traits that we do not like in them.

We must always remember that none of us are superhumans unless we have cleansed our souls from the burdens that weigh us down. This cleansing will help us release the old, outdated patterns and guide us into our higher hearts, where the higher truth can be acknowledged. The level of awareness that will take you there starts with your compassionate heart that not only knows that we are all trying our best, but also knows that our best is tainted with the fear of not being enough. If our best shows up as lazy, depressed, angry, irresponsible, withdrawn, and downright mean, it's because that is the best we can do when we lose connection to our spiritual heart.

If we could read the soul energy of those who made us feel bad about ourselves, then we would see how desperate their soul is for love. If we could read our own soul energy, we would see how we feared an inability to be loved. When we engage in higher understanding of the soul's journey in the physical world, we are free to see the innocence of our souls and the inability of others to free themselves from the trap.

Does changing your thoughts and feelings change the way you see yourself and the world? Absolutely! Is it easy to change the thoughts and feelings that you have become attached to in your life, some that go as far back as conception? No, it is not! Your patterns are ingrained in your soul. These patterns do not make up the real you. The real you does not participate in self-destructive behaviors. The false you, the one trapped in fear, is stuck in the patterns that create drama and suffering. It takes a higher level of awareness to understand these destructive patterns, heal them, and then release these lower energies from your soul.

To become the real you, you must start by seeing what you didn't want to look at in the past. Every time it popped up from your wounded soul, you found a way to avoid dealing with it. When you look at it now and see it from a higher level of truth, you will see it differently. You will see that others are unknowingly deficient in their emotional needs, so they unknowingly caused you to be deficient in yours. You will see how others got stuck in the trap and were able to pull you in because you were not aware of your divine self. You couldn't be in a place of awareness as a young child, but you can be now. This means you have some work to do to get back to the real you.

We all suffer because of a disconnect from the higher truth. When you regain the connection to the truth of who you are, you see the whole world in a different light. You become aware that there is a collective energy of fear that keeps us stuck in the drama and suffering of life. The only way to help change that is to bring back the compassion that comes from the spiritual heart. The real you lives from that higher place. This is growing up.

If you want to contribute to creating a better world, it starts with you. It starts with you growing up and becoming more conscious and aware of the truth behind your pain, the truth behind the people you blame for your pain, and the truth behind the reason you can't seem to get unstuck.

Nothing and no one can steal the light within you. You have chosen to dull your light because you felt unworthy of its greatness. You are a soul that has experienced the many challenges of physical life. They are experiences only, and not meant to own you, but to teach you who you are on a spiritual level.

When you are ready to invite your higher self forward, you will feel a sense of peace. Surrender to it. Let it help you through your soul-healing process, so you can engage fully with the truth of who you are.

When you are no longer holding anyone else responsible for your happiness, you have grown up. You have become the real you—the human soul that is connected to the spirit within.

It is only through higher understanding of how life works that you will be able to let go of all the lifelong attachments that kept you stuck. When you meet the real you, you will be able to set your soul free and blend deeper into your spirit.

When you realize who you are in your truest form, you won't let life throw you into a version of someone you are not. You will show up as your miraculous self because you will no longer be seeking the approval of those around you. You will shine so brightly that others will seek your guidance. Help them reach the higher truth and see the light within them.

It is your mission as a spiritual being to learn the higher truth and help others find it through you. This is becoming the real you.

CHAPTER 43

Becoming Responsible for Your Life

Old patterns that do not serve your soul in its highest form once had a purpose in your life. They were there to keep you connected to those you needed to take care of you. This was your survival strategy—so good job in keeping yourself safe. You are more intelligent than you think you are. You did the most responsible thing you could at the time. You adapted to their needs and expectations so you would be rewarded with love and safety. That was brilliant of you.

You are not that child anymore. You are in an adult body. Parts of you may still be in that child consciousness because you have not fully grown up, but that is not your fault. It wasn't your responsibility as a child to figure out how to grow up. It was the responsibility of the people who raised you. It was their responsibility to meet all of your childhood needs, create healthy childhood patterns, provide sufficient love and security, and give you the freedom to be your own person. In looking at the higher truth, you can now say, "It would have been great if they had known how to do that."

You now have to decide if you can be the responsible adult. A responsible adult will review all of their life experiences, take the lessons learned, and discard what will not serve their adult self. This means seeing the old survival patterns as obsolete. They have served their purpose, and that purpose is complete. There's a new purpose now, and that is to recreate your life in a way that serves a higher purpose. This is called becoming responsible.

No matter what you had to experience before this moment in time, you are still and always will be a miracle of life, a precious and innocent soul, and a part of the higher, loving consciousness that lives within all of us. That spark of light within you can grow into a grand illumination of love and compassion for yourself and others if you allow it. That, my dear, is freedom. It is true spiritual growth. That is what becoming the grown-up is. It is you taking responsibility for creating the life you deserve. It is you becoming responsible because you no longer want to look to others to save you.

A grown-up who is ready to grow up will start shedding the old, conditioned patterns and see the bigger picture through the light of spirit. I invite you now to see the grand illumination that awaits you when you engage with your higher heart and live from that genuine place within you.

If you can grasp the concept that someone's inability to be responsible has nothing to do with you, then you are becoming responsible. If you can reach that place of becoming responsible even though you didn't have the perfect childhood, then you are doing better than your caregivers could do. Be proud of that.

Loving Yourself Enough to Take Responsibility

You are, for certain, a product of all those who came before you. You took on their energetic patterns and became stuck in that energy. It's not so easy to release the energy that your body has become accustomed to over the years. Your body doesn't want to let any of that energy go. It is the energy your body survived on.

You can't destroy unwanted energy because energy doesn't die. What you can do with those energy imprints is give them the love and acceptance they need. Energy may not die, but it does shift, change form, and relax so it's not stuck in a contracted survival position. To recreate your life, you have to recreate the energetic imprints that were impressed upon your soul a long time ago. This means loving yourself enough to take responsibility for those imprints now.

If we don't recreate the energy that keeps us limited in our lives, then we become a magnet for the same energy. We also pass that energy on to others, especially other innocent souls that look to us for guidance.

When you shift your energy to a higher level, others around you begin to shift as well. Your responsibility to yourself, your loved ones, and the world is learning how to love yourself.

There is a place within you that is filled with love and light. That place in you knows who you are. Your ego may have created many strong self-protections. It is important to honor those protections because they kept you feeling safe. Now it is your divine obligation to go deeper into your soul and release your soul from the burdens of fear that created these protections. You are growing, you are evolving, and you are always being divinely guided. To continue your path forward, you must become aware of the energy that holds you back.

This is a call back to love. This is a call to honor your soul even though it is stuck in the fear of not being enough. It is the love of your spirit that can help your soul out of the darkness and into the light of the higher truth. This spirit within is the part of you that wants all the souls that walk this planet to free themselves from their heavy burdens. Your miraculous self is loving, compassionate, and understanding. Your true self is aware of your greatness and the potential greatness of those stuck in the trap.

You can't change the whole world, but you can change your energy into a higher vibration that contributes to healing the world. You can only do this if you are loving yourself enough to create change.

Loving yourself includes loving those shadow parts of you that you believed were unlovable. As long as you keep these parts of you from being heard, they will not heal, and you will not be fully loving you.

Loving yourself fully is part of your spiritual growth and evolution, so don't expect it to happen overnight. Learning how to get there is where you need to start. You must love yourself enough to take this important step in the process. Each time you heal a part of you that feels unloved, you bring more love into your soul. Each time you bring more love into your soul, you live more from the spirit within. The more you live from your spirit, the more responsible you become.

Loving yourself enough to take responsibility means forgiving yourself for your past mistakes, learning from your experiences, and releasing others from being responsible for you. No one is responsible for you now except you. Loving yourself enough means you stop focusing on what you wish could have been and start focusing on what could be.

Loving yourself enough to take responsibility for your healing is how you escape from the trap.

CHAPTER 44

Self-Forgiveness as a Self-Healing Tool

I know we hear a lot about forgiveness and how it heals the heart, the soul, and the world. If forgiveness is so healing, then why do we not forgive more often?

There is more to forgiveness than is understood. When we forgive authentically, we are not forgiving an act of unkindness. We are forgiving a soul in pain.

Most of the time, the people we need to forgive are just people who were able to trigger our own insecurities and deep sense of unworthiness. When they treated us with less than love, we felt that old, familiar feeling of not being enough. This could have caused us to become angry at them, although we are really angry with our own feelings of inadequacy. What we are not seeing is the whole picture. We only felt the suffering caused to us by another person who disregarded our feelings and triggered our insecurities. At that point, we lost all contact with our rational mind and went into our survival mind. The pain is so real that any act of forgiveness might release that pain. If that pain is released, we may forget how badly it hurt. That could make us vulnerable to another attack.

The refusal to forgive acts as a protector. It gives us a feeling of control in a situation in which we feel we lost control. It allows us to hold resentment and distrust against another as our weapon to destroy any further incoming attacks. The word "forgiveness" means we have been defeated by the enemy. We have given in because we are weak. By holding back on forgiveness, we believe we have taken back our power and will be fools no longer. We need to understand forgiveness in its true form.

If the word "forgiveness" is uncomfortable for you, then think of forgiveness as self-healing instead. Instead of forgiving someone, tell yourself you are self-healing from their inability to be in a place of love. You felt hurt because they didn't see you as valuable. That is what forgiveness is. Forgiveness is understanding that what others do and don't do has nothing to do with you. If you were hurt by someone, then forgiveness means forgiving yourself for believing that you were not worthy of their love and respect. Forgive yourself for those moments of self-disconnect. Come back into your spiritual heart. Give yourself some love and compassion. You are only human. You will hurt. Others will cause you pain. You have to decide whether it's OK to let them hold power over you, or whether you will do self-healing forgiveness.

The feelings that are being provoked in you were created a long time ago. The inability of someone to treat you with love and kindness stems from their feelings of unworthiness that were created for them a long time ago. We keep passing our negative energy around. This trap has a lot of power, and if you don't see the force behind it, you are going to keep falling deeper into it.

Not allowing ourselves to heal through forgiveness keeps us energetically attached to the people who hurt us.

When you practice authentic forgiveness, you are forgiving yourself for forgetting your inherent value. This is when you are able to stay in your higher truth, even if others keep trying to devalue you. When you are provoked by the unkind actions of another, then understand that this disregard for your feelings is not happening to you, it's happening through you. It's triggering an energetic imprint that's attached to your soul. It's that part of you that is afraid of not being loved. When you heal these parts of you, then you won't be triggered so easily. This takes work, but know that you are worth the time and effort it takes to get there. Part of the soul-healing process is learning self-forgiveness.

When you forgive, you are not letting anyone off the hook except yourself. If you are holding on to anger or resentment, then you have hooked yourself into someone else's inability to be in a place of love. This means you have fallen into their trap. When you do self-healing during a time when you feel hurt by another, you are telling yourself that you don't need to hook into their fears. The self-healing reminds you of the beautiful, innocent spirit you are, that you came from a place of love and no one can take that love from you. Any attachment to the pain caused by another means you have not resolved your own inner fears of unworthiness. It's OK to forgive yourself for not remembering your value.

When you are asked to forgive someone, you are being asked to remember that they made a mistake that has nothing to do with you. You are being asked to remember that you are worthy of respect even if someone didn't show you respect. When someone doesn't honor who you are as a human being, a soul with feelings, and a valuable asset to the world, they are showing you their inability to love themselves. They are not showing you your worth. True forgiveness of another is the act of self-forgiveness. It is the act of remembering that you are valuable and lovable even when others are not seeing that in you.

Forgiveness in Its Authentic Form

The word "forgive" is thrown around in the healing community as if it were something we should just do because it helps us heal. It is true that forgiveness helps to heal the soul, but without compassion in its highest form, forgiveness becomes a difficult process. This means forgiveness becomes a superficial attempt to let go of the anger or resentment that we believe we have a right to hold on to.

Before authentic forgiveness can take place, there must be true compassion. If we do not go beyond our intellectual mind and really feel compassion for those who feel unloved and unworthy, then we remain vulnerable to their lower vibrational energy. If we don't understand what causes someone to be unkind, then how can we truly forgive them for hurting us? If we don't understand that they are controlled by unconscious fears, then we will think they maliciously and intentionally wanted to hurt us because of who we are. It's because of who they believe they are. Their unkind acts tend to cause us to fear something might be wrong with us because we are unaware of their internal suffering. All we experience is their ego, which is protecting their fear of not being enough. Having compassion for their inability to grow up and see their own value is the way you can keep their fears from becoming your fears.

If you are holding the energy of guilt or shame for the wrong you have done to another, now is the time to go inside yourself and heal the wounds that caused you to disconnect from love. Now is the time to forgive yourself for not doing better. Now is the time to forgive yourself for getting stuck in the unworthiness trap and projecting your lack of self-love onto others. Now is the time to do better because you know better.

When you live from your spiritual heart, you feel compassion for those who can't experience love, including yourself. If someone can't experience love, they will not come from an authentic, loving place. You may be vulnerable as a sensitive human being, but you don't have to own their pain and you don't have to stay stuck in yours. That is where self-forgiveness becomes your self-healing tool. You are seeing the bigger picture. You can feel compassion for the inability of others to be kind. You show compassion for yourself for not knowing that there is a better way to resolve the matter. You remember that you are valuable and worthy of love. This allows you to be free of the low energy of others and allows you to learn how to do better than those who caused you pain.

Many people have asked me how I could forgive a father who intentionally tried to take my life from me. It wasn't easy to forgive a man with the mind of a killer, but it was not forgiveness of my father that gave me back my freedom. It was compassion for my father that gave me the ability to realize he was a soul filled with layers of pain accumulated over many years of childhood neglect, abuse, and fear. The person I needed to forgive was myself. I needed to forgive myself for believing that I was unworthy of his love and this world. I needed to forgive myself for not knowing the truth about who I am. I needed to forgive myself for falling into the same trap my father got stuck in.

After discovering the truth behind the stories that I had been telling myself, I realized that I was not the problem in my father's life. His soul was his problem. It was burdened with so much pain that it took him away from his true self and kept him in a brutal state of rage and hate. Although that doesn't make it OK for him to do what he did, I made the decision that I no longer needed to suffer for his inability to heal his wounds of unworthiness. I learned to be a better parent once I was able to let go of my entanglement with his suffering.

For my own healing, I had to find compassion for him and for myself. I had to send love and peace to his soul as well as the suffering soul of the little girl in me. Once I could feel compassion for both of us, I was able to release my attachment to my suffering and forgive myself for not knowing my value in this world.

> Dear Dad,
>
> You certainly put me to the test. I stayed angry for half my life. You damaged my heart and screwed up my mind. I felt unworthy and unlovable because you made me believe I was.
>
> I don't want to keep fighting the fight. It takes up all my energy.
>
> I realize now that I was not your enemy. You were your own enemy. You lost connection to your divine self, and you caused me to do the same. I connected the dots from your childhood to your adulthood and realized that you were still stuck in the childhood horror that consumed your soul.
>
> You have crossed over now. I didn't even get to say goodbye. You never met my children. I wish it could have been different, but it wasn't. It wasn't the life I wanted, but then again, it wasn't the life you wanted either.

I am sorry that you couldn't stop your suffering. I am sorry that you wanted to punish the world for it.

By getting rid of us, you thought you were getting rid of parts of yourself. Well, I am still here, Dad. I survived your attack. I will never forget that horrible day. I will never forget how my little body quivered in fear. I will never forget how much pain you caused me. I don't need to forget. I just need to forgive.

I am moving on now. I am forgiving myself for believing that I was not good enough for your love and acceptance. I am forgiving myself for believing I was unworthy of this world. I am doing the healing work I should have done many years ago.

Most importantly, I have released myself from the trap that relentlessly suffocated my soul. I hope that, wherever you are, you can find love in your heart and peace in your soul.

With all my love,
Your Daughter

CHAPTER 45

Compassion as the Ultimate Answer

For true forgiveness to take place, there must be feelings of compassion for those who have hurt you or someone you care about. Compassion means you understand, from a heartfelt level, that hurtful people are suffering from emotional trauma. When they are out of alignment with the wisdom of the heart, they live through the shadow aspects of the soul.

When souls have reached the point of destruction of themselves and others, we see them as villains of society. It is difficult to share our lives with people who are stuck in that lower level of consciousness, and we shouldn't have to. If they are disrupting our lives, we have to find a way to disconnect from their energy. As children, we could not escape the fierce shadow of the disconnected souls. This is why we have to undo the damage now. We have to understand how we got caught up in that pain and how we can heal through the spiritual heart of compassion.

Please understand that this is not about blaming the adults from your childhood. It is the opposite. It is about letting go of blame and instead embracing forgiveness, compassion, and the higher truth. This is what will help us get through our pain. We must unfreeze those frozen traumas within us, let out the pain by lovingly allowing it to express itself, and then step into the higher truth and begin replenishing our souls with the love and compassion we deserve.

The Voiceless Soul

No matter how enlightened one is, being around the energy of suffering souls can be distressing. Removing yourself from them does not mean you don't care about them. It only means that you care about the wellness of your soul. Compassion for self and others is the ultimate answer to healing. To continuously engage with their toxic behavior means you are stuck in the trap with them. Your innocent soul can free itself by entering the space of the spiritual heart.

There are many souls that have not been able to evolve in this lifetime. Your lessons in life are to not let them stagnate your soul growth. When you practice compassion, you accept each soul where they are on their journey. By accepting souls where they are on their journey, you are not judging them, you have no expectations of them, and you are not wrapped up in their drama.

I know it's not easy to feel compassion for anyone who has done something awful to you. A normal human reaction would be anger, resentment, and a need to see them suffer. It is a natural human response to want to balance the scale so you don't feel cheated, slighted, or at a disadvantage to anyone.

Here's the thing, sweet miracle of life: they are already suffering.

If they are unkind, uncaring, and unloving people, then they are disconnected from their source of love. They are in immense pain in their hearts, and their souls feel depleted. They are the people who are missing out on the joys of life because they don't feel deserving of anything good. That is why they continue to create the bad. They only know what they believe to be true.

Trauma of the soul can cause a lot of damage, and we have to recognize the truth behind the damage being done. Otherwise, we will stay in the unworthiness trap, and the damage will continue. When you practice empathy and understanding, you will not need to forgive anyone for their sins. Their shortcomings will not be personal to you. The only necessary forgiveness is self-forgiveness for becoming entangled in their energy.

Kelly Tallaksen

The best revenge you can have on anyone who has hurt you is to move on and leave that negative energy behind you. Life is not always peachy, but you know that already. You don't have to carry someone else's load. Compassion will help you release the burdens that others have projected onto you. There is a place for compassion in every situation. You must be in the higher truth to know that a spiritual heart is what is needed, not judgment or fear.

Compassion in Its Highest Form

Compassion in its highest form is being able to feel the emotional pain of others and express empathy for their suffering.

My dad spent part of his early childhood life in an orphanage. He did not grow up feeling loved by anyone. He did not grow up doing what little boys do. He grew up believing he was a throwaway child.

Then the authorities in the orphanage reinforced his belief. Life in the orphanage meant no one wanted you, and most of the time no one did. He was alone and despondent. He was forced to do hard labor and fight for his life at a very young age. He was mentally, emotionally, physically, and sexually abused. His anger grew more and more over the years. Then it turned to rage as he stayed stuck in the drama that was so familiar to him. The world to him was a very dark and unsafe place, where love did not exist. My dad had no idea what love meant. He only knew his pain, and so it was his pain that became my pain.

I had to understand his suffering so I could release my attachment to it. I had to feel sincere compassion for his fractured soul so I could stop making his inability to love himself about me. I have compassion for the little boy in him who only wanted to belong in this world, who only wanted to matter to someone. I know he wanted to love us, but the force of darkness in his soul overpowered his desire for love. When the fears become that controlling, they deplete the energy that leads to the higher truth.

I have compassion for my mom, who spent her whole life feeling unloved by her mother. I was told by my mom's sister that my mother was treated differently from the other siblings. She was treated like she was not worthy of her mother's love because her complexion was much darker than the complexion of the other children. I could not understand why my mother would be saddened her whole life because of this.

I get it now. I have compassion for that little girl who just wanted to feel her mother's love. I found out later that my grandmother on my mother's side of the family was shunned by others because of her darker complexion. My grandmother was not rejecting my mother. She was rejecting the part of herself that she saw in my mother. This was not something my mother could have known as a child. This was something my mother never learned in her adulthood. This was why my mother unknowingly spent most of her life not honoring herself. This was why my mother was energetically attracted to men like my dad.

We all have experiences of trauma, and we all suffer on some level from the disconnect that trauma causes. Understanding the higher truth and healing those broken connections will be your true savior. I had to heal the disconnect I felt with both my mom and my dad. I did this through learning the truth about their lives and writing letters from a place of higher understanding. I did not need to send the letters to them. I just needed to release the pain of disconnect from my soul.

Compassion in its highest form means going above intellectual thinking and being in a higher truth. You must be able to understand from a higher level of awareness that their struggles are caused by their inability to be in alignment with spirit. This is the higher knowing that we must reach so we can stay in our spiritual hearts.

If we continue to feel disconnected from the important people in our lives because of our anger or resentment toward them, we will suffer on a soul level. We will remain energetically entwined with the pain they projected onto us.

If we practice this higher form of compassion, where we know from a higher level of consciousness that all souls are good souls until burdened by their painful experiences, then we can heal our own souls.

That is the journey we are on.

CHAPTER 46

Reconnecting to Spirit Through the Spiritual Heart

The consciousness of your spiritual heart is your spirit. It is connected to a universal source that is all-loving, all-compassionate, and all-forgiving. It is a form of higher intelligence. This higher intelligence is within all of us, but we have lost touch with it along the journey. This intelligence expands through a field of energy into the cosmos and keeps us in alignment with our true source of love. When your heart is open and you are in tune with the heart's vibrational energies, you will realize that life may not be perfect, but your spirit is.

Spirit is who you are in your wholeness. Spirit is your unburdened soul in ultimate freedom, where you can explore this world with curiosity, depth, and soul-centered awareness. Spirit is the soul in its true, divine source. When the soul lets go of the heaviness of complexes and burdens, it is free to soar into the spirit of life, becoming one with the energy of higher truth, higher love, and compassion in its highest form. By staying in the spiritual heart, we are blended with spirit.

Since your primary caregivers were your first teachers in your physical life, your trust in life comes from their ability to help you keep your spiritual heart open and aligned with the higher truth. If your primary caregivers lived mostly from an ego-protected consciousness, then you may have lost connection to your true essential self.

The Voiceless Soul

An important lesson for you in this lifetime is to understand that your primary caregivers were not your first spiritual teachers. Your first spiritual teacher is your Creator. You are initially a child of the divine, and that makes you a divine being. You have been given opportunities by your Creator to grow and evolve into the highest spiritual truth. The fastest way to do that is to have experiences that will challenge your soul. Within each trauma experience is a chance to learn a spiritual lesson and take the soul to a higher level of conscious.

If your experiences have left your soul feeling numb, then you must see your experiences in a different way. If you won't reach for the higher truth, then you have given up on your right to experience what love really is. This means you have also given up on your heritage and your divine gifts.

This is not why you are here. You are here to expand your spiritual heart and live and teach from a level of love. It cannot be done through the ego mind, the intellectual mind, or the wisdom you find in a book. It can only be done through spiritual lessons built on patience, kindness, forgiveness, understanding, acceptance, compassion, and truth. You must heal the burdens of the soul by bringing these spiritual lessons from your heart into your soul, so you can come back into spiritual alignment and live like the divine being you are.

Soul healing goes beyond human survival consciousness. When healing your soul, you must be able to enter the spiritual heart and reconnect to the divine love that is within you. In the following chapters, I share the ways in which you can do that.

Meet Your Challenges with an Open Heart

The spiritual heart is the sacred center of your physical body. It emits an energy that links to the highest form of love. The heart begins to beat about twenty-two days after conception. Many researchers believe the heart has a brain of its own.

The HeartMath Institute, a nonprofit organization that pursues cutting-edge heart-brain science, indicates that the heart has a brain of its own and communicates with the brain via the nervous system.[5] The heart is also known for its intuitive guidance, which many people rely on in making decisions—hence the saying "Follow your heart."

It is further suggested that the heart sends more signals to the brain than the brain sends to the heart. These signals influence emotional processing as well as higher cognitive faculties like attention, perception, memory, and problem-solving.

We are intuitive beings from the beginning of life in the womb. What we feel from the heart has a great impact on the soul.

We have to do more than think our way through life. We must also feel our way through life. This includes understanding others from the spiritual heart and not the head. The brain likes to overthink every situation. We must unblock our hearts so we can put more loving and intuitive energy into difficult situations and find the deeper truth in them.

Every difficult challenge needs a warm heart, higher understanding, and clear level of intellect. We must be able to keep our spiritual heart open when we are using our rational mind to resolve an emotional issue. This will keep us from inviting too much ego consciousness into the matter. This will help us heal our emotional conflicts and keep us spiritually connected to ourselves and others.

This is spiritual growth.

Dear Mom and Dad,

From my adult, intellectual mind, I know you did the best you could. The little girl in me, however, struggled for years trying to figure out what was wrong with me. My feelings

---

[5] https://www.heartmath.org/research/science-of-the-heart/heart-brain-communication/

of shame have held me back from achieving the goals I dreamed of. My fears of abandonment caused tension in my relationships. My thoughts of unworthiness kept me in my victimhood. I felt damaged. I felt disconnected. I felt alone.

I am OK now. I have learned many great things. You have taught me how to survive, and now I am learning how to do more than survive. I am learning how to stay in my spiritual heart and live my life from a higher place of love and understanding. I am now able to let go of the burdens of pain I held on to for so long. I am growing in my ability to let go of what I cannot control. I am learning from your mistakes and my own.

It is with this understanding and higher awareness, together with the healing of my deepest wounds, that I can now say, from the deepest part of my liberated soul, that you did the best you could with what you had. You were lost and confused and didn't know how to help yourself. You were deficient in the very things I needed from you.

I unknowingly let your wounds become my wounds. My biggest lesson was to learn my value so I could live in my higher truth. I understand now that it is my responsibility to remember who I am.

I am sorry for both of you. I am sorry you didn't have the knowledge or resources to heal your pain.

I'm sorry you didn't get a chance in this lifetime to experience love the way you needed to. I'm sorry no one was there for you during your darkest moments. I'm sorry you didn't know how to love me the way I needed you to. I'm sorry that you were so burdened by anger that your souls ached for relief. I didn't know you were suffering, just like you didn't know the suffering you were causing me. I hope you can forgive yourselves.

My spiritual heart is open, and I am sending love to both of you—the love you always needed. Your pain has stifled your souls' evolution because you couldn't see the higher truth. I finally did. Your struggles are no longer my struggles. They are my lessons for spiritual growth.

I am now in a place of knowing. By looking at the bigger picture, I can see the innocence in all of us. I now feel your divine essence. I now see you in the higher truth. Your light is so beautiful. I pray for you to see it the way I do.

Forever in my heart,
Your Daughter

CHAPTER 47

We are Born Creators

We are now, as grown-ups, the true creators of our lives. For us to reach that level of awareness and take action toward the life we choose to live, we must release those who keep us in limitation. We release others by releasing our negative bond with them. The only way to do that is to remember the miracle that you are, to have compassion for others' inability to love themselves, and to remove yourself from the unworthiness trap they pulled you into.

Life may have been created for you from the beginning, but you are wiser, stronger, and more courageous than ever before. You have survived all of it, and now you are here and able to share your story through a wider lens. You can see the bigger picture and tell your story from a place of higher truth.

Changing the way you tell your story changes the energy of the story. This energy is what affects every level of your soul. Let the energy be of pure light, love, and compassion. Let yourself create from a higher level of truth, so you don't get pulled back down.

You have a masterpiece waiting to be created from the deepest part of your soul. Feel yourself expressing this masterpiece through higher intentions filled with a higher sense of purpose. You are not here for anything less than that. You can free your soul's heavy energy by expressing yourself from a level of higher understanding and not from the level of fear.

By reaching into your spiritual heart, you begin to see the reason you have been held back from your greatness. You will see how you unknowingly lived through a false self.

When you reach the higher truth, you bring love to the fears trapped in your soul, allowing your soul to release their energetic power as you see them for what they really are. You now see the truth: fear is a consciousness that gets tangled within the soul when the soul experiences the energy of nonlove. As you learn this truth, you give your soul the freedom to reconnect to the essence of divine love.

Use your hard-earned strength, wisdom, and courage in ways that bring you closer to your spiritual heart. Share your high energy with others and stay true to the spirit within.

I hope this book made you feel a little lighter in your soul. I hope you continue to heal and stay true to yourself. You can do better than your caregivers could do. You can do better because you know better. Be in that space, and you will be the hero the world is looking for.

This is the generation of love. Let's make it flourish!

CHAPTER 48

Healing through Expressions from the Soul

Generation after generation, grown-ups have struggled with life.

Today, we are more aware, but we are not feeling deeply enough into our souls to become aware enough to create change. The way to free yourself from the emotions that hold you in the trap is through expressions from the soul. The soul has been trying to speak through you, but it was expressing from the fear of not being enough. Sit down and just breathe in the higher truth and higher knowing that there is nothing wrong with you. Things were difficult for you because things were difficult for others. The energy of struggle is not easy to transform when you are disconnected from the spiritual heart. When you breathe in the higher truth, then you can express your pain from a higher level of understanding. This is what will free your soul. True expression will help you release the stuck energy that keeps you immobilized.

Since spirit is all-loving, you can meet your challenged relationships with the energy of the divine essence within you. This is how your soul can heal from the pain of disconnected love. You must reach that higher knowing that we are all in the same trap and we are all worthy of being freed from it. It must start with you, and then hopefully others will follow. You cannot control the path for others, but you can be the example of higher truth.

Kelly Tallaksen

Speaking Out with Compassion

We must speak out from our hearts, without judgment or criticism of self or others. When we speak from a higher place of love, we stop reliving the same old untruths that keep us stuck. We must do this with the knowing that it's a trap and we all got caught in it—not because we are bad and not because we are not smart enough, but because we are human. We must know we are ready to rise above the low-level critical thoughts that have been consuming our souls. We must be ready to take action. We must heal the old story and begin the story of who we really are. Your soul is not free until you set it free. Once you do that, your spiritual heart leads your soul into a higher vibration of spirit. You just melt into that higher knowing that we are all deserving of love. This is the ultimate truth that we all came here to learn.

Expressing from Higher Knowledge

Every adult has an unheard child within them. All those emotionally immature adults are acting through the immature child within them. They are trying to be heard—but like a child, they do not know how to communicate without the fear of rejection.

If my younger self could have spoken up and expressed my true feelings, then I would have felt heard. I would have released the energy that was disrupting my spiritual growth. Being able to express what is bubbling inside of us prevents a buildup of toxic emotions that can sabotage our dreams, our gifts, and our relationships. Expression of our needs is the most important. Suppression of our needs is what keeps us stuck in the trap and desperately seeking completion outside of ourselves. Getting to the ultimate higher truth provides the last piece of the untold story.

As adults, we can allow the younger, innocent, and unheard self that lives within us to express through our adult self all of the feelings that were buried a long time ago. Release of these heart-heavy feelings is like releasing the lid on a boiling pot of water. Don't wait for the explosion. As you express your fears, your worries, and your self-sabotaging thoughts, and as you let yourself feel the heartfelt emotions behind them, keep in mind that the people you hold responsible for what comes up for you were also experiencing these low vibrational thoughts and feelings. Always know that you have strength, you have courage, and you have a voice. Use all of them. Remember to speak only from that higher level of knowledge that comes from the spiritual heart.

When you are expressing from higher knowledge, it does not mean holding in anger or rage. These are not bad emotions; they are human emotions that need to be expressed. Repression of these emotions is what keeps us from loving ourselves. You have every right to express all your anger, fears, worries, resentments, and distrust. You are a spiritual being with human emotions that deserve a voice. Do not be ashamed to express all that you feel inside. All feelings are important. All emotions must be felt.

We can only feel our true emotions when we allow ourselves to go deeper into our souls. From this deep place within, we can openly express ourselves through the physical act of writing, as described at the end of this chapter.

When we express ourselves from a higher truth, it does not mean we express only loving thoughts and mushy phrases of forgiveness and compassion. Our higher truth is acknowledging that we have lower thoughts and feelings that need to come up for healing. Our higher truth is acknowledging that the hurt parts of us are lovable, valuable, and significant parts of who we are. The forgiveness and compassion expressions are the parts of us that come alive when we release ourselves from the need for others to validate our worth. When we see the bigger picture and speak from that higher level of understanding, we see others as children with burdened souls, not as the adults who were trying to break our spirit.

Healing through Expression

We've all been bitten by the unworthiness bug. Some of you have been bitten pretty hard and some maybe got just a pinch. No matter the size of the bite, the pain is real, and we all feel it differently. There is hope for all of us.

Our first step is to acknowledge that we have this core wound that is sucking the joy from our lives. The feelings of unworthiness stop us in our tracks. We are better than that, but we forgot our value and significance in this world. We forget that we have a soul purpose that leads to greatness for ourselves and others.

A simple step-by-step process will help you regain your strength and reach that level of understanding that was not available to you as a child. It will help you remember that you are a miraculous being of light that is on a spiritual mission as you explore the physical realm. You are here to learn, discover, seek the higher truth, and find your way back to your spiritual heart. The physical journey has taken you off track, and you are now being called back to divine truth.

These days, there are many healing techniques to choose from, and it's wonderful to see so many people engaging with them. Many of us are trying to let go of what holds us back, find our true selves, and live life with a full heart. I applaud our efforts to reconnect with our truth.

As you will notice in the letters that I have written to the people who I feel have hurt me, I have grown up enough to accept their shortcomings. I went from a hurt and confused soul to a protective ego consciousness to the higher truth as I opened my spiritual heart. There is something deeply healing about expressing everything you could not express before. Releasing those heavy thoughts, feelings, and emotions from your soul is like letting out the darkness that is ravaging your life-force energy.

If you are new to inner healing work, the process I am sharing with you will jump-start your healing journey. If you are already doing some inner healing work, this process will boost your healing efforts. This process, together with your understanding of how life was created for you (and your right to recreate it), will help you get out of the unworthiness trap and fully accept your mission on this planet as a light being that is here to spread the message of love.

The Voiceless Soul

Since our souls are aching to release the heavy emotions that were suppressed a long time ago, I found it deeply healing to express these emotions through writing letters from heart-level consciousness. The healing comes from the full expression of these emotions, so they are no longer creating negative energy in the soul. Writing letters to those who have caused you pain, including those parts of you that kept you in your pain, is the way you get out of denial and into the truth of the matter.

Writing down our thoughts and feelings helps us to understand them better. You want to release the soul from the disruptive energy of the ego consciousness before you begin to write. It is important to raise the level of consciousness within the soul by moving the soul energy into the spiritual heart. This will connect you to your divine truth, which comes from the spirit within. The process below will help you connect to your spiritual heart and open up the consciousness of love and compassion within you.

Through writing, we can express the things we have been afraid to say. Writing is a way to release pent-up emotional energy that got stored in our bodies when we were stuck in emotional trauma. It's like lifting a huge weight from our souls.

All you will need is a pen and paper (or a journal), the personal notes you created in the back of this book, the energy of your breath, and the willingness to open your heart.

The breath represents life force energy. The breath can take us deeper inside ourselves.

To connect with your soul's energy and bring it through the spiritual heart, take some long, deep breaths. As you exhale the breath, direct your breath into the center of your heart. As you do that, imagine the breath flowing into the heart and back out again. Imagine your heart opening and expanding with each breath. Do this several times. Once you feel yourself connecting with the heart consciousness, you will feel yourself being guided deeper into your soul with the love of spirit that lives within the heart energy field. Once you feel that deep connection with your spirit, look at your personal notes in the back of the book and use them to help you write your letters.

When you begin to write your letters, feel free to express everything you feel. In your spirit energy, you are inviting the burdens of the soul to come forward for clearing, cleansing, and healing, while spirit holds these soul burdens in a place of love and compassion. Do not hold anything back. Express any anger, frustration, shame, guilt, sadness or distrust and cuss if you feel the need to. This is your soul releasing old energy that no longer serves you.

For healing to take place, it's important to close each letter with the understanding and acceptance that comes from your spiritual heart. When you bring forgiveness and compassion into your writing, you are engaging with higher vibrational energies. You are reconnecting to the higher truth. You are reconnecting to the broken pieces of your life through a higher understanding. You are healing your fragmented soul by feeling compassion for other fragmented souls. This helps you heal your broken connections without giving up a piece of your soul.

When all of your soul burdens feel cleansed, cleared, and healed, your soul will reach the vibration of spirit. This is your true self. You are one with the energy and spirit of all that is. You will live life through this energy, through your miracle body, and through your highest truth.

Start writing, and let the burdens that weigh you down be freed from your soul. Below are sample letters you can use as a guide. These are samples only. Your expressions must come from your open heart and the depths of your soul.

Express yourself from your wounded soul first, and then bring in your spiritual heart filled with love and compassion.

Your first step is to decide who you wish to write a letter to. (Examples: mom, dad, adoptive mother, adoptive father, primary caregiver, teacher, sibling, lover, spouse, partner, friend, other.)

The Voiceless Soul

To decide who you need to express yourself to, you can take the following steps:

1. Find a comfortable space where you can sit down and close your eyes.
2. Take a few deep breaths and exhale slowly into your heart center.
3. As you breathe into your heart, let your eyes get soft and relaxed, and then let them close.
4. With each new exhale, imagine your heart opening and expanding.
5. As your heart opens, imagine a field of awareness opening up all around your heart.
6. Allow each breath that you exhale to expand that field of energy around your heart. Then feel it expanding around your entire body.
7. As that field of energy around your body expands from the heart, focus on the person who is able to provoke an emotional charge in you. You are only invoking their soul energy, which means this person can be in a physical body or someone who has crossed over. Let that person come into your awareness through this field of energy. Be mindful of the energy they are projecting as they come into your field. Don't absorb their energy, just feel it. You may see the person or you may just feel them. You will have a sense that they are there. The heart is very intuitive.
8. As you become aware of their energy, give that energy a feeling. Does it feel angry? Sad? Lonely? Betrayed? Just let the feeling surface. You will feel their burdens through the energy they are projecting.
9. Feel them or just sense them being in front of you. Now, go back in time with them. See them or sense them getting younger and smaller until they reach an age under ten years old.
10. Notice how the defects in their soul were created for them by their unhealed childhood traumas caused by fear of nonlove.
11. Now hold that image in your mind and open your eyes.

You are ready to express yourself to them on paper. Express to them what you felt as you became aware of the energy they were carrying. This is their soul's energy. Express in writing how their energy affected you. Express every painful feeling that they projected onto you because of their unhealed soul traumas. Acknowledge that you didn't have the voice to express your true feelings before, but now you do.

It's important to express how they were unable to meet your childhood emotional needs. Explain how your unmet needs caused you to feel unworthy and how those feelings of unworthiness played out in your life. Explain in your letters how your suppressed emotions and feelings of unworthiness caused you to limit yourself in this lifetime. List those areas of your life and the consequences to those self-limited beliefs. This helps you acknowledge that you have kept yourself small because you were stuck in their trap.

The final step in your letters is when you can go into that higher place of love within you. You can begin by acknowledging that we are all stuck in the same trap. Maybe you didn't think of it that way before, but after reading this book, you realize that there is a real emotional trap that we are all capable of falling into. Maybe you were able to feel their childhood pain when you imagined a younger version of them. Maybe you were able to see or feel their innocence as a child and how they continued to live in fear as an adult.

Acknowledge that the person (or part of you) addressed in your letter is stuck in the trap that caused you to fall into it. Acknowledge that you have grown and evolved from that dark place inside the trap. Include in your letter your higher understanding about this person (or part of you) that you are addressing. Be sure to include how you understand that this was not intentional, even though it was hurtful and wrong.

Explain in your letter that you are healing now because you are living your life through your spiritual heart, which is that place of love and compassion within you. Acknowledge in your letter that by living from this higher truth, you now have the ability to release yourself from this debilitating trap, and you hope that one day they can do the same. If the letter is to a part of yourself, bring enough love and compassion to that part of you so you can pull that part of you from the trap and integrate this innocent part of you back into your spiritual heart.

Close your letter by stating that you now agree to release all of your attachments to anger, resentment, jealousy, sadness, guilt, shame, fear, distrust, and whatever other emotions you have suppressed, because you are now living from a higher place of truth. Make a heartfelt promise to yourself to live by this higher truth. You now know that it is the only way you can free yourself from the trap and live like the miracle you are.

Use these sample letters as guides. Use your own words when expressing your feelings. Let your words flow from your hurt soul while you are engaged with the spiritual heart, so the energy of these burdens can be released without fear, judgment or resistance. Stay in your spiritual heart to create peace around the disconnect from love. Remember, your spirit is always with you on this journey.

***

Sample Letter from Adult Self to Parent/Primary Caregiver

Dear _____,

When you _____ or when you don't _____, it makes me feel _____. I was just a little _____ (boy/girl) and I have been holding your baggage all these years. I thought there was something wrong with me. I thought I was _____. I felt _____ and _____.

I spent years feeling unfairly treated. This has caused many problems in my life because _____. [*Be specific with your thoughts and feelings.*] My soul lost connection to your soul when you made me feel unworthy of your love. That disconnect has caused me to disconnect from my own spiritual heart. I stopped trusting life. I gave up my joy and happiness because of your inability to help me love and honor myself. I feel wronged by you in many ways. [*Use your own words, thoughts, feelings, and emotions.*]

I did some growing up. I am doing deep soul-healing work. I am becoming more aware of the higher truth.

I realize now that we are all being sucked into a big trap because we are sensitive emotional beings. I realize now that there was nothing wrong with me. I was guided by grown-ups who did not fully grow up. It stifled my emotional growth and kept me from seeing my miraculous self. I was stuck in my ego fears and self-protection. I am willing to let that go now. You were stuck in your pain. You were guided by people that were stuck in their pain.

I have chosen to be the hero and get out of the trap. For me to do that, I must be able to have enough love and compassion in my heart to be able to forgive you for not doing better.

I have reached that level of higher truth, and I will now apply it to my healing.

I choose to forgive you for not having the awareness that you needed to get out of the trap. I choose to forgive your inability to grow up. I realize now that you did not intentionally want to make me feel unworthy. You were projecting onto me your childhood trauma without realizing how much pain you were in. Most importantly, I forgive myself for believing I was not worthy of your love.

What I know now is that the hurt child in you is what kept you from loving yourself. Your inability to love yourself has caused a disconnect between us. You are a child who attempted to raise a child. It was not the ideal situation.

I am ready to see the bigger picture. Now it is up to me, as an adult, to grow up and recreate the life I desire and deserve. I finally realize, from a deep-feeling level, that you did do the best you could, even though your best was not enough for me.

It is now my responsibility to release you from the responsibility to make me feel worthy. I am releasing myself from your burdens, so I can focus my energy on my life and my goals.

I hope you find your way back to your spiritual heart, so you can release your inner suffering as I did. You will feel light and free again.

That is who you are underneath all those burdens of pain. [*If this person has crossed over, wish them healing for their soul, as crossing over does not release soul burdens. We must choose to release them.*]

I have learned many lessons from my experiences. I embrace them all with gratitude.

Sincerely,

Sample Letter to Others

To: Every boss who belittled me and made me feel inadequate
Every boyfriend/girlfriend who made me feel unworthy of them
Every teacher who made me feel stupid and unable to succeed
Every caregiver who failed to encourage me to thrive
Every friend who could not support my highest good
Every relative who made me feel like I did not belong

I forgive you. By forgiving you, I forgive myself for believing that your inability to be kind and loving was a reflection of me. I want you to know that I forgive myself for forgetting who I am.

I hope you can get out of the trap that keeps you from knowing who you are. I hope you can release all your attachments to those who have hurt you.

I have grown. I have learned. I have reached a higher level of truth. I am no longer under your control. I feel empowered and free. I have found the gift of higher knowing. I am able to release all negative energetic bonds with you.

I hope you can learn how to set yourself free. I did, and it feels liberating. I feel deeply connected to who I am. I live my life from the higher knowing that I am a beautiful, sensitive, innocent soul on a spiritual path that is choosing to live from the spiritual heart. I wish the same for you.

Sending love and compassion to your soul,
Me

Sample Letter from Adult Self to Younger Self

Dear Little Me,

I am sorry you felt _____. I want you to know that you are _____, _____, lovable, valuable, and important to me.

(Mom/Dad/other) _____ was not able to provide you with what you needed because he/she did not feel it within herself/himself. You deserved to get all your childhood needs met. Unfortunately, you did not because (Mom/Dad/other) _____ did not. They were stuck in the unworthiness trap, and they unknowingly pulled you into it.

(Mom/Dad/other) _____ did not know how to heal her/his soul traumas and unknowingly made you feel _____. You are still innocent. You are a perfect soul, a miracle of life that came into this world to love and be loved. I will always love you and will always take care of you. You are never alone in this world.

Let's hope that (Mom/Dad/other) _____ finds his/her way back to his/her spiritual heart. He/she is lost and disconnected and suffers deep within his/her soul. We can heal together by having compassion for (Mom/Dad/other) _____ and praying for him/her to heal what needs to be healed.

You were always strong and brave. You held all those emotions inside of you, and you still turned out pretty awesome. I am so proud of you. I am proud that you are a part of me. I need your strength and bravery now so we can let go of the past and live the life we deserve. You are a divine being. You are a miracle. You are me, and I love you.

With all my love,
Your Current Self

Letter from Adult Self to Adult Self

Dear Me,

I am so proud of you for taking the time and energy to heal your old wounds. It was not easy for you to navigate this journey while you were feeling _____.

Now that you have a higher understanding of how people get hurt and then unknowingly project it onto others, you have evolved. You have discovered the truth about human consciousness, and you have a higher understanding of where it went wrong.

You have reached the higher truth, and this is what has set you free. You are no longer being controlled by the energy of the unworthiness trap. You are stepping back into your true, divine self. You are remembering the miracle that you are.

I am looking forward to a harmonious and balanced future. Thank you for doing the work to heal your soul.

With all my love,
Me

***

Your voice is important. It must be heard. Everything you feel inside, everything you held back that needed to be expressed, must be expressed.

When you express yourself through writing, you are putting your words into a material format so they can have the substance they deserve.

Your feelings matter. You matter. Express yourself freely.

CHAPTER 49

Embracing Your Spirit

Tell me, what is it you plan to do with your one wild and precious life?

—Mary Oliver

In all that we do and in all that we are, we must embody the energy of the soul and take in with gratitude the essence of this consciousness that lives within us. We must understand from a level of heart consciousness that the burdens of pain that disrupt the pure energy of the soul are nothing more than thought forms based in fear. These thought forms are continuously pulling us into the unworthiness trap, causing self-destructive behaviors, and disconnecting us from the energy of spirit.

The physical body, the soul, and the spirit are blended together in consciousness. A disruption in any one of the levels of consciousness will cause a disruption in the entire field of energy within you and around you.

You are here to learn many great things. Every experience has brought you growth if you understood the lesson within it.

I know we can easily get stuck in that lower place. We can read book after book, attend every power seminar around the world, seek out professional help, and still feel like we are stuck. This is because our burdens are heavy and not so easily lifted. This is not anyone's fault. The soul is a sensitive energy body, and the ego thrives on safety. Sometimes it's difficult to heal that conflict when you don't know there is one.

When you begin to release your burdens through soul expression, you are moving forward in your evolution. You are acknowledging that you know there is a higher truth you must seek. This in itself calls you forward.

You are no accident. You are here for a divine purpose. You are here to help change the world. We are moving toward a spiritual evolution, because we have been in a spiritual crisis for too long. You are part of a huge awakening of humanity. You chose this book for a reason. Your soul was calling for help. Many souls are being called to heal their shadow wounds, step it up in consciousness, and gather into a higher energy for a collective healing of the world. Not everyone is hearing the call. I believe you are. That is why you have read this far in the book without discarding it as another play on useless words of encouragement. You are ready to embrace your spirit. Be proud of yourself. You are truly a miraculous being of light and love.

I wish you all the best on your journey. May you always reach for the higher truth, stay in your true power, and live like the miracle you are.

Put your hand over your heart and feel into it. Say the words, "It is time to step into the higher truth." And now step into your awesomeness. What an amazing feeling that is.

Welcome back to your true, divine self.

> Dear Innocent Soul,
>
> You are doing well on your journey. You have been challenged by the lessons of nonlove, and you have succeeded in finding the higher truth. Welcome back, I have missed you.
>
> Please know that your suffering has not been in vain, dear one. It is the suffering of nonlove that brought you

closer to me. It is the disconnect with your divine self that brought you back to your spiritual heart.

Your journey continues with a higher understanding about life. This understanding will help you navigate the journey with clarity, compassion, connection, and, most importantly, self-love. I will continue to guide you along this sacred journey with the highest and purest love.

I wish you many blessings, dear one. You are the true hero whom your ancestry has been praying for. You are a true hero who can bring more compassion into the world. There are many more heroes out there. Let's help them find their calling.

With love, light, and peace,
Your Spirit

My mother made her transition to the other side while I was writing this book. I had so many hopeful ideas for helping her get out of the trap. No matter what I said or did, she always responded to me like a hurt child who didn't understand how her life could be different. This left me with feelings of helplessness that I continue to struggle with today. I feel like I failed her. I had all this knowledge about living from the heart, letting go of the past, knowing who you are, and being in higher consciousness. Yet I couldn't help my own mother.

It took me time to realize that when someone is stuck in the trap, it might be because they are afraid to let go of it. I could not make her believe in herself or convince her that she had the ability to rewrite her life script. I could only believe in myself and my ability to heal. I had to let go of my need to change her life so I could feel better about mine.

By accepting and loving her, even with her inability to love me the way I wanted to be loved, I have set myself free from the trap. The most I can do for her or anyone else is share my own story of trauma to triumph and hope they see the bigger picture in their lives.

CHAPTER 50

A Special Acknowledgement to My Clients

I have had the opportunity to meet many amazing souls in their physical existence. They have walked into my office holding onto a bit of hope that they will finally be able to heal their wounded selves and feel passionate about life again. They have expressed their pain through tears and words of despair. I could feel their energy. I could see the fear of the unknown in their eyes. They were nervous, yet optimistic as they held onto my words of encouragement as their long-awaited moment to emotional freedom. I took my clients through a deep spiritual journey not only to meet with their wounded parts, but to see the bigger picture around them. This was the first step towards their emotional healing.

I want to express my deepest gratitude for their strength and courage during their healing process. It was not easy for them to step into that place that they have been avoiding their whole lives. Every painful remembrance of the past led them deeper into their souls where they eventually felt their innocence. Their ability to see the bigger picture from a higher level of awareness helped them forgive those that caused them pain. My clients, by engaging with their spiritual hearts, were able to acknowledge the innocence of those that got caught up in the trap and unknowingly pulled my clients into it. They were able to forgive those parts of themselves that couldn't see their true value.

Every client session was a learning experience for my clients and for myself. I have learned the importance of understanding the higher truth.

Kelly Tallaksen

With permission of two of my clients, I share with you here their personal stories from troubled and disconnected child to triumphant, thriving adult. Both of these remarkable women have found peace for their souls through writing their stories from a place of courage, wisdom, compassion, and understanding. They came to me to experience the inner journey so they could connect deeper with their souls.

A few months before the completion of this book, my client Marika shared with me her autobiography. Marika expressed her feelings with truth and passion. She told me how writing her story from a higher level of understanding has helped her heal from the past.

Marika's story is one of trauma, survival, and full expression of her deepest pain. Her energy is enriching and ambitious. She is intelligent, kind-hearted, generous, and deeply connected to love. Despite her inability to connect as a child, she has grown into her spirit through a higher understanding of life.

This is Marika's story.

***

I was born in Hungary on August 27, 1947, to parents who had just survived the most horrific and subhuman conditions of our times—the Holocaust. My parents had just survived the loss of most of their families, rides in cattle cars, beatings, starvation, and other dehumanizing acts of the Nazis.

I was born to a father who weighed under one hundred pounds at liberation. I was born to a father whose first wife and two-year-old daughter had been murdered in the Holocaust. I was given the name Marika, the same name as my father's first daughter.

I was born to a mother who had been deprived of dignity and of a coat in the bitter winter. She had endured baldness, nudity, and ill-fitting shoes. I was born to a mother who had feelings of contamination and was living life through a masked depression after just surviving Auschwitz. She probably never expected to give birth to a healthy child.

I feel as though the great expectations for my life began way before my birth. Even at that point, a little voice was saying in my head, "You can't cause them any more pain. Protect them, protect them."

I have memories of feeling very much loved and adored by my parents, in a self-sacrificing way. The message of being "the very special child" was conveyed to me. My parents always had a very loving and devoted marriage, conveying outward affection. That provided me with a certain sense of stability and security. Their devotion to and love for each other was so great that I felt very much left out.

Feelings of inadequacy, guilt, and shame started to creep in simultaneously with the birth of my sister Eva in 1949, before I was two and half years old.

Maintaining the very special position of the very special child was the most important thing to me. I was always very outspoken, frustrated to the point of stuttering until the age of five. I felt dissatisfied and misunderstood by the world around me.

My parents had been victims of the Nazis during the Holocaust, and now we were victims of a country being run by communists. Their lives were about survival, not enjoyment. Their lives were about work, not play. I remember in my child's mind making a vow: "I will never bring my parents any more pain. Protect them, protect them."

Rather than playing pretend with dolls, my thoughts and fantasies were of the recent Holocaust. While other children in the world were carefree, my world comprised fantasies of loss, death, human suffering, and anguish. The suppression of the times was suppressing my opportunity to be outspoken, my desire to fantasize, my desire to be creative, and my opportunity to develop appropriately and live a normal childhood.

During the Hungarian revolution in 1956, my family left for a life of freedom and opportunities—me on my father's back, my sister Eva being carried by my mother across uncertain, threatening, and dangerous borders. After spending four very emotionally significant months in Austria with other displaced families, living in indecision as to whether to go to Israel, we came to the USA and settled in Delaware. My father had one hundred American dollars and didn't speak a word of English.

Adjustment for my sister, my parents, and I was difficult. How could I express these difficulties with adjustment? How could I express daily problems with friends and fellow students at school? How could my normal, appropriate problems as a teenager compare with what my parents had suffered? Comparing my pain and measuring up to the pain of my parents became all mixed up for me in those formative years, leaving me with strong feelings of guilt, shame, and insecurities about myself.

While girls my age were going through prepubescence, worrying about boys and clothes, once again I found myself not being able to have age-appropriate problems and worries. I still remembered the little voice in my head, saying, "Don't bring them any more pain. Protect them."

My youngest sister, Carol, was born a few years after we arrived in the USA. I was twelve and a half years old at the time. I remember wanting to Americanize and just be like all the other girls my age. The last thing I wanted was to have a mother who was pregnant and then a baby sister. It once again made me different and apart from those people to whom I most desperately wanted to conform.

The remainder of my teenage years living in Wilmington were spent feeling inadequate. I wanted desperately to be aesthetically beautiful and popular, although I felt damaged and wounded. I wanted to be the smartest, most successful, happiest girl I knew, once again not leaving room for expression of feelings about my life.

I thought I could run away and start all over with new people and a new place when I went to a junior college on Long Island. I lived in the dorms and studied dental hygiene. I pretended I was prepared for this separation from my parents, again living a life without true expression.

It was in my second semester at SUNY Farmingdale that I met and fell head over heels in love with my (eventual) husband, Alex. I met Alex a year after the death of his father; the irony of meeting up in a context of pain and loss became even more significant as my life progressed.

Alex and I were married in 1970. I felt like I was on top of the world. I was enthusiastic about sharing a life with my beloved, about gaining a family of three brothers, and especially about duplicating the intimacy and loving selflessness of my parents, whose married relationship was the only one I had known.

The problem was that Alex wasn't my father. I insisted on holding on to the values of my parents, which were so ingrained in me. The reality of this fact was to cause me much pain and anguish in the years ahead.

I was working full-time as a dental hygienist while Alex finished his studies, during which time I became pregnant with my first son. In the latter part of my pregnancy Alex's brother Paul died as a result of drug addiction, once again leaving our family with pain and loss.

Jack, my older and most beautiful son, was born on July 24, 1974, in Brooklyn, New York, where we were living at the time. Mothering, trying to appear happy to my friends, and maintaining my seemingly happy marriage were very emotional times for me.

In 1977, we moved to Bellmore, Long Island, to a single-family home. I was at this point in my life committed to making everything about my life appear perfect and beautiful on the outside. I still had no room for expression of my internal turmoil. I played the role of the happy married daughter, tied to predetermined expectations. I still heard, "Never bring them any more pain. Protect them."

On April 5, 1978, my younger and again most beautiful, healthy son Adam was born. Having two children, living in suburbia, trying to keep up with the neighbors, and maintaining a marriage in which my husband was not living up to my expectations overwhelmed me. It was during this overwhelmed part in my life that my brother-in-law Brian, Alex's younger brother, died of complications from drug addiction. Yet again this left behind a legacy of loss and pain.

In 1980, at the age of 34, I finally moved toward self-expression, honesty, introspection, and less pretense when I started working with a professional therapist. I started working through the burdened feelings of shame and guilt and insecurity that were intertwined in my life. For the first time in my life, I allowed some of my inner pain to be expressed. For the first time in my life, I was doing something for myself.

I was in the process of working through some of my suppressed feelings. I was in the process of making change to connect with people in a more meaningful way. I was in the process of trying to give my children opportunities for more self-expression. Then my younger son Adam was diagnosed with cancer at the age of six.

His diagnosis on the day of my thirty-seventh birthday was the turning point in my life. Living through the many months of his illness was like reliving the Holocaust with my parents. The stigma connected with cancer brought back feelings of contamination and victimization that were felt by my parents in the Holocaust. I felt the painful treatments for Adam's cancer in my veins and flesh.

Living on after Adam's passing in 1986 at the age of eight was an act of survival, void of enjoyment, very similar to my parents' lives and so familiar to me.

Love of family and the importance of my Judaism have been major parts of my recovery. I am always actively working on and striving for healthier boundaries. I have built strongly connected and communicative relationships with my parents, sisters, husband, and surviving son. I am always actively working on a most loving, honest, and expressive relationship with myself. I am always actively working on developing a stronger sense of self. Allowing more self-acceptance and more self-caring into my life doesn't come naturally to me.

In my striving for survival, I have reached out for honesty, openness, and truth. In my striving for survival, I have reached out for more creativity and expression.

Writing the very painful and unspeakable aspects of my life in this autobiography is my way of living up to this honesty. In my journey for survival, I have implemented many modalities for help. I reached out for help from the Compassionate Friends and Children of Holocaust Survivors support group. I have taken responsibility for my fulfillment, contentment, and, yes, happiness. Fitness of body and mind, returning to school, and acquiring my BS in counseling have given me great feelings of accomplishment. I feel lucky to have enthusiasm and passion for walking and dancing in my life.

Writing this autobiography and speaking the unspeakable are part of my journey. I am so glad to have the opportunity to partake in an art therapy course as part of my journey toward thriving and not just surviving.

**

Marika is very active in helping children with cancer through fundraising efforts and other projects. Marika continues to bring her love of life into the world.

By referral from Marika, Karen Flyer became a client. Karen has survived many soul traumas. Hearing her story made my life seem relatively simple. Karen found healing of her soul through writing. She is the author of *Loss and Found*, a moving and provocative story of death, sexual abuse, and addiction. She has triumphed through these struggling times by being in her truth. She was able to express her pain and find a way to accept and heal what her father stole from her—her dignity and her self-respect.

I am honored to have had the opportunity to get to know Karen on a personal level. After reading her book, I found a renewed interest in tending to my soul and remembering the reason we are all here.

Except from Karen's book:

> "He got sick, and his heart just stopped working," my mother tried to explain, turning to Omama with a questioning look as if she were seeking an alibi to corroborate a story. Omama nodded her head in concurrence without saying a word, though her expression told me all I needed to know—my mother was telling the truth. She was not playing a callous childhood game of trickery; she was not teasing me with a belated April Fool's joke. This was real. Suddenly, the waves of sadness cascading over me accelerated into the more weighty feeling of guilt. The sensation of a sharp kitchen knife stabbing me in the gut nearly caused me to double over; luckily, I was sitting on the bed and not standing, for I certainly would have swooned like a southern belle and fainted onto the hard floor. At that moment, a grave realization hit me like a rock: I had broken my daddy's heart with the mean thoughts that passed through my mind the day before our last trip to Maine."

About Karen Flyer:

Growing up is extraordinarily difficult for some girls. Some lose a parent at any early age. Some suffer from depression. Some battle anorexia. Some are sexually abused. Some turn to drugs, alcohol or sexual promiscuity in order to dull their pain. Karen Flyer experienced all of these tragedies during her tumultuous childhood and adolescence. Karen suffered through fear of abandonment and a constant struggle to prove herself worthy of love. It was when she realized her own self-worth that she finally found peace.

Karen expresses that although she had friends around her, she felt cut off from the world. To safe-guard her feelings, she was forced to build a wall of self-preservation around herself.

Between her angst and her drive to be perfect, she found little time to be happy growing up. Karen talks about learning to love and live again after years of struggle.

Finally, Karen learns to look back at her troubled childhood and see the gift in her experiences.

Karen, despite her traumatized soul, graduated as valedictorian of her high school and near the top of her class at Duke University. She went on to earn her MBA and pursue a successful career in marketing. She has published numerous articles for trade organizations and currently lives on Long Island, New York, with her husband and two children.

Karen is an inspiration for all those who have suffered a difficult childhood. Her book is well-written and deeply healing for the soul.

A SPECIAL ACKNOWLEDGMENT TO THE WOUNDED SOULS OF MY PARENTS

I miss my mom and sometimes feel sorry that we didn't reach that deep connection with each other. I wanted so much to get closer to her heart. I wanted so much for her to get out of her woundedness and be the mother I needed.

With all the healing work I did, I felt more connected to what is real. I no longer saw my mom as a weak woman, but more of a brave soul who had to endure so much pain. A part of me was angry because I couldn't fix her. I couldn't make her understand that she was worthy of love even though her whole life she felt unloved.

Mom was always a loving and caring mother, even though she was lost in her pain. She sacrificed her younger years to make sure we had the best life she could give us. She could have easily turned us over to social services when they were trying to take us away. She could have started a new life and never looked back. Her beautiful heart would not let her do that. Her inability to leave my dad was due to her inner child desperately seeking love and approval, even from a man who abused her.

Mom worked hard and loved us the best way she knew how. As a child, I felt neglected by Mom because she was always leaving for somewhere. I realize now that she had no choice. She worked hard for us. She was truly an amazing woman.

I am proud to call her Mom.

Rest in peace, beautiful soul.

***

My dad was a deep soul. He was intelligent to the point of insanity. He spent much of his time reading about the stars, space, and the planets. Sadly, he suffered from such deep trauma that he lost connection with himself, his family, and the world. Maybe that's why he was so focused on the universe. It was not part of the world that treated him badly. I tried to spend time with him as an adult but found it difficult to sustain a relationship. Part of the problem was me. I did not see the bigger picture. I wanted to have a dad. I wanted to get close to him, but my childhood memories kept me at a distance.

Dad passed away when my first daughter was two years old. I cried all night long. Many people couldn't understand my pain. They couldn't understand why his death did not make me happy. The only story I had told them was how my dad was a villain and I was the victim. I cried because a part of me was longing to be loved by him—and now it was too late.

Sometimes, I wish he were here because I would love to have a deep conversation with him about the universe. I want him to see how well I am doing. I want him to see the real me so maybe he could be the real him. As much as I want the chance to fix things, I have learned to let go of what couldn't be fixed and focus now on what could be.

Rest in peace, beautiful soul.

**

I now know that both my parents are watching over me. They are proud of how I turned my life around. They are healing now. I am sending them love through my spiritual heart.

**

A LETTER TO MY GROWN-UP SELF

Dear Grown-Up Me,

I am proud of all the soul-healing work you have done. I applaud your courage and your consistent hard work in writing this book. You have expressed your deepest pain to the world in an effort to help others see the truth about the human experience and our debilitating disconnect from love.

I am proud of you for never giving up, even though many times you thought you should. I am proud of you for listening to your heart when you spoke of the plight of others. Your ability to stay focused on the wellness of your body, soul, and spirit shows how much strength you have gained over the years.

I am proud of your efforts to share your knowledge and help others regain their connection to spirit. You have worked hard to find balance in your life, and you are now being rewarded for staying true to your divine calling.

I especially want to mention that I am proud of you for trying to be the best mom you could. Even though you have made mistakes during your learning process, your ability to forgive yourself so you can do better is an important step in your spiritual growth.

Keep on learning, keep on giving, and keep on sharing your light, and you will continue to do well on your journey.

Love and light,
Me

REFERENCES

Past Life Therapy - Special Edition with Past Life Therapy Center, by Morris Netherton, Ph.D. and Dr. Thomas Paul - published February 25, 2013

Healing Lost Souls, by William J. Baldwin, Ph.D. - Hampton Roads Publishing (June 1, 2003)

Windows to the Womb - Revealing the Conscious Baby from Conception to Birth, by David Chamberlain - North Atlantic Books; 1st edition (January 15, 2013)

The Aware Baby, by Aletha J. Solter - Aware Parenting Institute; Revised ed. edition (May 1, 2001)

Welcoming Consciousness, by Wendy Anne McCarthy, Ph.D., RN - Wondrous Beginnings Publishing (October 15, 2012)

Born Scared, by Julia Ingram, MA - Julia Ingram; 1st edition (March 18, 2014)

Psychology of the Future, by Stanislav Grof, MD - State University of New York Press; 1st edition (July 14, 2000)

The Trauma of Birth, by Otto Rank - Martino Fine Books (September 14, 2010)

Remarkable Healings, by Shakuntala Modi, Ph.D. - Hampton Roads Publishing; First Printing edition (April 1, 1998)

Birthpsychology.com - The Association of Prenatal and Perinatal Psychology and Health (APPPAH)

The Mind of Your Newborn Baby, by David Chamberlain - North Atlantic Books; 3rd ed. edition (April 2, 1998)

HeartHealth – The Vulnerability of Being, by Mark Sircus, Ac, OMD - IMVA Publications (April 8, 2014)

Toxic Parents – Overcoming Their Hurtful Legacy and Reclaiming Your Life, by Dr. Susan Forward with Craig Buck - Bantam; Reprint edition (January 2, 2002)

Alchemical Quotes Paulo Coelho, by Sreechinth C – Google Play Books

The Body Keeps the Score, by Bessel van der Kolk, M.D.- Penguin Books; Reprint edition (September 8, 2015)

Adventures of the Soul - Journeys Through the Physical and Spiritual Dimensions, by James Van Praagh, Hay House Inc.; Reprint edition (March 8, 2016)

Letting Go - The Pathway to Surrender, by David R. Hawkins, M.D., Ph.D. - Hay House Inc.; 2nd ed. edition (January 15, 2014)

Homecoming – Reclaiming and Championing Your Inner Child, by John Bradshaw - Bantam; Illustrated edition (February 1, 1992)

Human Development and Trauma - How Childhood Shapes into Who We Are as Adults, by Darius Cikanavicius - Independently published (March 15, 2018)

The Courage to Heal Workbook - For Women and Men Survivors of Sexual Abuse, by Laura Davis - Harper Perennial; 1st edition (February 28, 1990)

The Soul of Leadership Unlocking Your Potential for Greatness, by Deepak Chopra -Harmony; 1st edition (December 28, 2010)

Chapter _____
My Personal Notes and Feelings:

Chapter _____
My Personal Notes and Feelings:

Chapter _____
My Personal Notes and Feelings:

Chapter _____
My Personal Notes and Feelings:

Chapter _____
My Personal Notes and Feelings:

Chapter _____
My Personal Notes and Feelings:

Chapter _____
My Personal Notes and Feelings:

Chapter _____
My Personal Notes and Feelings:

Chapter _____
My Personal Notes and Feelings:

Chapter _____
My Personal Notes and Feelings:sss

Made in the USA
Monee, IL
27 June 2021